Contents

W9-CEO-272

How To Use This Guide

You will find this guide is a cinch to use. Information is presented in an easy to understand format, flowing logically from state to state and highway to highway. Take a few minutes to read this section and you will have no problem quickly finding whatever information you seek.

Guidebook Layout

- United States rest areas appear first, followed by Canadian rest areas.
- Within the U.S. and Canada, areas are presented by state or province in alphabetical order.
- A map is shown for each state or province on which rest areas (and service stations with RV dump facilities) are depicted.
- Within each state, the facilities at areas along interstate highways are presented first, followed by facilities at those along U.S. highways and then state highways.
- In each highway category, highways are listed from lowest number to highest.
- For north-south highways, areas are listed from south to north; areas along east-west highways are listed from west to east.
- Following the rest area listings, information is presented on truck stops/service stations with RV sanitary dump facilities, if applicable.

General Information

Information for each state or province begins with a "header block" identifying that state or province and providing a few miscellaneous facts.

Example

KANSAS
"Sunflower State"

Capital: Topeka	Largest City: Wichita
Population: 2,477,574	Area: 81,787 sq. mi.
Highest Point: 4,039 ft.	Lowest Point: 680 ft.
Date of Statehood: January 29, 1861	

Symbols

Picnic Tables ──────────────

Modern Rest Rooms ──────────

Drinking Water ─────────────

Outside Night Lights ──────────

Handicapped Facilities ─────────

Public Telephone ────────────

RV Sanitary Dump Station ────────

Welcome/Information Center ───────

Note: ⊡ indicates non-flushing toilet facility.

Abbreviations

Gas

AM	Amoco	BP	B P Oil	CH	Chevron
CS	Coastal Serv.	ES	Esso	EX	Exxon
EZ	EZ Go	GF	Gulf	MO	Mobil
PC	Petro-Can	PH	Phillips 66	SH	Shell
		SN	Sunoco	TX	Texaco

Food

AA	Auntie Ann's	AR	Arby's	BBB	Bob's Big Boy
BJ	Ben & Jerry's	BK	Burger King	BR	Breyers
BY	Benny's BBQ	CF	Coffee Shop	CV	Carvel Ice Cream
DD	Dunkin' Donuts	DN	Denny's	ET	Entenmann's
GB	Gormet Bean	GH	Gift Shop	GS	General Store
HD	Hardee's	HN	Horton's	KFC	Kentucky Fr Ch
KG	Kings	MA	Marriott	MC	MAC
McD	McDonald's	MF	Mrs. Fields'	MI	Mamma Ilardo's
MS	Mr. Sub	NA	Nathans's	OM	Oscar Mayer
POP	Popeye's	PT	Pretzel Time	RAX	RAX
RR	Roy Rogers	SB	Sbarro	SK	Snack Bar
TB	Taco Bell	TC	TCBY	WD	Wendy's

Other

AS	Archaeological Site	BL	Boat Launch	C	Camping
CR	Corral/Horse area	F	Fishing	FG	Firegrills or pits
GT	Gazebo/travel info	HM	Historical Marker	PA	Play Area
PW	Pet Walk	SC	Sculpture	SP	State Park
TP	Truck Parking	TR	Hiking Trails	VM	Vending Machine
VP	Vista Point	WR	Weather Radio		

ISBN 0-937877-25-5

REST AREA GUIDE

TO THE
UNITED STATES AND CANADA

By Bill Cima

ISBN Number: 0-937877-25-5

The "header block" is followed by **General Information** presented in three categories: Additional Information on Services, Rules for Usage, and Driving in that particular state or province.

Additional Information on Services contains information on rest area and welcome center hours, toll road plazas and tourist information telephone number.

Example

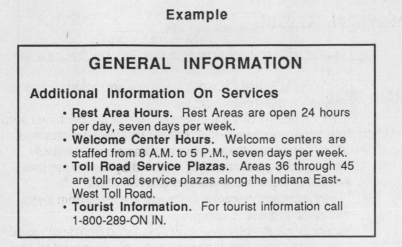

GENERAL INFORMATION

Additional Information On Services

- **Rest Area Hours.** Rest Areas are open 24 hours per day, seven days per week.
- **Welcome Center Hours.** Welcome centers are staffed from 8 A.M. to 5 P.M., seven days per week.
- **Toll Road Service Plazas.** Areas 36 through 45 are toll road service plazas along the Indiana East-West Toll Road.
- **Tourist Information.** For tourist information call 1-800-289-ON IN.

The **Rest Area Usage Rules** lists specific rules for this state or province which were not covered in the Rules and Regulations section on page 9.

Example

Rest Area Usage Rules
- **Overnight Parking.** No overnight parking.
- **Camping.** Camping is not permitted.
- **Stay Limit.** No published limit.

Driving in... presents some of the motorist laws that may be of interest to you. Be aware that these laws change from time to time and that some of the states and provinces presently have bills before congress seeking alterations.

5

Example

Driving In Indiana

- **Emergencies.** For highway emergencies call State Police Headquarters at 1-317-232-8250.
- **Open Container.** No open container law.
- **Seat Belts.** Seat belts are required for all occupants. Children 3 and under must be in a child restraint system.
- **Helmets.** Motorcycle operators and passengers 18 and under must wear helmets.
- **Road Conditions.** Dial 1-317-232-8300.

State Maps

For each state or province, a skeletal map is provided on which the approximate location of rest areas is depicted by the placement of numbers. The approximate location of truck stops/service stations equipped with RV sanitary dump facilities is shown using letters.

Example

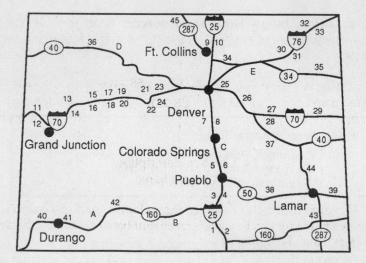

Rest Area Listings. A typical rest area listing follows:

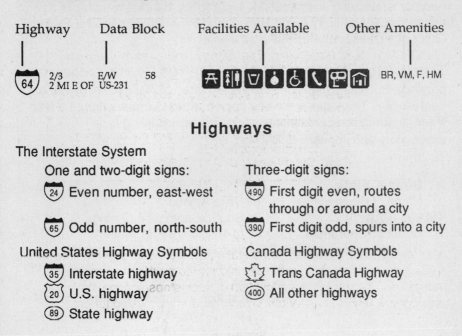

Highway   Data Block   Facilities Available   Other Amenities

64   2/3   E/W   58   BR, VM, F, HM
    2 MI E OF US-231

Highways

The Interstate System

One and two-digit signs:

24 Even number, east-west

65 Odd number, north-south

United States Highway Symbols

35 Interstate highway

20 U.S. highway

89 State highway

Three-digit signs:

490 First digit even, routes through or around a city

390 First digit odd, spurs into a city

Canada Highway Symbols

1 Trans Canada Highway

400 All other highways

Data Block

Direction(s) served

Rest area reference numbers corresponding to numbered map locations —— 2/3   E/W   58 —— Milepost marker number. If in parenthesis, indicates exit number or nearest exit number.

2 MI E OF US-231

Location description or rest area name

Note: If two numbers are listed in the milepost marker position, they correspond to the two rest area reference numbers listed at the beginning of the data block respectively.

Facilities and Other Amenities

See the inside front cover for symbols and abbreviations. Primary rest area facilities are depicted with symbols. These include picnic tables, restrooms, drinking water, outside night lights, handicapped facilities telephone, RV sanitary dump station, and information/welcome center. Other amenities are listed using abbreviations.

Truck Stop/Service Station Listings. Within each state or province, truck stops/service stations are listed alphabetically by city or nearest city. The letter preceding each business corresponds to a map letter depicting its approximate location. A typical listing is self-explanatory and appears as follows:

A. Buena Vista

Name of Business:	Buena Vista Amoco
Location:	US-24 South (South side of city).
Hours of Operation:	7 A.M. to 10 P.M. (8 P.M. winter).
RV Information:	$2.00 charge for use of RV Dump ($5.00 if fuel not purchased). Waterfill and diesel fuel available. No propane.
Station Type:	Service station with mini-mart (Amoco).

8

Rules and Regulations

Rest Areas were developed to provide the traveler with a means of relieving fatigue through a brief stay at a pleasant and relaxing area. Every state or province has its own set of rules and regulations governing use. These rules are designed to provide for the safety and health of users.

Listings in this book should be treated as intermediate stopping points, not destinations. Rest area systems were developed to help you reach your destination in a more safe and restful manner. They provide a peaceful environment in which you can relieve driving fatigue for a few hours before proceeding to your destination. If you seek a prolonged stay, you should consider a campground, park or similar facility.

The primary rule of rest area usage is to be respectful of the rights of others and of the environment. By so doing, you may help prevent an accident and also keep the rest area pleasant for others.

Below are listed general rules which apply to nearly all areas listed in this publication. Specific rules in addition to these are listed for the individual states or provinces to which they apply.

ACTIVITIES

Meetings. Public meetings, assemblies or other gatherings, distribution of merchandise or literature, and circulating petitions for signature are all prohibited activities.

Outside Activities. No parking is allowed to engage in any activity off of the rest area, such as, cross-country skiing, off-road vehicle use, fishing, hiking, camping or hunting unless otherwise specified.

Repairs. Routine servicing is not permitted. Minor repairs to make the unit operable are allowed.

Selling. Any commercial selling or advertising of any nature is prohibited without prior written permission of the controlling agency. This includes preparation and/or distribution of food and beverage, including coffee, for public consumption for free, donation or sale.

Solicitation. Any solicitation of voluntary donations for any purpose is prohibited.

Transfer of Cargo. Transfer of cargo or trailers is not permitted. Further, uncoupling a unit is also not allowed.

PERSONAL BEHAVIOR

Alcohol. Most states do not allow consumption or distribution of alcoholic beverages at rest areas.

Demeanor. Acts of indecent exposure and lewd motions or actions are prohibited. Loitering or loafing within or around toilet facilities or other buildings or using the area as place to loiter or hitchhike is prohibited. Users shall not block vehicular or pedestrian traffic.

Emergencies. In matters of safety and orderliness, persons shall obey reasonable requests made by authorized rest area personnel.

Fires. Most areas do not allow fires. If permitted, fires must be confined to designated areas and containers and must be extinguished after use.

Firearms. Exhibiting, use, or discharge of firearms, pellet guns, B-B guns or other weapons is prohibited. This also is a prohibition against fireworks.

Garbage. All garbage and trash should be properly deposited in designated trash containers and the area of use cleaned before leaving. Disposal of waste other than travel trash by vehicles in transit is prohibited.

Nature. Plants and wildlife must not be disturbed.

Noise. The use of noise-producing instruments, megaphones, loudspeakers or other similar devices which are used to amplify sound is not permitted.

Parking. Vehicles must be parked only in designated parking areas. Generally, this means on paved surfaces and not on grass.

Pets and Other Animals. All animals must be totally under control. In general, this means that household pets must be kept on a leash and other larger animals must be confined to the vehicle, enclosures or other adequate restraint.

Property. Moving or defacing any property is prohibited.

Restroom Facilities. Clothes or dishes may not be washed in restroom sinks. Electrical outlets in restrooms may not be used to brew coffee or to cook meals. Electric hand dryers may not be used in restrooms to dry dishes, clothing, etc.

Sanitary Waste. Sanitary waste must be disposed of only in designated RV sanitary dump stations.

Signs. Signs or any other material must not be attached in any way to any tree or structure.

State Utilities. The unauthorized use of water, electrical and gas utilities is prohibited.

Water Usage. Water intended for human consumption may not be polluted or contaminated in any way. Hydrants or water faucets may not be used for cleaning fish, food or clothing.

United States Rest Areas

ALABAMA

"Yellowhammer State"

Capital: Montgomery   Largest City: Birmingham
Population: 4,040,587   Area: 50,708 sq. mi.
Highest Point: 2,407 ft.   Lowest Point: Sea Level
Date of Statehood: December 14, 1819

GENERAL INFORMATION

Additional Information On Services

- **Rest Area Hours.** Rest Areas are open 24 hours per day, seven days per week.
- **Welcome Center Hours.** Welcome centers are open 24 hours per day, seven days per week.
- **Tourist Information.** For tourist information call 1-800-ALABAMA.

Rest Area Usage Rules

- **Overnight Parking.** No overnight parking.
- **Camping.** Camping is not permitted.
- **Stay Limit.** No usage time limit.

Driving In Alabama

- **Emergencies.** For highway emergencies dial 1-800-525-5555 to reach the nearest State Trooper post or call 911 (may not be operable in all counties).
- **Open Container.** Some counties in Alabama are "dry" counties. In these counties, no alcoholic containers, open or closed, are allowed in the passenger area of the vehicle. Open container laws in other counties are governed by local ordnance.
- **Seat Belts.** Children 5 and under must be in safety restraints. Children 4 and 5 may use safety belts instead of federally approved child restraints.
- **Helmets.** Motorcycle and motor-driven cycle riders must wear helmets and shoes. Operators must be licensed.
- **Road Conditions.** Dial 1-205-242-4378.

ALABAMA REST AREAS

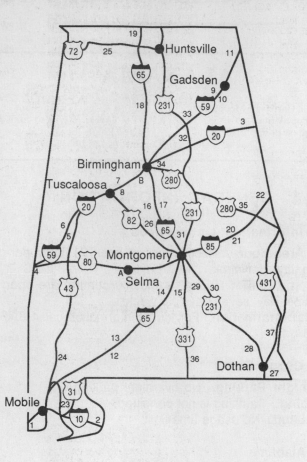

	1 E 2 MI E OF MISSISSIPPI LINE	🏕🚹🚰🍼♿📞📺🏠	PW, TP, WR
	2 W 1 MI W OF FLORIDA LINE	🏕🚹🚰🍼♿📞📺🏠	PW, TP, WR
	3 W 2 MI W OF GEORGIA LINE	🏕🚹🚰🍼♿📞📺🏠	PW, TP, WR
	4 N MISSISSIPPI LINE	🏕🚹🚰🍼♿📞📺🏠	PW, TP, WR
	5/6 N/S 2 MI S OF ST RTE 14	🏕🚹🚰🍼♿📞📺	PW, TP, WR
	7/8 N/S 11 MI E OF TUSCULOOSA	🏕🚹🚰🍼♿📞📺	PW, TP, WR
	9/10 N/S 17 MI S OF GADSDEN	🏕🚹🚰🍼♿📞📺	PW, TP, WR
	11 S GEORGIA LINE	🏕🚹🚰🍼♿📞📺🏠	PW, TP, WR

Route	Exit	Dir	Location	Amenities		PW, TP, WR
65	12	N	12 MI SW OF EVERGREEN	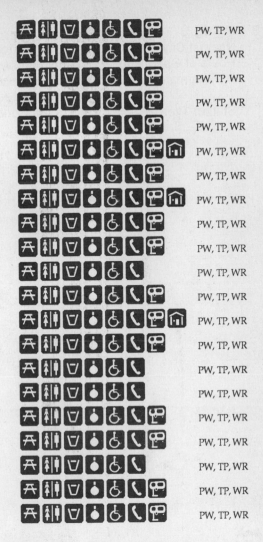		PW, TP, WR
	13	S	8 MI SW OF EVERGREEN			PW, TP, WR
	14/15	N/S	2 MI N OF GREENVILLE			PW, TP, WR
	16/17	N/S	6 MI N OF CLANTON			PW, TP, WR
	18	N/S	7 MI S OF CULLMAN			PW, TP, WR
	19	S	1 MI S OF TENNESSEE LINE			PW, TP, WR
85	20/21	E/W	12 MI SW OF AUBURN			PW, TP, WR
	22	W	1 MI W OF GEORGIA LINE			PW, TP, WR
31	23	S	5 MI S OF BAY MINETTE			PW, TP, WR
43	24	N	1 MI S OF WAGARVILLE			PW, TP, WR
72	25	E	3 MI E OF ROGERSVILLE			PW, TP, WR
82	26	N	2 MI NW OF MAPLESVILLE			PW, TP, WR
231	27	N	FLORIDA LINE			PW, TP, WR
	28	S	6 MI S OF OZARK			PW, TP, WR
	29/30	N/S	1 MI S OF PINE LEVEL			PW, TP, WR
	31	S	1 MI S OF WETUMPKA			PW, TP, WR
	32/33	N/S	I-59 INTERSECTION			PW, TP, WR
280	34	W	7 MI E OF BIRMINGHAM			PW, TP, WR
	35	W	5 MI W OF OPELIKA			PW, TP, WR
331	36	N	6 MI N OF FLORALA			PW, TP, WR
431	37	S	10 MI S OF EUFAULA			PW, TP, WR

ALABAMA TRUCK STOPS WITH RV DUMP

A. Clean Machine of Alabama

Nearest City/Location:	Selma, US-80 W, in city (1 block from Holiday Inn).
Hours of Operation:	6 A.M. to 10 P.M.
RV Information:	No charge for use of RV Dump. Waterfill, propane and diesel fuel available.
Station Type:	Truck stop (Citgo).

B. **Flying J Travel Plaza,**
Nearest City/Location: Bessemer, I-20 & I-59, Exit 104.
Hours of Operation: 24 hours per day.
RV Information: No charge for use of RV Dump. Waterfill, propane and diesel fuel available.
Station Type: Truck stop (Conoco)

ALASKA

"The Last Frontier"

Capital: Juneau	**Largest City:** Anchorage
Population: 550,043	**Area:** 591,004 sq. mi.
Highest Point: 20,320 ft.	**Lowest Point:** Sea Level

Date of Statehood: January 3, 1959

GENERAL INFORMATION

Additional Information On Services

- **Rest Area Hours.** Alaska does not maintain a system of rest areas. This listing consists of state parks along selected roads. Some of these park units are campgrounds, others are day use areas. Some day use areas are closed at night and most of these units are not maintained during winter: i.e., latrines and water pumps are closed and the area is not plowed.
- **RV Accommodations.** Most campsites accommodate RV's up to 35 ft in length. Electrical hook-ups are not available.
- **Latrines.** All latrines are primitive, vaulted type.
- **Facility Type.** Abbreviations after the name of each location indicate the following facility types:
  SRS State Recreation Site
  SRA State Recreation Area
  SHP State Historic Park
  SHS State Historic Site
  ST State Trail
- **Tourist Information.** For tourist information call 1-907-465-2010 for Juneau and 1-907-563-2167 for Anchorage.

Rest Area Usage Rules

- **Overnight Parking.** Overnight parking is permitted.
- **Camping.** Camping is permitted. Fees vary from $6 to $12 per night. Annual camping passes are available.
- **Stay Limit.** Most sites with camping have 15 day stay limits. Limit at site #35 is 5 days, at #9 and # 40 is 7 days and at #6 is 4 days.
- **Horseback Riding.** Horseback riding is allowed in designated areas.
- **Discharge of Firearms.** Check with park office for area closures and for 1/4 or 1/2 mile restrictions near developed

facilities. Target shooting is prohibited.

Driving In Alaska

- **Emergencies.** For highway emergencies call 911 (may not be operable in all counties) or dial the local police or local number for the highway patrol.
- **Open Container.** Open containers of alcoholic beverages in the passenger compartment of the vehicle are not permitted.
- **Seat Belts.** Seat belts are required for all occupants. Children 4 and under must be in a child restraint system.
- **Helmets.** Motorcycle operators and passengers 18 and under must wear helmets.
- **Road Conditions.** Dial 1-800-478-7675.

ALASKA REST AREAS

ALASKA HIGHWAY

1	N/S	1309	🏕️ T 🗑️	♿	C, TR
TOK RIVER SRS					
2	N/S	1332	🏕️ T 🗑️	♿	BL, C
MOON LAKE SRS					
3	N/S	1415	🏕️ T 🗑️	♿	BL, C, F
CLEARWATER SRS					

CHENA HOT SPGS RD

4	N/S	27	🏕️ T 🗑️	♿	C, F, TR
CHENA RIVER SRA					

ELLIOTT HIGHWAY

5	E/W	11	🏕️ T 🗑️	♿	BL, C, F
LOWER CHATANIKA RIVER					

GLENN HIGHWAY

6	E/W	12	🏕️ T 🗑️	♿	C, F, TR
EAGLE TIVER CAMPGROUND					
7	E/W	26	T		TR
THUNDERBIRD FALLS TR ST					
8	E/W	36	🏕️ T 🗑️	♿	F, TR
KEPLER-BRADLEY LAKES SRA					
9	E/W	55	🏕️ T 🗑️	♿	C, F, TR
MOOSE CREEK SRS					
10	E/W	76	🏕️ T 🗑️		C
KING MOUNTAIN SRS					
11	E/W	85	🏕️ T		BL, C, F
LONG LAKE SRS					
12	E/W	101	🏕️ T 🗑️	♿	C, TR
MATANUSKA GLACIER SRS					
13	E/W	137	🏕️ T		BL, C, F, TR
LITTLE NELCHINA SRS					

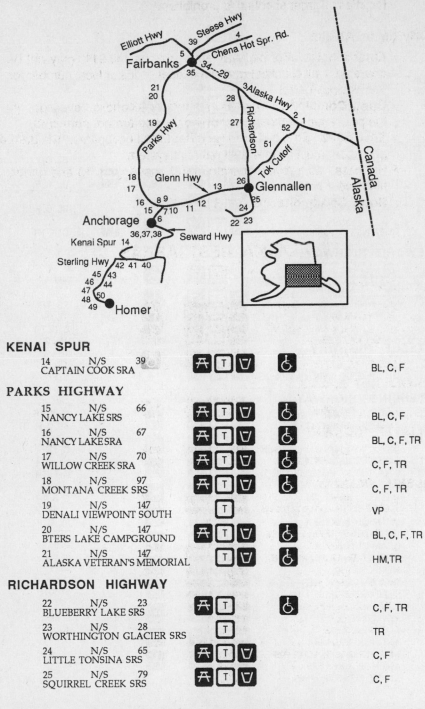

KENAI SPUR

14 N/S 39 CAPTAIN COOK SRA	🏕	T	🥤	♿	BL, C, F

PARKS HIGHWAY

15 N/S 66 NANCY LAKE SRS	🏕	T	🥤	♿	BL, C, F
16 N/S 67 NANCY LAKE SRA	🏕	T	🥤	♿	BL, C, F, TR
17 N/S 70 WILLOW CREEK SRA	🏕	T	🥤	♿	C, F, TR
18 N/S 97 MONTANA CREEK SRS	🏕	T	🥤	♿	C, F, TR
19 N/S 147 DENALI VIEWPOINT SOUTH		T			VP
20 N/S 147 BTERS LAKE CAMPGROUND	🏕	T	🥤	♿	BL, C, F, TR
21 N/S 147 ALASKA VETERAN'S MEMORIAL		T	🥤	♿	HM, TR

RICHARDSON HIGHWAY

22 N/S 23 BLUEBERRY LAKE SRS	🏕	T		♿	C, F, TR
23 N/S 28 WORTHINGTON GLACIER SRS		T			TR
24 N/S 65 LITTLE TONSINA SRS	🏕	T	🥤		C, F
25 N/S 79 SQUIRREL CREEK SRS	🏕	T	🥤		C, F

#	Dir	Mile	Name	Facilities	Activities
26	N/S	117	DRY CREEK SRS	🏕 T 🚰 ♿	C, F, TR
27	N/S	200	FIELDING LAKE, SRS	🏕 T	BL, F, C
28	N/S	238	DONNELLY CREEK, SRS	🏕 T 🚰	C, TR
29	N/S	267	DELTA SRS	🏕 T 🚰	C
30	N/S	274	BIG DELTA SHP	🏕 T 🚰 ♿	HM, TR
31	N/S	278	QUARTZ LAKE SRA	🏕 T 🚰 ♿	BL, C, F, TR
32	N/S	305	BIRCH LAKE SRS	🏕 T	BL, C, F
33	N/S	321	HARDING LAKE SRA	🏕 T 🚰 ♿ 📞	BL, C, F, TR
34	N/S	323	SALCHA RIVER SRS	🏕 T 🚰	BL, C, F
35	N/S	—	CHENA RIVER SRS	🏕 T 🚰 ♿ 📞	C, F, TR

SEWARD HIGHWAY

#	Dir	Mile	Name	Facilities	Activities
36	N/S	115	POTTER SECTION HOUSE SHS	T 🚰 ♿	HM
37	E/W	111	MC HUGH CREEK PICNIC SITE	🏕 🚰 ♿	FG, TR, VP
38	E/W	101	BIRD CREEK CAMPGROUND	🏕 T 🚰 ♿	C, F, TR

STEESE HIGHWAY

#	Dir	Mile	Name	Facilities	Activities
39	E/W	39	UPPER CHATANIKA RIVER SRS	🏕 T 🚰	C, F

STERLING HIGHWAY

#	Dir	Mile	Name	Facilities	Activities
40	E/W	79	BING'S LANDING CG SRS	🏕 T 🚰 ♿	BL, C, F, TR
41	E/W	81	IZOAK WALTON CAMPGROUND	🏕 T 🚰 ♿	C, TR
42	E/W	85	SCOUT LAKE CAMPGROUND	🏕 T 🚰 ♿	C, F, TR
43	N/S	109	KASILOF RIVER SRS	🏕 T 🚰 ♿	C, F, TR
44	N/S	110	JOHNSON LAKE SRA	🏕 T 🚰 ♿	BL, C, F
45	N/S	117	CLAM GULCH SRA	🏕 T 🚰 ♿	C, F
46	N/S	135	NINILCHIK SRA	🏕 T 🚰 ♿	C, F
47	N/S	138	DEEP CREEK SRA	🏕 T 🚰 ♿	BL, C, F
48	N/S	151	STARISKI SRA	🏕 T 🚰 ♿	C
49	N/S	157	ANCHOR RIVER SRA	🏕 T 🚰 ♿	C, F
50	N/S	162	ANCHOR RIVER SRS	🏕 T 🚰 ♿	C, F

TOK CUTOFF

51	N/S	64			
PORCUPINE CREEK		SRS			C, F, TR
52	N/S	109			
EAGLE TRAIL SRS					C, HM, TR

ARIZONA

"Grand Canyon State"

Capital: Phoenix	**Largest City:** Phoenix
Population: 3,665,228	**Area:** 113,417 sq. mi.
Highest Point: 12,633 ft.	**Lowest Point:** 70 ft.

Date of Statehood: February 14, 1912

GENERAL INFORMATION

Additional Information On Services

- **Rest Area Hours.** Rest Areas are open 24 hours per day, seven days per week.
- **Welcome Center Hours.** The welcome center at Painted Cliffs is staffed 8 hours per day.
- **Tourist Information.** For tourist information call 1-800-247-4000. Arizona travel information is available at 1-800-842-8257.

Rest Area Usage Rules

- **Overnight Parking.** Overnight parking is permitted so long as travelers remain within the vehicle.
- **Camping.** Camping or sleeping outside of vehicle is not permitted.
- **Stay Limit.** No published limit.

Driving In Arizona

- **Emergencies.** For highway emergencies call 911 or dial 1-800-525-5555 to reach the Arizona Highway Patrol.
- **Open Container.** Open containers of alcoholic beverages in the passenger compartment of the vehicle are not permitted.
- **Seat Belts.** Seat belts are required for all occupants. Children 4 and under or less than 40 poinds must be in a child restraint system.
- **Helmets.** Motorcycle operators and passengers must wear helmets.
- **Road Conditions.** Dial 1-602-252-1010, ext. 7623.
- **Dust Storms.** For dust storm alerts, tune AM radio to 550/620/910.
- **First Aid.** First aid stations are located throughout the state and can also furnish emergency communications, such as telephone and radio.

ARIZONA REST AREAS

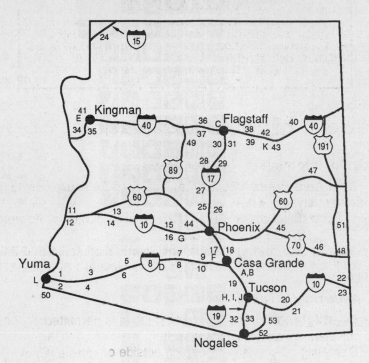

(8)	1/2 E/W 22 LIGURTA				
	3/4 E/W 56 MOHAWK	⛙ 🚻 🚰 🚾 ♿ ☎	GT, TP, VM
	5/6 E/W 84 SENTINEL	⛙ 🚻 🚰 🚾 ♿	GT, TP, VM
	7/8 E/W 123 GILA BEND	⛙ 🚻 🚰 🚾	TP
	9/10 E/W 150 TABLE TOP	⛙ T 🚰	TP
(10)	11/12 E/W 4 EHRENBERG	⛙ 🚻 🚰 🚾 ♿ ☎	TP
	13/14 E/W 52 BOUSE WASH	⛙ 🚻 🚰 🚾 ♿ ☎	GT, TP, VM
	15/16 E/W 86 BURNT WELLS	⛙ 🚻 🚰 🚾 ♿ ☎	GT, TP, VM
	17/18 E/W 183 SACATON	⛙ 🚻 🚰 🚾 ♿ ☎	GT, TP, VM
	19 E 217 PICACHO	⛙ 🚻 ♿	TP
	20/21 E/W 320 TEXAS CANYON	⛙ 🚻 🚰 🚾 ♿ ☎	GT, TP, VM
	22/23 E/W 388 SAN SIMON	⛙ 🚻 🚰 🚾 ♿	GT, TP, VM

Route	No.	Dir	Mile	Name	Notes
15	24	N	18	CEDAR POCKET	TP
17	25/26	N/S	228	DESERT HILLS	TP
	27	S	252	SUNSET POINT	GT, TP, VM
	28/29	N/S	298	MC GUIREVILLE	GT, TP, VM
	30/31	N/S	326	CHRISTENSEN	GT, TP, VM
19	32/33	N/S	34	CANOA RANCH	GT, TP, VM
40	34/35	E/W	22	HAVILAND	GT, TP, VM
	36/37	E/W	182	PARKS	GT, TP, VM
	38/39	E/W	236	METEOR CRATER	GT, TP, VM
	40	W	358	PAINTED CLIFFS	GT, TP, VM
BUS. 40	41	E/W	56	KINGMAN	
	42	E/W	225	WINSLOW	
	43	E/W	225	HOLBROOK	
60	44	E/W	117	HASSAYAMPA	GT
	45	E/W	243	SALT RIVER CANYON	GT
	46	E/W	385	SPRINGERVILLE	GT
34	47	E/W	338	SAFFORD	GT
	48	E/W	378	DUNCAN	GT
89	49	N/S	345	HELLS CANYON	
95	50	N/S		SAN LUIS	
191	51	N/S	162	CLIFTON	GT
82	52	N/S	19	PATAGONIA	
83	53	N/S	32	SONOITA	

ARIZONA SERVICE STATIONS WITH RV DUMP FACILITIES

A. Eloy

Name of Business: Truck Stops of America
Location: I-10, Exit 200 (Toltec Rd.)

Hours of Operation: 6 A.M. to 10 P.M.
RV Information: No charge for use of RV Dump. Waterfill and diesel fuel available. No propane.
Station Type: Truck Stop (EXXON).

B. Eloy
Name of Business: Flying J Travel Plaza
Location: I-10, Exit 208 (Sunshine Blvd.)
Hours of Operation: 24 hours per day.
RV Information: No charge for use of RV Dump. Waterfill, propane and diesel fuel available.
Station Type: Truck Stop (Conoco).

C. Flagstaff
Name of Business: Little America Truck Stop
Location: I-40, Exit 198 (Butler Avenue).
Hours of Operation: 24 hours per day.
RV Information: No charge for use of RV Dump. Waterfill and diesel fuel available. No Propane.
Station Type: Truck Stop (Sinclair).

D. Gila Bend
Name of Business: Holt's Texaco Truck Stop
Location: I-8, Exit 119 (Butterfield Trail).
Hours of Operation: 24 hours per day.
RV Information: No charge for use of RV Dump. Waterfill and diesel fuel available. No Propane.
Station Type: Truck Stop (Texaco).

E. Kingman
Name of Business: Flying J Travel Plaza
Location: I-40, Exit 53 (Andy Devine Ave.).
Hours of Operation: 24 hours per day.
RV Information: No charge for use of RV Dump ($2.00 if fuel not purchased). Waterfill and diesel fuel available. No Propane.
Station Type: Truck Stop (Conoco).

F. Stanfield
Name of Business: Vija Truck Stop
Location: I-8, Exit 151 (Highway 84).
Hours of Operation: 24 hours per day.
RV Information: $6.00 charge for use of RV Dump. Waterfill,

Arizona ■■■■■■■■■■■■■■■■■ 23

propane and diesel fuel available. Saguaro
RV Park is part of same facility.

Station Type: Truck Stop (Independent).

G. Tonopah

Name of Business: Minute Mart Texaco
Location: 1-10, Exit 94 (411th Avenue).
Hours of Operation: 24 hours per day.
RV Information: No charge for use of RV Dump ($3.00 if fuel
not purchased). Waterfill and diesel fuel
available. Propane available from 6A.M. to 6
P.M. only.
Station Type: Truck Stop (Texaco)

H. Tucson

Name of Business: Mr. T's Truck Stop
Location: I-10, Exit 268 (Craycroft).
Hours of Operation: 24 hours per day.
RV Information: No charge for use of RV Dump. Waterfill,
propane and diesel fuel available.
Station Type: Truck Stop (Independent).

I. Tucson

Name of Business: Tucson Truck Terminal (RV dump in
conjunction with Mr. T's).
Location: I-10, Exit 268 (Craycroft).
Hours of Operation: 24 hours per day.
RV Information: No charge for use of RV Dump. Waterfill,
propane and diesel fuel available.
Station Type: Truck Stop (Independent).

J. Tucson

Name of Business: Terminal Stations (RV dump is actually part of
Wilmont Bizaar and Swap Meet).
Location: I-10, Exit 269 (Wilmont).
Hours of Operation: 24 hours per day.
RV Information: $2.00 charge for use of RV Dump. Waterfill
and diesel fuel available. No propane.
Station Type: Truck Stop (Texaco).

K. Winslow

Name of Business: Giant Express
Location: I-40, Exit 253.

Hours of Operation:	24 hours per day.
RV Information:	No charge for use of RV Dump. Waterfill, propane and diesel fuel available.
Station Type:	Truck Stop (Independent).

L. Yuma

Name of Business:	Barney's Texaco
Location:	I-40, Exit 253 (4th Avenue and 29th Street).
Hours of Operation:	6 A.M. to 10 P.M.
RV Information:	No charge for use of RV Dump ($3.00 if less than 8 gal. of fuel purchased). Waterfill and diesel fuel available. No propane.
Station Type:	Service station with mini-mart (Texaco).

ARKANSAS

"The Land of Opportunity"

Capital: Little Rock	**Largest City:** Little Rock
Population: 2,350,725	**Area:** 51,945 sq. mi.
Highest Point: 2,750 ft.	**Lowest Point:** 55 ft.

Date of Statehood: June 15, 1836

GENERAL INFORMATION

Additional Information On Services

- **Rest Area Hours.** Rest areas are open 24 hours per day, seven days per week.
- **Welcome Center Hours.** Welcome centers are manned 8 A.M. to 5 P.M. in the winter months and 7 A.M. to 7 P.M. from May through September.
- **Truck Parking.** Rest areas 14 and 15 have separate buildings, facilities and parking for truckers.
- **Tourist Information.** For tourist information call 1-800-NATURAL or 1-501-682-7777.

Rest Area Usage Rules

- **Overnight Parking.** Overnight parking is permitted for safety reasons only.
- **Camping.** Overnight camping is not allowed.
- **Stay Limit.** No usage time limit.

Driving In Arkansas

- **Emergencies.** For highway emergencies call 911 or dial the local police or local number for the state police.
- **Open Container.** Drinking in public places, e.g., parks, highways, rest areas, parking lots, etc., is illegal. However, there is no open container law.
- **Seat Belts.** All front seat occupants must wear seat belts. Children 5 and under must be in safety restraints. Children 4 and 5 may use safety belts instead of federally approved child restraints.
- **Helmets.** Motorcycle riders must wear helmets.
- **Road Conditions.** Dial 1-501-569-2000.

ARKANSAS REST AREAS

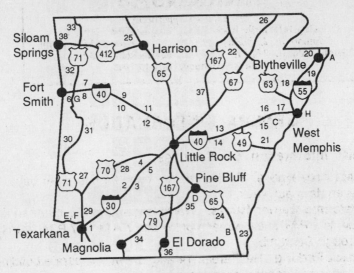

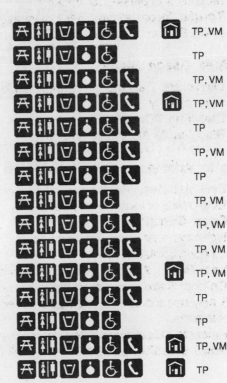

(30) 1 E TEXARKANA	⛵	🚻	🗑	🍼	♿	☎	🏠	TP, VM
2/3 E/W 17 MI S OF ARKADELPHIA	⛵	🚻	🗑	🍼	♿			TP
4/5 E/W 7 MI SE OF MALVERN	⛵	🚻	🗑	🍼	♿	☎		TP, VM
(40) 6 E 2 MI E OF STATE LINE	⛵	🚻	🗑	🍼	♿	☎	🏠	TP, VM
7/8 E/W 1 MI W OF OZARK	⛵	🚻	🗑	🍼	♿	☎		TP
9/10 E/W 6 MI E OF LAMAR	⛵	🚻	🗑	🍼	♿	☎		TP, VM
11/12 E/W 1 MI E OF MORRILTON	⛵	🚻	🗑	🍼	♿	☎		TP
13/14 E/W 46 MI E OF LITTLE ROCK	⛵	🚻	🗑	🍼	♿			TP, VM
15 E 5 MI W OF FORREST CITY	⛵	🚻	🗑	🍼	♿	☎		TP, VM
16 W 2 MI E OF FORREST CITY	⛵	🚻	🗑	🍼	♿	☎		TP, VM
17 W 6 MI W OF WEST MEMPHIS	⛵	🚻	🗑	🍼	♿	☎	🏠	TP, VM
(55) 18 S 27 MI N OF W MEMPHIS	⛵	🚻	🗑	🍼	♿			TP
19 N 22 MI S OF BLYTHEVILLE	⛵	🚻	🗑	🍼	♿			TP
20 S 2 MI N OF BLYTHEVILLE	⛵	🚻	🗑	🍼	♿	☎	🏠	TP, VM
(49) 21 W 3 MI W OF STATE LINE	⛵	🚻	🗑	🍼	♿	☎	🏠	TP

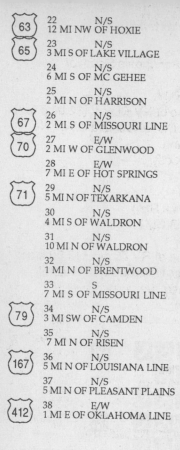

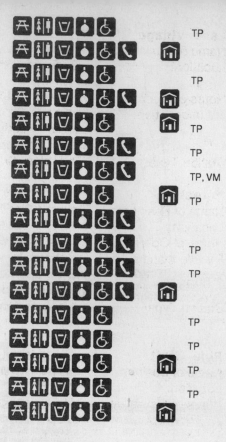

Route	#	Direction / Location	Facilities	Notes
63	22	N/S – 12 MI NW OF HOXIE		TP
65	23	N/S – 3 MI S OF LAKE VILLAGE		
	24	N/S – 6 MI S OF MC GEHEE		TP
	25	N/S – 2 MI N OF HARRISON		
67	26	N/S – 2 MI S OF MISSOURI LINE		TP
70	27	E/W – 2 MI W OF GLENWOOD		TP
	28	E/W – 7 MI E OF HOT SPRINGS		TP, VM
71	29	N/S – 5 MI N OF TEXARKANA		TP
	30	N/S – 4 MI S OF WALDRON		
	31	N/S – 10 MI N OF WALDRON		TP
	32	N/S – 1 MI N OF BRENTWOOD		TP
	33	S – 7 MI S OF MISSOURI LINE		
79	34	N/S – 3 MI SW OF CAMDEN		TP
	35	N/S – 7 MI N OF RISEN		TP
167	36	N/S – 5 MI N OF LOUISIANA LINE		TP
	37	N/S – 5 MI N OF PLEASANT PLAINS		TP
412	38	E/W – 1 MI E OF OKLAHOMA LINE		

ARKANSAS SERVICE STATIONS WITH RV DUMP FACILITIES

A. Blytheville

Name of Business: Blytheville Truck Plaza
Location: I-55, Exit 63 (U.S. 61).
Hours of Operation: 24 hours per day.
RV Information: No charge for use of RV Dump ($5.00 if fuel not purchased). Waterfill and diesel fuel available. No propane. Knights of the Road RV Park is adjacent, but RV dump station is with Truck Stop.
Station Type: Truck stop (Citgo).

B . Lake Village
Name of Business: Al's All In One
Location: US 65 and US 82 (1/2 mile South of junction).
Hours of Operation: 5:30 A.M. to 10 P.M.
RV Information: No charge for use of RV Dump ($2.00 if fuel not purchased). Diesel fuel available. No waterfill or propane.
Station Type: Truck stop (Conoco).

C . Palestine
Name of Business: Brewer's Fina Kwik Stop
Location: I-40, Exit 233 (AR 261).
Hours of Operation: 24 hours per day.
RV Information: No charge for use of RV Dump ($2.00 if not staying at RV park on property). Waterfill, propane and diesel fuel available.
Station Type: Truck stop (Fina).

D . Pine Bluff
Name of Business: Big Red Travel Plaza
Location: I-365, Exit 34 (US 270).
Hours of Operation: 24 hours per day.
RV Information: No charge for use of RV Dump. Propane and diesel fuel available. No waterfill.
Station Type: Truck stop (Fina).

E . Texarkana
Name of Business: Texarkana 76 Auto/Truck Plaza
Location: I-30, Exit 223A (State Line Avenue).
Hours of Operation: 24 hours per day.
RV Information: No charge for use of RV Dump. Waterfill and diesel fuel available. No propane.
Station Type: Truck stop (Unocal 76)

F . Texarkana
Name of Business: Flying J Travel Plaza
Location: I-30, Exit 7
Hours of Operation: 24 hours per day.
RV Information: No charge for use of RV Dump. Waterfill, propane and diesel fuel available.
Station Type: Truck stop (Conoco)

G. Van Buren

Name of Business:	Van Buren 76 Auto/Truck Center
Location:	I-40, Exit 5 (AR 59).
Hours of Operation:	24 hours per day.
RV Information:	No charge for use of RV Dump. Diesel fuel available. No waterfill or propane.
Station Type:	Truck stop (Unocal 76)

H. West Memphis

Name of Business:	Flying J Travel Plaza
Location:	I-40, Exit 280 (Club Rd.) and I-55, Exit 4 (Club Rd.).
Hours of Operation:	24 hours per day.
RV Information:	No charge for use of RV Dump. Waterfill, propane and diesel fuel available.
Station Type:	Truck stop (Conoco)

CALIFORNIA

"Golden State"

Capital: Sacramento	**Largest City:** Los Angeles
Population: 29,760,021	**Area:** 156,361 sq. mi.
Highest Point: 14,494 ft.	**Lowest Point:** -282 ft.

Date of Statehood: September 9, 1850

GENERAL INFORMATION

Additional Information On Services

- **Rest Area Hours.** Rest areas open 24 hours per day.
- **Welcome Center Hours.** Welcome center at rest area 28 is open from May through October, 9 A.M. to 7 P.M. Welcome center at reat area 89 is open summer only.
- **Tourist Information.** For tourist information call 1-800-862-2543.

Rest Area Usage Rules

- **Overnight Parking.** No overnight parking.
- **Camping.** Camping is not permitted.
- **Stay Limit.** Parking limited to 6 hours.
- **Tents.** Pitching of tents or similar apparatus is prohibited.
- **Fires.** Building or maintaining campfires or other open fires is prohibited.
- **Barbecues.** Small portable butane, propane or charcoal hibachis, barbecues or braziers may be used if placed on the ground or on designated stands.

Driving In California

- **Emergencies.** For highway emergencies call 911 (may not be operable in all counties) or dial the local police or local number for the highway patrol.
- **Open Container.** Open containers of alcoholic beverages in the passenger compartment of the vehicle are not permitted.
- **Seat Belts.** Seat belts are required for all occupants. Children 4 and under or less than 40 lbs. must be in a child restraint system.
- **Helmets.** Motorcycle riders must wear helmets.
- **Road Conditions.** Dial 1-916-653-7623.

CALIFORNIA REST AREAS

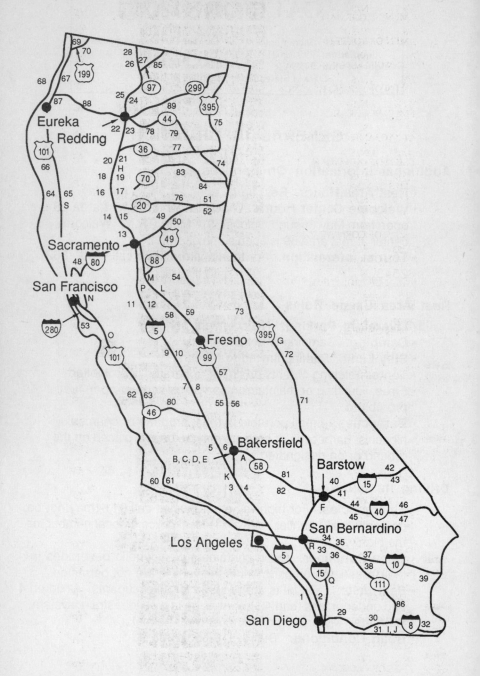

California

Route	Mile	Dir	Location	Facilities	
5	1/2	N/S	6 MI N OF OCEANSIDE	⛱ 🚻 ♨ 🍼 ♿ ☎ 🅿	TP
	3/4	N/S	4 MI N OF GORMAN	⛱ 🚻 ♨ 🍼 ♿ ☎ 🅿	TP
	5/6	N/S	2 MI N OF ROUTE 58	⛱ 🚻 ♨ 🍼 ♿ ☎	TP
	7/8	N/S	1 MI N OF LASSEN AVE.	⛱ 🚻 ♨ 🍼 ♿ ☎	TP
	9/10	N/S	1 MI N OF FRESNO CO LINE	⛱ 🚻 ♨ 🍼 ♿ ☎	TP
	11/12	N/S	1 MI S OF I-580 JCT	⛱ 🚻 ♨ 🍼 ♿ ☎ 🅿	TP
	13	S	AT SACRAMENTO METRO AP	⛱ 🚻 ♨ 🍼 ♿ ☎	TP
	14/15	N/S	1 MI N OF DUNNIGAN	⛱ 🚻 ♨ 🍼 ♿ ☎	TP
	16/17	N/S	2 MI S OF MAXWELL	⛱ 🚻 ♨ 🍼 ♿ ☎	TP
	18/19	N/S	2 MI S OF ARTOIS	⛱ 🚻 ♨ 🍼 ♿ ☎ 🅿	TP
	20/21	N/S	1 MI N OF CORNING RD	⛱ 🚻 ♨ 🍼 ♿ ☎	TP
	22/23	N/S	4 MI N OF RED BLUFF	⛱ 🚻 ♨ 🍼 ♿ ☎	TP
	24	N	9 MI N OF PROJECT CITY	⛱ 🚻 ♨ 🍼 ♿ ☎	TP
	25	S	1 MI N OF LAKEHEAD	⛱ 🚻 ♨ 🍼 ♿ ☎	TP
	26/27	N/S	6 MI N OF WEED	⛱ 🚻 ♨ 🍼 ♿ ☎	TP
	28	N/S	10 MI N OF YREKA	⛱ 🚻 ♨ 🍼 ♿ ☎ 🏠	TP
8	29	E/W	3 MI E OF PINE VALLEY	⛱ 🚻 ♨ 🍼 ♿ ☎ 🅿	TP
	30/31	E/W	6 MI W OF EL CENTRO	⛱ 🚻 ♨ 🍼 ♿ ☎ 🅿	TP
	32	E/W	20 MI W OF ARIZONA ST LINE	🚻 ♨ 🍼	TP
10	33	E	1 MI W OF CALIMESA	⛱ 🚻 ♨ 🍼 ♿ ☎	TP
	34	W	3 MI W OF BEAUMONT	⛱ 🚻 ♨ 🍼 ♿ ☎	TP
	35/36	E/W	1 MI W OF WHITEWATER	⛱ 🚻 ♨ 🍼 ♿ ☎	TP
	37/38	E/W	15 MI E OF INDIO	⛱ 🚻 ♨ 🍼 ♿ 🅿	TP
	39	E/W	15 MI W OF BLYTHE	⛱ 🚻 ♨ 🍼 ♿ ☎ 🅿	TP
15	40/41	N/S	30 MI E OF BARSTOW	⛱ 🚻 ♨ 🍼 ♿ ☎	TP
	42/43	N/S	26 MI W OF NEVADA LINE	⛱ 🚻 ♨ 🍼 ♿ ☎	TP
40	44/45	E/W	9 MI E OF NEWBERRY	⛱ 🚻 ♨ 🍼 ♿ ☎	TP
	46/47	E/W	45 MI W OF NEEDLES	⛱ 🚻 ♨ 🍼 ♿ ☎	TP
80	48	W	7 MI E OF VALLEJO	⛱ 🚻 ♨ 🍼 ♿ ☎	TP

Route	#	Dir	Location	Facilities	
	49/50	E/W	BTN SAW MILL & GOLD RUN	🛉 restroom, water, trash, handicap, phone, RV	TP
	51/52	E/W	DONNER PASS	picnic, restroom, water, trash, handicap, phone	TP
280	53	N	NEAR SAN FRANCISCO RES	picnic, restroom, water, trash, handicap, phone	TP
49	54	N/S	4 MI S OF ANGELS CAMP	picnic, restroom	TP
99	55/56	N/S	2 MI N OF TIPTON	picnic, restroom, water, trash, handicap, phone	TP
	57	N/S	30 MI N OF TIPTON	picnic, restroom, water, trash, handicap, phone, RV	TP
	58/59	N/S	2 MI S OF TURLOCK	picnic, restroom, water, trash, handicap, phone	TP
101	60/61	N/S	S END OF GAVIOTA TUNNEL	picnic, restroom, water, trash, handicap, phone	TP
	62/63	N/S	8 MI N OF SAN MIGUEL	picnic, restroom, water, trash, handicap, phone	TP
	64	N	8 MI S OF LAYTONVILLE	picnic, restroom, water, trash, handicap, phone	TP
	65	S	11 MI S OF LAYTONVILLE	picnic, restroom, water, trash, handicap, phone	TP
	66	N/S	3 MI S OF CUMMINGS	picnic, restroom, water, trash, handicap, phone	TP
	67	N	.5 MI S OF PATRICKS PT	picnic, restroom, water, trash, handicap, phone, RV	TP
	68	S	1 MI S OF SEAWOOD DR	picnic, restroom, water, trash, handicap, phone	TP
199	69/70	N/S	3 MI S OF OREGON LINE	picnic, restroom, water, trash, handicap, RV	TP
395	71	N/S	17 MI S OF RTE 395/190 JCT	picnic, restroom, water, trash, handicap, phone, RV	TP
	72	N/S	10 MI N OF INDEPENDENCE	picnic, restroom, water, trash, handicap, phone, RV	TP
	73	N/S	2 MI S OF CRESTVIEW	picnic, restroom, water, trash, handicap, phone	TP
	74	N/S	8 MI N OF MILFORD	picnic, restroom, water, trash, handicap, phone	TP
	75	N/S	12 MI S OF RAVENDALE	picnic, restroom, water, handicap	
20	76	E/W	4 MI E OF WASHINGTON JCT.	picnic, restroom, handicap	TP
36	77	E/W	4 MI E OF CHESTER	picnic, restroom, water, trash, handicap	TP
44	78	E/W	3 MI E OF SHINGLETOWN	picnic, restroom, water, trash, handicap	TP
	79	E/W	28 MI NW OF SUSANVILLE	picnic, restroom, water, trash	TP
46	80	E/W	1 MI E OF RTE 41/46 JCT	picnic, restroom, water, trash, handicap, phone	TP
58	81/82	E/W	4 MI W OF BORON	picnic, restroom, water, trash, handicap, phone, RV	TP
70	83	E/W	7 MI E OF QUINCY	picnic, restroom, water, trash, handicap, phone	TP
	84	E/W	3 MI E OF PORTOLA	picnic, restroom, water, trash, handicap, phone	TP
97	85	N/S	20 MI N OF WEED	picnic, restroom, water, trash, handicap, phone	TP

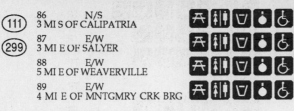
CAILFORNIA SERVICE STATIONS WITH RV DUMP FACILITIES

A. Arvin

Name of Business:	Truckstops of America
Location:	I-5, Lake Isabella Exit.
Hours of Operation:	24 hours per day.
RV Information:	No charge for use of RV Dump. Waterfill and diesel fuel available. No propane.
Station Type:	Truck stop (BP Gas).

B. Bakersfield

Name of Business:	Texaco Star Mart
Location:	White Lane and Gosford (between I-5 and US-99).
Hours of Operation:	24 hours per day.
RV Information:	No charge for use of RV Dump ($6.00 if fuel not purchased). Waterfill and diesel fuel available. No propane.
Station Type:	Service station with mini-mart (Texaco)

C. Bakersfield

Name of Business:	Bruce's Buttonwillow 76 Truck Stop
Location:	I-5, CA-58 Exit.
Hours of Operation:	24 hours per day.
RV Information:	No charge for use of RV Dump. Waterfill and diesel fuel available. No propane.
Station Type:	Truck stop (Unocal 76).

D. Bakersfield

Name of Business:	Texaco Star Mart
Location:	CA-99, Olive Drive Exit East.
Hours of Operation:	24 hours per day.
RV Information:	No charge for use of RV Dump ($6.00 if fuel

not purchased). Waterfill and diesel fuel available. No propane.

Station Type: Service station with mini-mart (Texaco).

E. Bakersfield

Name of Business: Flying J Travel Plaza
Location: US 99, Merced Exit (11 mi. N of Bakersfield).
Hours of Operation: 24 hours per day.
RV Information: No charge for use of RV Dump. Waterfill, propane and diesel fuel available.
Station Type: Truck stop (Conoco).

F. Barstow

Name of Business: Rip Griffin Travel Center
Location: I-15, Lenwood Rd. Exit (mile marker 69).
Hours of Operation: 24 hours per day.
RV Information: No charge for use of RV Dump. Waterfill, propane and diesel fuel available.
Station Type: Truck stop (Texaco).

G. Bishop

Name of Business: Inyo Shell Y-Mart
Location: US-395 and US-6.
Hours of Operation: 24 hours per day.
RV Information: No charge for use of RV Dump. Waterfill and diesel fuel available. No propane.
Station Type: Truck stop (Shell).

H. Corning

Name of Business: Burns Brothers Travel Stop
Location: I-5, South Avenue Exit.
Hours of Operation: 24 hours per day.
RV Information: No charge for use of RV Dump ($3.00 if fuel not purchased). Waterfill, propane and diesel fuel available.
Station Type: Truck stop (Independent).

I. El Centro

Name of Business: 111 Truck Plaza
Location: I-8, CA-111 Exit.
Hours of Operation: 24 hours per day.
RV Information: No charge for use of RV Dump. Diesel fuel available. No waterfill or propane.

Station Type: Truck stop (Texaco).

J. El Centro
Name of Business: Imperial 8 Travel Center
Location: I-8, 4th Street Exit South.
Hours of Operation: 24 hours per day.
RV Information: $3.00 charge for use of RV Dump. Waterfill,
                     propane and diesel fuel available.
Station Type: Truck stop (Independent).

K. Frazier Park
Name of Business: Flying J Travel Plaza
Location: I-5, Frazier Park Exit.
Hours of Operation: 24 hours per day.
RV Information: No charge for use of RV Dump. Waterfill,
                     propane and diesel fuel available.
Station Type: Truck stop (Conoco).

L. Livingston
Name of Business: M & M Mini Market
Location: CA-99, Shank's Exit (south for two blocks).
Hours of Operation: 5 A.M. to Midnight.
RV Information: No charge for use of RV Dump (a donation to
                     the Lion's Club is requested). Waterfill
                     available. No propane or diesel fuel.
Station Type: Service station with mini-mart (Beacon).

M. Lodi
Name of Business: Flame Liquor
Location: CA-12, between Kettleman Lane and Ham
                     Lane.
Hours of Operation: 6 A.M. to 11 P.M.
RV Information: $3.00 charge for use of RV Dump. Waterfill
                     and diesel fuel available. No propane.
Station Type: Service station with mini-mart (EXXON).

N. Oakland
Name of Business: San Francisco-Oakland Truck Stop
Location: I-880, 66th Avenue Exit (3/4 mile S of
                     Coliseum).
Hours of Operation: 6 A.M. to 6 P.M.
RV Information: $10.00 charge for use of RV Dump. Waterfill,
                     propane and diesel fuel available.

California ━━━━━━━━━━━━━━━━━━━━━━━━━━━━

Station Type: Truck stop (Unocal 76).

O. Salinas

Name of Business:	Sidhu Unocal 76
Location:	US-101, Airport Blvd. Exit.
Hours of Operation:	24 hours per day.
RV Information:	No charge for use of RV Dump ($5.00 if fuel not purchased). Waterfill, propane and diesel fuel available.
Station Type:	Service station with mini-mart (Unocal 76).

P. Santa Nella

Name of Business:	Pea Soup Anderson Texaco
Location:	I-5, Santa Nella Exit.
Hours of Operation:	6 A.M. to 2 A.M.
RV Information:	No charge for use of RV Dump. Waterfill and diesel fuel available. No propane.
Station Type:	Service station with mini-mart (Texaco).

Q. Temecula

Name of Business:	Bob's Unocal 76
Location:	I-15, Rancho California Rd. Exit West.
Hours of Operation:	5 A.M. to midnight.
RV Information:	No charge for use of RV Dump ($5.00 if fuel not purchased). Waterfill and diesel fuel available. No propane.
Station Type:	Truck stop (Unocal 76)

R. Thousand Palms

Name of Business:	Flying J Travel Plaza
Location:	I-10, Ramon Road Exit.
Hours of Operation:	24 hours per day.
RV Information:	No charge for use of RV Dump. Propane and diesel fuel available. No waterfill.
Station Type:	Truck stop (Conoco)

S. Ukiak

Name of Business:	Chevron
Location:	US-101, Perkins Street Exit West.
Hours of Operation:	24 hours per day.
RV Information:	No charge for use of RV Dump. Waterfill and diesel fuel available. No Propane.
Station Type:	Service station with mini-mart (Chevron).

COLORADO

"Centennial State"

Capital:	Denver	**Largest City:**	Denver
Population:	3,294,394	**Area:**	103,794 sq. mi.
Highest Point:	14,433 ft.	**Lowest Point:**	3,350
	Date of Statehood:	August 1, 1876	

GENERAL INFORMATION

Additional Information On Services

- **Rest Area Hours.** Rest Areas are open 24 hours per day, seven days per week. RV dump stations are often closed in the winter.
- **Welcome Center Hours.** Welcome centers are staffed from 9 A.M. to 5 P.M. seven days per week between October and May. The remainder of the year, centers are staffed daily from 8 A.M. to 6 P.M.
- **Tourist Information.** For tourist information call 1-800-433-2656.

Rest Area Usage Rules

- **Overnight Parking.** No overnight parking.
- **Camping.** Camping is not permitted.
- **Stay Limit.** No published limit.

Driving In Colorado

- **Emergencies.** For highway emergencies call 911 (may not be operable in all counties) or dial the local police or local number for the highway patrol.
- **Open Container.** No state-wide open container law, but some jurisdictions treat open containers as an offense.
- **Seat Belts.** Seat belts are required for all front seat occupants. Children 4 and under must be in a child restraint system.
- **Helmets.** Helmets are not required for motorcyclists.
- **Road Conditions.** Dial 1-303-639-1234 throughout Colorado and
1-303-639-1111 within two hours of Denver.

COLORADO REST AREAS

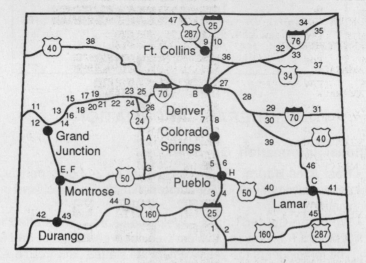

(25)	1/2 RUGBY	N/S	37	🅰 🚻	🚰 ♿	🏕				TP
	3/4 BRANTZELL	N/S	81	🅰 🚻	🚰 ♿					TP
	5/6 PINON	N/S	113	🅰 🚻 🚮	🚰 ♿	🏕				TP
	7/8 LARKSPUR	N/S	170	🅰 🚻 🚮	🚰 ♿	📞				TP
	9/10 POUDRE RIVER	N/S	266	🅰 🚻 🚮	🚰 ♿	📞				TP
(70)	11/12 FRUITA	E/W	19	🅰 🚻 🚮	🚰 ♿	📞 🏕 🏠				TP
	13/14 RIFLE	E/W	90	🅰 🚻 🚮	🚰 ♿	📞 🏕 🏠				TP
	15/16 GLENWOOD SPRINGS	E/W	115	🅰 🚻 🚮	🚰 ♿	📞				TP
	17/18 E OF GLENWOOD SPRINGS	E/W	119	🅰 🚻 🚮	🚰 ♿					TP
	19/20 GRIZZLY CREEK	E/W	121	🅰 🚻 🚮	🚰 ♿					TP
	21 HANGING LAKE	E	126	🅰 🚻	🚰 ♿					TP
	22 BAR RANCH	E	128	🅰 🚻 🚮	🚰 ♿					TP
	23/24 EDWARDS	E/W	163	🅰 🚻 🚮	🚰 ♿	🏕				TP
	25/26 VAIL PASS	E/W	193	🅰 🚻 🚮	🚰 ♿	📞				TP
	27 BENNETT	W	306	🅰 🚻 🚮	🚰 ♿	📞				TP

Route	Exit	Dir.	Mile	Facilities	
	28 DEER TRAIL	W	331	(picnic, restroom, water, fuel, handicap, phone)	TP
	29/30 ARRIBA	E/W	383	(picnic, restroom, water, fuel, handicap, phone, RV)	TP
76	31 BURLINGTON	W	437	(picnic, restroom, water, fuel, handicap, phone, RV, shelter)	TP
	32/33 PREWITT RESEVOIR	E/W	108	(picnic, restroom, water, fuel, handicap)	TP
	34 TAMARACK	E/W	155	(picnic, restroom, water, fuel, handicap, phone, RV)	TP
	35 TAMARACK	E/W	155	(picnic, restroom, water, fuel, handicap, phone)	TP
34	36 .4 MI W OF RTE 144	E/W		(picnic, restroom, water, fuel)	TP
	37 2 MI E OF ECKLEY	E/W		(picnic, restroom, water, fuel)	TP
40	38 12 MI E OF CRAIG	E/W		(picnic, restroom, water, fuel)	TP
	39 8 MI E OF HUGO	E/W		(picnic, restroom, water, fuel)	TP
50	40 9 MI E OF LA JUNTA	E/W		(picnic, restroom, fuel, handicap, RV)	TP
	41 4 MI E OF HOLLY	E/W		(picnic, restroom, fuel, handicap, RV)	TP
160	42 2.5 MI W OF MESA VERDA ENT	E/W		(picnic, restroom, water, fuel)	TP
	43 .5 MI W OF BAYFIELD	E/W		(picnic, restroom, water, fuel)	TP
	44 5 MI E OF SOUTH FORK	E/W		(picnic, restroom, water, fuel, phone)	TP
	45 RTE 287 JCT	E/W		(picnic, restroom, water)	TP
287	46 2 MI E OF EADS	N/S		(picnic, restroom, water, fuel)	TP
	47 AT WYOMING STATE LINE	N/S		(picnic, restroom, water, fuel)	TP

COLORADO SERVICE STATIONS WITH RV DUMP FACILITIES

A. Buena Vista

Name of Business:	Buena Vista Amoco
Location:	US-24 South (South side of city).
Hours of Operation:	7 A.M. to 10 P.M. (8 P.M. winter).
RV Information:	$2.00 charge for use of RV Dump ($5.00 if fuel not purchased). Waterfill and diesel fuel available. No propane.
Station Type:	Service station with mini-mart (Amoco).

B. Denver/Wheat Ridge

Name of Business: Denver West Travel Center
Location: I-70, Ward Road Exit (mile marker 262).
Hours of Operation: 24 hours per day.
RV Information: No charge for use of RV Dump ($5.00 if fuel not purchased). Waterfill and diesel fuel available. No propane.
Station Type: Truck stop (Sinclair).

C. Lamar

Name of Business: The Pit Stop
Location: US-287 & US 50.
Hours of Operation: 6 A.M. to 10 P.M.
RV Information: No charge for use of RV Dump. Waterfill, propane and diesel fuel available.
Station Type: Service station with mini-mart (Diamond Shamrock).

D. Monte Vista

Name of Business: Monte Vista Co-op
Location: US-160, 1/2 mile east of Monte Vista.
Hours of Operation: 7 A.M. to 7 P.M. (6 P.M. in winter).
RV Information: No charge for use of RV Dump. Waterfill, propane and diesel fuel available.
Station Type: Truck stop (Farmland Co-op).

E. Montrose

Name of Business: Sun Valley Truck Stop
Location: US-50 North (North side of city limits).
Hours of Operation: 24 hours per day.
RV Information: No charge for use of RV Dump. Waterfill and diesel fuel available. No propane.
Station Type: Truck stop (Texaco)

F. Montrose

Name of Business: Blair's Truck Stop
Location: US-50 East (in city).
Hours of Operation: 24 hours per day.
RV Information: No charge for use of RV Dump. Waterfill and diesel fuel available. No propane.
Station Type: Truck stop (Conoco).

G. Poncha Springs

Name of Business: Shavano Snack Mart Truck Stop
Location: US-50 & US-285.
Hours of Operation: 7 A.M. to 9 P.M.
RV Information: No charge for use of RV Dump. Waterfill and diesel fuel available. No propane.
Station Type: Truck stop (Amoco).

H. Pueblo

Name of Business: Cliff Brice Station
Location: Pueblo Blvd., South of Thacher.
Hours of Operation: 6 A.M. to 11:15 P.M.
RV Information: No charge for use of RV Dump. Waterfill and diesel fuel available. No propane.
Station Type: Service station with mini-mart (Diamond Shamrock).

CONNECTICUT

"Constitution State"

Capital: Hartford	Largest City: Bridgeport
Population: 3,287,116	Area: 4,862 sq. mi.
Highest Point: 2,380 ft.	Lowest Point: Sea Level

Date of Statehood: January 9, 1788

GENERAL INFORMATION

Additional Information On Services

- **Rest Area Hours.** Rest areas are open 24 hours per day, seven days per week.
- **Welcome Center Hours.** Welcome centers are staffed May through October, from approximately 10 A.M. to 6 P.M., seven days per week.
- **Tourist Information.** For tourist information call 1-800-CT-BOUND.

Rest Area Usage Rules

- **Overnight Parking.** No overnight parking.
- **Camping.** Camping or sleeping outside of vehicle is not permitted.
- **Stay Limit.** No published limit.

Driving In Connecticut

- **Emergencies.** For highway emergencies call 911.
- **Open Container.** No open container law.
- **Seat Belts.** Operator and front seat passengers must wear seat belts. Children under the age of four must be in a child restraint system. For children between ages 1 and 4 years old, a safety belt in the rear seat may be used instead of a child restraint system.
- **Helmets.** No motorcycle helmet law.
- **Road Conditions.** Dial 1-203-594-2650.
- **Snow Tires.** Studded snow tires may only be used from November 15 through April 30.

CONNECTICUT REST AREAS

 84

1 E 2 MI E OF NEW YORK LINE										TP
2 E/W 8 MI E OF WATERBURY										TP
3/4 E/W 23 MI NE OF HARTFORD										TP

91

5 S 6 MI S OF MERIDEN										TP
6 N 3 MI N OF MERIDEN										TP

95

7 S 16 MI E OF NEW LONDON								TP

CONNECTICUT SERVICE STATIONS WITH RV DUMP FACILITIES

A. New Haven

Name of Business:	New Haven 95 East Truck Stop
Location:	I-95, Exit 56.
Hours of Operation:	24 hours per day.
RV Information:	$3.00 charge for use of RV Dump. Waterfill and diesel fuel available. No propane.
Station Type:	Truck Stop (Independent).

DELAWARE

"Diamond State"

Capital: Dover   Largest City: Wilmington
Population: 666,168   Area: 1,982 sq. mi.
Highest Point: 442 ft.   Lowest Point: Sea Level
Date of Statehood: December 7, 1787

GENERAL INFORMATION

Additional Information On Services

- **Rest Area Hours.** Rest Areas are open 24 hours per day, seven days per week.
- **Welcome Center Hours.** Welcome centers are staffed from 8 A.M. to 8 P.M. seven days per week during the summer. The remainder of the year, centers are staffed daily from 8 A.M. to 5 P.M.
- **Service Plaza.** Rest area 2 is a tollroad service plaza.
- **Tourist Information.** For tourist information call 1-800-282-8667 in Delaware and 1-800-441-8846 from outside Delaware.

Rest Area Usage Rules

- **Overnight Parking.** Overnight parking is allowed, but not encouraged.
- **Camping.** Camping or sleeping outside of vehicle is not permitted.
- **Stay Limit.** No published limit.

Driving In Delaware

- **Emergencies.** For highway emergencies call 911 (may not be operable in all counties) or dial the local police or local number for the highway patrol. Police also monitor CB channel 9.
- **Open Container.** No open container law, but it is an offense to drink and drive.
- **Seat Belts.** Seat belts are required for all front seat occupants. Children 3 and under must be in a child restraint system.
- **Helmets.** Motorcycle operators and passengers must wear helmets and eye protection
- **Road Conditions.** Dial 1-302-739-5851.

DELAWARE REST AREAS

Dover

1   N/S
2 MI S OF SMYRNA

2   N/S
BETWEEN RTE 896 & RTE 273

TP

BBB, EX, MO,
MF, RR, SB,
SK, TB, TP

FLORIDA

"Sunshine State"

Capital: Tallahassee	**Largest City:** Jacksonville
Population: 12,937,926	**Area:** 54,090 sq. mi.
Highest Point: 345 ft.	**Lowest Point:** Sea Level

Date of Statehood: March 3, 1845

GENERAL INFORMATION

Additional Information On Services

- **Rest Area Hours.** Rest Areas are open 24 hours per day, seven days per week.
- **Welcome Center Hours.** Welcome centers are staffed from 8 A.M. to 5 P.M. seven days per week .
- **Toll Road Service Plazas.** Areas 63 through 70 are service plazas along Florida's Turnpike.
- **Tourist Information.** For tourist information call 1-904-487-1462.

Rest Area Usage Rules

- **Overnight Parking.** No overnight parking.
- **Camping.** Camping or sleeping outside of vehicle is not permitted.
- **Stay Limit.** Parking limited to 3 hours.

Driving In Florida

- **Emergencies.** For highway emergencies call 911 or dial 1-904-488-8676 to reach highway patrol headquarters.
- **Open Container.** Open containers of alcoholic beverages in the passenger compartment of the vehicle are not permitted.
- **Seat Belts.** Operator and front seat passengers under 16 years of age must wear seat belts. Children age five and under must be in a child restraint system. For children three and under, this restraint must be a separate carrier.
- **Helmets.** Motorcycle riders must wear helmets.
- **Road Conditions.** Dial local or state police.

FLORIDA'S REST AREAS

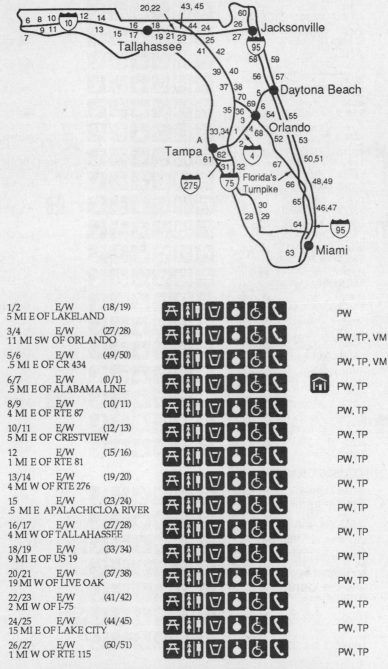

4	1/2 E/W (18/19) 5 MI E OF LAKELAND	🏕 🚻 🚰 🍼 ♿ ☎					PW
	3/4 E/W (27/28) 11 MI SW OF ORLANDO	🏕 🚻 🚰 🍼 ♿ ☎					PW, TP, VM
	5/6 E/W (49/50) .5 MI E OF CR 434	🏕 🚻 🚰 🍼 ♿ ☎					PW, TP, VM
10	6/7 E/W (0/1) .5 MI E OF ALABAMA LINE	🏕 🚻 🚰 🍼 ♿ ☎			🏠		PW, TP
	8/9 E/W (10/11) 4 MI E OF RTE 87	🏕 🚻 🚰 🍼 ♿ ☎					PW, TP
	10/11 E/W (12/13) 5 MI E OF CRESTVIEW	🏕 🚻 🚰 🍼 ♿ ☎					PW, TP
	12 E/W (15/16) 1 MI E OF RTE 81	🏕 🚻 🚰 🍼 ♿ ☎					PW, TP
	13/14 E/W (19/20) 4 MI W OF RTE 276	🏕 🚻 🚰 🍼 ♿ ☎					PW, TP
	15 E/W (23/24) .5 MI E APALACHICLOA RIVER	🏕 🚻 🚰 🍼 ♿ ☎					PW, TP
	16/17 E/W (27/28) 4 MI W OF TALLAHASSEE	🏕 🚻 🚰 🍼 ♿ ☎					PW, TP
	18/19 E/W (33/34) 9 MI E OF US 19	🏕 🚻 🚰 🍼 ♿ ☎					PW, TP
	20/21 E/W (37/38) 19 MI W OF LIVE OAK	🏕 🚻 🚰 🍼 ♿ ☎					PW, TP
	22/23 E/W (41/42) 2 MI W OF I-75	🏕 🚻 🚰 🍼 ♿ ☎					PW, TP
	24/25 E/W (44/45) 15 MI E OF LAKE CITY	🏕 🚻 🚰 🍼 ♿ ☎					PW, TP
	26/27 E/W (50/51) 1 MI W OF RTE 115	🏕 🚻 🚰 🍼 ♿ ☎					PW, TP

I-75

Exit	Dir	(Mile)	Location	Services
28/29	N/S	(21)	5 MI W OF FT. MYERS	PW, TP, VM
30	N/S	(28)	5 MI N OF PUNTA GORDA	PW, TP, VM
31/32	N/S	(45/46)	1.5 MI N OF MANATEE RIVER	PW, TP, VM
33/34	N/S	(57/58)	12 MI N OF TAMPA	PW, TP, VM
35/36	N/S	(61/62)	7 MI S OF BUSHNELL	PW, TP, VM
37/38	N/S	(67/68)	6 MI S OF OCALA	PW, TP, VM
39/40	N/S	(73/74)	5 MI S OF GAINESVILLE	PW, TP
41/42	N/S	(79/80)	17 MI S OF LAKE CITY	PW, TP
43	S	(84/85)	11 MI N OF I-10	PW, TP
44	N	(84/85)	8 MI N OF I-10	PW, TP
45	S		1 MI S OF GEORGIA LINE	PW, TP

I-95

Exit	Dir	(Mile)	Location	Services
46/47	N/S	(61/62)	3 MI S OF STUART	PW, TP
48/49	N/S	(66/67)	3 MI N OF FT. PIERCE	PW, TP
50/51	N/S	(69/70)	5 MI S OF PALM BAY	PW, TP
52/53	N/S	(81/82)	2 MI N OF RTE 46	PW, TP, VM
54/55	N/S	(84/85)	3 MI S OF I-4	PW, TP, VM
56/57	N/S	(92/93)	5 MI N OF US-1	PW, TP, VM
58/59	N/S	(96/97)	14 MI N OF ST AUGUSTINE	PW, TP
60	S		3.5 MI S OF GEORGIA LINE	PW, TP

I-275

Exit	Dir	(Mile)	Location	Services
61	N/S	(1/2)	NORTH END OF SKYWAY BDGE	PW, TP
62	N/S	(2/3)	1 MI E OF US-41	PW, TP

FLORIDA'S TURNPIKE

Exit	Dir	Mile	Location	Services
63	N/S	19	SNAPPER CREEK SERVICE PL	BK, DD, RR, EX, TP
64	N/S	65	POMPANO SERVICE PLAZA	MF, POP, SB, SH, SK, TC, TP
65	N/S	94	WEST PALM BEACH SERVICE PL	BBB, BK, MO, NA, SH, TC, TP
66	N/S	144	FORT PIERCE SERVICE PLAZA	BK, MF, SB, SH, TC, TP
67	N/S	184	FORT DRUM SERVICE PLAZA	BBB, BK, NA, TC, TP, TX
68	N/S	229	CANOE CREEK SERVICE PLAZA	BK, CH, MF, POP, TP
69	N/S	263	TURKEY LAKE SERVICE PLAZA	BK, SB, MO, TC, TP

FLORIDA SERVICE STATIONS WITH RV DUMP FACILITIES

A. Tampa

Name of Business: Tampa 301 Truck Stop
Location: I-4, Exit 6.
Hours of Operation: 24 hours per day.
RV Information: No charge for use of RV Dump ($15.00 if fuel not purchased). Waterfill, propane and diesel fuel available.
Station Type: Truck Stop (Citgo).

GEORGIA

"Peach State"

Capital:	Atlanta	Largest City:	Atlanta
Population:	6,478,216	Area:	58,073 sq. mi.
Highest Point:	4,784 ft.	Lowest Point:	Sea Level

Date of Statehood: January 2, 1788

GENERAL INFORMATION

Additional Information On Services

- **Rest Area Hours.** Rest Areas are open 24 hours per day, seven days per week.
- **Welcome Center.** Welcome centers are staffed from 8:30 A.M. until 5:30 P.M. seven days per week. Restrooms are open from 7:30 A.M. until 11:30 P.M., seven days a week. Both services are closed on Thanksgiving, Christmas and New Year's day.
- **Vending Machines.** All areas have vending machines. Vending machines are open between 7:30 A.M. and midnight, seven days a week.
- **Tourist Information.** For tourist information call 1-404-656-3590.

Rest Area Usage Rules

- **Overnight Parking.** No overnight parking.
- **Camping.** Camping or sleeping outside of vehicle is not permitted.
- **Stay Limit.** No published limit.

Driving In Georgia

- **Emergencies.** For highway emergencies call 911 or dial 1-404-624-6077 for the state patrol.
- **Open Container.** Open containers of alcoholic beverages in the vehicle are not permitted unless in the possession of a passenger or in the trunk or other locked compartment inaccessible to the operator.
- **Seat Belts.** Seat belts are required for all front seat occupants. Children 4 and under must be in a child restraint system. For children 3 and 4 years old, a seat belt may be substituted for the restraint system.

- **Helmets.** Motorcycle riders must wear helmets.
- **Road Conditions.** Dial 1-404-656-5267.

GEORGIA REST AREAS

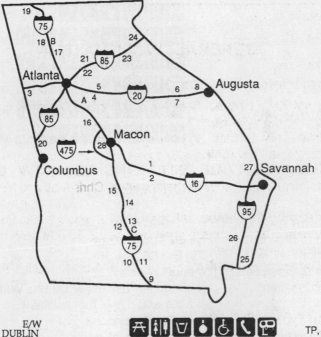

16	1/2 E/W W OF DUBLIN		🏕️🚻♿️🍼♿️📞🚏	TP, VM
20	3 E ALABAMA LINE	3	🏕️🚻♿️🍼♿️📞🚏🏠	TP, VM
	4/5 E/W MADISON	108	🏕️🚻♿️🍼♿️📞🚏	TP, VM
	6/7 E/W APPLING	182	🏕️🚻♿️🍼♿️📞🚏	TP, VM
	8 W SOUTH CAROLINA LINE	203	🏕️🚻♿️🍼♿️📞🚏🏠	TP, VM
75	9 N FLORIDA LINE	4	🏕️🚻♿️🍼♿️📞🚏🏠	TP, VM
	10/11 N/S ADEL	49	🏕️🚻♿️🍼♿️📞	TP, VM
	12/13 N/S ASHBURN	86/76	🏕️🚻♿️🍼♿️📞🚏	TP, VM
	14 N VIENNA	111	🏕️🚻♿️🍼♿️📞🚏	TP, VM
	15 S UNADILLA	120	🏕️🚻♿️🍼♿️📞🚏	TP, VM
	16 S FORSYTH	181	🏕️🚻♿️🍼♿️📞🚏🏠	TP, VM

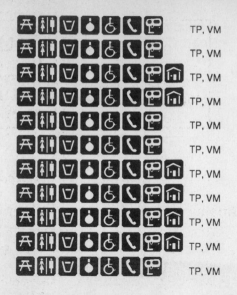

17	N	324	ADAIRSVILLE	TP, VM
18	S	336	RESACA	TP, VM
19	S	365	CHATTANOOGA	TP, VM
(85) 20	N	5	ALABAMA LINE	TP, VM
21/22	N/S	109	LAWRENCEVILLE	TP, VM
23	N	160	CARNESVILLE	TP, VM
24	S	177	SOUTH CAROLINA LINE	TP, VM
(95) 25	N	1	FLORIDA LINE	TP, VM
26	S	43	DARIEN	TP, VM
27	S	112	SOUTH CAROLINA LINE	TP, VM
(475) 28	N	8	MACON	TP, VM

GEORGIA SERVICE STATIONS WITH RV DUMP FACILITIES

A. Jackson

Name of Business:	Flying J Travel Plaza
Location:	I-75, Exit 66 (GA 36).
Hours of Operation:	24 hours per day.
RV Information:	No charge for use of RV Dump. Waterfill, propane and diesel fuel available.
Station Type:	Truck Stop (Conoco).

B. Resaca

Name of Business:	Flying J Travel Plaza
Location:	I-75, Exit 133.
Hours of Operation:	24 hours per day.
RV Information:	No charge for use of RV Dump. Waterfill, propane and diesel fuel available.
Station Type:	Truck Stop (Conoco).

C. Tifton

Name of Business:	Tifton Travel Center
Location:	I-75, Exit 16 (South Central Avenue).
Hours of Operation:	24 hours per day.
RV Information:	No charge for use of RV Dump. Waterfill, propane and diesel fuel available.
Station Type:	Truck Stop (Shell).

IDAHO
"Gem State"

Capital:	Boise	**Largest City:**	Boise
Population:	1,108,229	**Area:**	83,557 sq. mi.
Highest Point:	12,622 ft.	**Lowest Point:**	770 ft.

Date of Statehood: July 3, 1890

GENERAL INFORMATION

Additional Information On Services

- **Rest Area Hours.** Rest Areas are open 24 hours per day, seven days per week. Areas 2, 26 and 31 may be closed in winter.
- **Welcome Center Hours.** Welcome centers are staffed seven days per week from 9 A.M. to 7 P.M. May 1st through Labor Day and from 9 A.M. to 4 P.M. Labor Day to May 1st.
- **Vending Machines.** Most rest areas have vending machines and some have newspaper vending.
- **Tourist Information.** For tourist information call 1-800-635-7820.

Rest Area Usage Rules

- **Overnight Parking.** Overnight parking permitted.
- **Camping.** Camping or sleeping outside of vehicle is not permitted.
- **Stay Limit.** Parking limited to 8 hours at interstate facilities, 16 hours at all others.
- **Motorcycles.** Motorcycles may not be driven on trails within the rest area.

Driving In Idaho

- **Emergencies.** For highway emergencies call 911 (may not be operable in all counties) or dial 1-800-233-1212 for the state police.
- **Open Container.** Open containers of distilled alcoholic beverages (liquor, wine, etc.) are not permitted in the vehicle. Open containers of brewed alcoholic beverages (beer) are permitted generally, but certain cities have ordnances prohibiting these also.

- **Seat Belts.** Seat belts are required for all front seat occupants. Children 4 and under or less than 40 pounds must be in a child restraint system.
- **Helmets.** Motorcycle operators and passengers18 and under must wear helmets.
- **Road Conditions.** Dial 1-208-336-6600.

IDAHO REST AREAS

Route	No.	Dir.	Mile	Name	Amenities
15	1	N	7	CHERRY CREEK	PW, TP, WR
	2	S	25	MALAD SUMMIT	PW, TP, WR
	3/4	N/S	59	INKOM	PW, TP
	5/6	N/S	101	BLACKFOOT	AS, PW, TP, TR, WR
	7	N/S	167	DUBOIS	PW, TP
84	8	E	1	SNAKE RIVER VIEW	PW, TP, VP, WR
	9/10	E/W	62	BLACKS CREEK	HM, PW, TP
	11/12	E/W	133	BLISS	PW, TP
	13/14	E/W	173	US-93 JCT	PW, TP
	15/16	E/W	229	COTTERELL	PW, TP
	17/18	E/W	269	JUNIPER	PW, TP
86	19	E	19	COLDWATER HILL	HM, PW, TP, VP, WR
	20	W	31	MASSACRE ROCKS	HM, PW, TP, VP, WR
90	21/22	E/W	8	HUETTER	PW, WR
12	23	E/W	28	LENORE	BL, HM, PW, TP
20	24	E/W	178	TIMMERMAN	PW, TP
	25	E/W	265	BIG LOST RIVER	HM, PW
	26	E/W	357	CLARK HILL	PW, TP, VP, WR
26	27	E/W	184	HAGERMAN	PW
30	28	N/S	101	MIDVALE HILL	PW, TP
95	29	N/S	189	SHEEP CREEK	FG, PW, TP

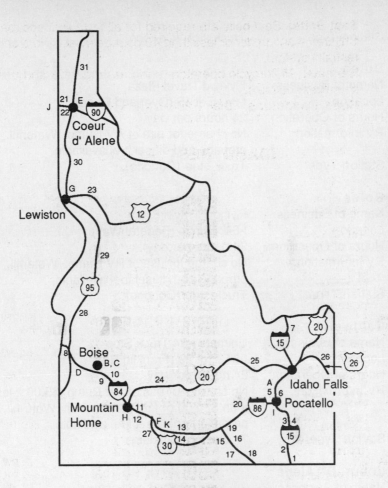

30	N/S	371	PW, TP, TR
MINERAL MOUNTAIN			
31	N/S	452	PW
HOODOO CREEK			

IDAHO SERVICE STATIONS WITH RV DUMP FACILITIES

A. Blackfoot

Name of Business:	Flying J Travel Plaza
Location:	I-15, Exit 93 (Burgender Road).
Hours of Operation:	24 hours per day.
RV Information:	No charge for use of RV Dump. Waterfill, propane and diesel fuel available.

Station Type: Truck stop (Conoco).

B. Boise

Name of Business:	Flying J Travel Plaza
Location:	I-84, Exit 15 (Overland Road).
Hours of Operation:	24 hours per day.
RV Information:	No charge for use of RV Dump. Waterfill, propane and diesel fuel available.
Station Type:	Truck stop (Conoco).

C. Boise

Name of Business:	Flying J Travel Plaza
Location:	I-84, Exit 54 (Federal Way).
Hours of Operation:	24 hours per day.
RV Information:	No charge for use of RV Dump. Waterfill, propane and diesel fuel available.
Station Type:	Truck stop (Conoco).

D. Caldwell

Name of Business:	Unimarc I-84 Truck Stop
Location:	I-84, Exit 29 (Franklin Rd.).
Hours of Operation:	24 hours per day.
RV Information:	No charge for use of RV Dump ($5.00 if less than $20.00 of fuel purchased). Waterfill, propane and diesel fuel available.
Station Type:	Truck stop (Sinclair).

E. Coeur D' Alene

Name of Business:	Big Y Truck Stop
Location:	I-90, Exit 15 (Sherman Avenue).
Hours of Operation:	24 hours per day.
RV Information:	No charge for use of RV Dump. Waterfill, propane and diesel fuel available.
Station Type:	Truck stop (Independent).

F. Jerome

Name of Business:	Honker's Mini Mart.
Location:	I-84, Exit 168 (South Lincoln).
Hours of Operation:	24 hours per day.
RV Information:	No charge for use of RV Dump ($5.00 if fuel not purchased). Waterfill, propane and diesel fuel available.
Station Type:	Truck stop (Sinclair).

G. Lewiston

Name of Business:	Flying J Travel Plaza
Location:	US-12 & US-95.
Hours of Operation:	24 hours per day.
RV Information:	No charge for use of RV Dump. Waterfill, propane and diesel fuel available.
Station Type:	Truck stop (Conoco).

H. Mountain Home

Name of Business:	Pilot Travel Center
Location:	I-84, Exit 95 (US-20).
Hours of Operation:	24 hours per day.
RV Information:	No charge for use of RV Dump. Diesel fuel available. No waterfill or propane.
Station Type:	Truck stop (Pilot Oil).

I. Pocatello

Name of Business:	Cowboy Hitching Post
Location:	I-86, Exit 61 (US-91, Yellowstone Road.
Hours of Operation:	24 hours per day.
RV Information:	No charge for use of RV Dump. Waterfill, propane and diesel fuel available.
Station Type:	Truck stop (Conoco).

J. Post Falls

Name of Business:	Flying J Travel Plaza
Location:	I-90, Exit 2 (Pleasant View).
Hours of Operation:	24 hours per day.
RV Information:	No charge for use of RV Dump. Waterfill, propane and diesel fuel available.
Station Type:	Truck stop (Conoco).

K. Twin Falls

Name of Business:	Petro 2 #82
Location:	I-84, Exit 173 (US-93)
Hours of Operation:	24 hours per day.
RV Information:	$1.00 charge for use of RV Dump ($3.00 if fuel not purchased). Waterfill, propane and diesel fuel available.
Station Type:	Truck stop (Chevron).

ILLINOIS

"Prairie State"

Capital: Springfield   Largest City: Chicago
Population: 11,450,000   Area: 55,748 sq. mi.
Highest Point: 1,235 ft.   Lowest Point: 279 ft.
Date of Statehood: December 3, 1818

GENERAL INFORMATION

Additional Information On Services

- **Rest Area Hours.** Rest areas are open 24 hours per day, seven days per week.
- **Welcome Center Hours.** Welcome centers are staffed approximately 8 hours per day.
- **Toll Road Oases.** Areas 50 and 52 through 57 are Toll Road Oases.
- **TDD.** Telecommunications device for the deaf available at 6, 7, 14, 15, 22, 23, and 51.
- **Tourist Information.** For tourist information call 1-800-223-0121.

Rest Area Usage Rules

- **Overnight Parking.** Overnight parking permitted.
- **Camping.** Camping and erection of tents is not permitted.
- **Stay Limit.** No published limit, but length of stay may be limited when capacities of the facilities are approached or exceeded.
- **Fires.** Wood and charcoal fires are prohibited. Commercial or camping type gas stoves are permitted.
- **Aquatic Activities.** Swimming, bathing or fishing in any waters within or adjacent to the rest area is prohibited.

Driving In Illinois

- **Emergencies.** For highway emergencies call 911 (may not be operable in all counties) or dial the local police or local number for the highway patrol.
- **Open Container.** Open containers of alcoholic beverages in the vehicle are not permitted.
- **Seat Belts.** Seat belts are required for all front seat occupants. Children 4 and under must be in a child restraint system. Children 4 through 6 must be in a child restraint system or seat belt.

- **Helmets.** No motorcycle helmet law.
- **Road Conditions.** Dial 1-800-452-IDOT.

ILLINOIS REST AREAS

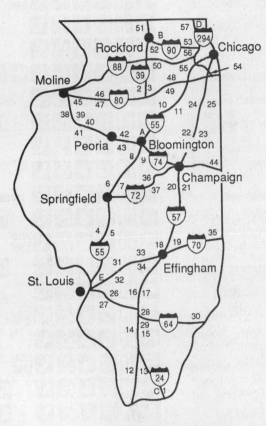

	1 N 37
24	2 MI N OF KENTUCKY LINE
39	2/3 N/S 16 MI N OF LA SALLE
55	4/5 N/S 65 25 MI S OF SPRINGFIELD
	6/7 N/S 102 5 MI N OF SPRINGFIELD
	8/9 N/S 149 10 MI S OF BLOOMINGTON
	10/11 N/S 194 3 MI S OF PONTIAC

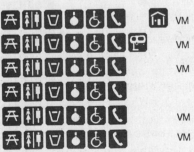

Route	Exit	Dir	Mile	Location	Facilities
57	12	S	32	32 MI N OF MISSOURI LINE	VM
	13	N	32	32 MI N OF MISSOURI LINE	VM
	14/15	N/S	76	REND LAKE	VM
	16/17	N/S	114	2 MI S OF SALEM	VM
	18/19	N/S	166	4 MI N OF EFFINGHAM	VM
	20/21	N/S	221	14 MI S OF CHAMPAIGN	
	22/23	N/S	268	18 MI N OF RANTOUL	VM
	24/25	N/S	332	17 MI N OF KANKAKEE	VM
64	26	W	25	25 MI E OF ST. LOUIS	VM
	27	E	25	25 MI E OF ST. LOUIS	VM
	28/29	E/W	84	4 MI E MT VERNON	VM
	30	W	130	1 MI W OF INDIANA LINE	
70	31	W	27	27 MI E OF ST. LOUIS	VM
	32	E	27	27 MI E OF ST. LOUIS	VM
	33/34	E/W	87	8 MI W OF EFFINGHAM	VM
	35	W	149	7 MI W OF INDIANA LINE	VM
72	36/37	E/W	50	12 MI E OF DECATUR	
74	38/39	E/W	28	28 MI SE OF ROCK ISLAND	VM
	40/41	E/W	62	12 MI E OF GALESBURG	VM
	42/43	E/W	114	14 MI W OF BLOOMINGTON	VM
	44	W	208	7 MI W OF DANVILLE	VM
80	45	E	1	1 MI E OF IOWA LINE	
	46/47	E/W	51	5 MI W OF PRINCETON	VM
	48/49	E/W	118	8 MI W OF I-55 JCT	VM
88	50	E/W	107	DEKALB OASIS	McD, MO
90	51	S	2	2 MI S OF WISCONSIN LINE	VM
	52	E/W	54	BELVIDERE OASIS	McD, MO
	53	E/W	5	DES PLAINES OASIS	McD, MO
294	54	N/S	1	LINCOLN OASIS	BK, POP, MO

62

55	N/S	26		WD, MO
HINDALE OASIS				
56	N/S	38		BK, MO
O'HARE OASIS				
57	N/S	60		WD, MO
LAKE FOREST OASIS				

ILLINOIS SERVICE STATIONS WITH RV DUMP FACILITIES

A. Bloomington
Name of Business: Bloomington 76 Auto/Truck Plaza
Location: I-55 & 74, Exit 160A (Market Street, IL-9).
Hours of Operation: 24 hours per day.
RV Information: No charge for use of RV Dump. Waterfill and diesel fuel available. No propane.
Station Type: Truck Stop (Unocal 76).

B. Hampshire
Name of Business: Elgin West Truck Stop
Location: I-90, Hampshire-Marengo Exit (US-20, mile marker 36).
Hours of Operation: 24 hours per day.
RV Information: No charge for use of RV Dump. Waterfill and diesel fuel available. No propane.
Station Type: Truck Stop (Unocal 76).

C. Metropolis
Name of Business: Metropolis Truck/Travel Plaza
Location: I-24, Exit 37 (US-45).
Hours of Operation: 24 hours per day.
RV Information: $5.00 charge for use of RV Dump. Diesel fuel available. No waterfill or propane.
Station Type: Truck Stop (BP).

D. Rusell
Name of Business: Truckstops of America
Location: I-94, Exit 1 (Russell Road)
Hours of Operation: 24 hours per day.
RV Information: No charge for use of RV Dump. Waterfill and diesel fuel available. No propane.
Station Type: Truck Stop (Mobil).

E. Troy

Name of Business:	St. Louis East Truck Plaza
Location:	I-55 & 70, Exit 18 (Edwardsville Road, IL 162)
Hours of Operation:	24 hours per day.
RV Information:	No charge for use of RV Dump. Waterfill, propane and diesel fuel available.
Station Type:	Truck Stop (Unocal 76).

INDIANA
"Hoosier State"

Capital: Indianapolis   Largest City: Indianapolis
Population: 5,544,159   Area: 36,097 sq. mi.
Highest Point: 1,257 ft.   Lowest Point: 320 ft.
Date of Statehood: December 11, 1816

GENERAL INFORMATION

Additional Information On Services

- **Rest Area Hours.** Rest Areas are open 24 hours per day, seven days per week.
- **Welcome Center Hours.** Welcome centers are staffed from 8 A.M. to 5 P.M., seven days per week.
- **Toll Road Service Plazas.** Areas 36 through 45 are toll road service plazas along the Indiana East-West Toll Road.
- **Tourist Information.** For tourist information call 1-800-289-ON IN.

Rest Area Usage Rules

- **Overnight Parking.** No overnight parking.
- **Camping.** Camping is not permitted.
- **Stay Limit.** No published limit.

Driving In Indiana

- **Emergencies.** For highway emergencies call 911 (may not be operable in all counties) or dial State Police Headquarters at 1-317-232-8250.
- **Open Container.** No open container law.
- **Seat Belts.** Seat belts are required for all front seat occupants. Children 3 and under must be in a child restraint system. Children 3 through 5 must be in a child restraint system or seat belt.
- **Helmets.** Motorcycle operators and passengers 18 and under must wear helmets.
- **Road Conditions.** Dial 1-317-232-8300.

INDIANA REST AREAS

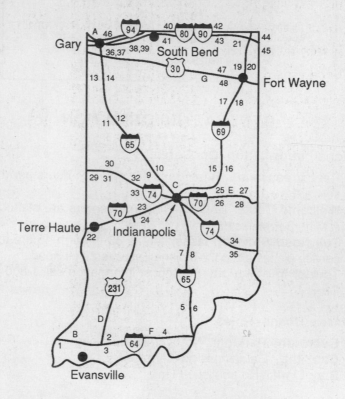

🛡️ **64**	1 E 6 7 MI E OF ILLINOIS LINE	🏕️	🚻	🗑️	🍼	♿	📞	🏠	TP, VM
	2/3 E/W 58 2 MI E OF US-231	🏕️	🚻	🗑️	🍼	♿	📞		TP, VM
	4 W 112 2 MI W OF GEORGETOWN INT	🏕️	🚻	🗑️	🍼	♿	📞		TP, VM
🛡️ **65**	5/6 N/S 22 3 MI N OF HENRYVILLE	🏕️	🚻	🗑️	🍼	♿	📞		TP, VM
	7/8 N/S 73 3 MI S OF TAYLORSVILLE	🏕️	🚻	🗑️	🍼	♿	📞		TP, VM
	9/10 N/S 149 5 MI N OF LEBANON	🏕️	🚻	🗑️	🍼		📞		TP, VM
	11/12 N/S 195 23 MI N OF LAFAYETTE	🏕️	🚻	🗑️	🍼		📞		TP, VM
	13/14 N/S 231 23 MI S OF MERRIVILLE	🏕️	🚻	🗑️	🍼	♿	📞		TP, VM
🛡️ **69**	15/16 N/S 50 1 MI N OF US-35	🏕️	🚻	🗑️	🍼	♿	📞		TP, VM
	17/18 N/S 91 18 MI S OF FT. WAYNE	🏕️	🚻	🗑️	🍼	♿	📞		TP, VM

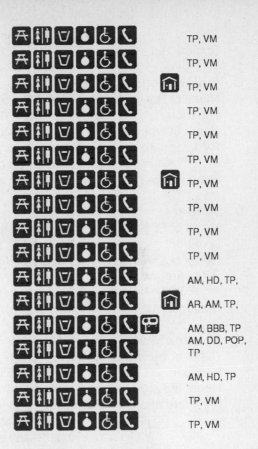

Exit	Dir	Mile	Facilities	Codes
19/20	N/S	124	5 MI S OF AUBURN	TP, VM
21	S	145	4 MI S OF ANGOLA	TP, VM
22	E	1	1 MI E OF ILLINOIS LINE	TP, VM
23/24	E/W	64	5 MI W OF PLAINFIELD EXIT	TP, VM
25/26	E/W	107/114	E OF GREENFIELD EXIT	TP, VM
27/28	E/W	144	5 MI E OF RICHMOND	TP, VM
29	E	1	1 MI E OF ILLINOIS LINE	TP, VM
30/31	E/W	22	22 MI E OF ILLINOIS LINE	TP, VM
32/33	E/W	56	4 MI W OF LIZTON	TP, VM
34/35	E/W	152	20 MI W OF OHIO LINE	TP, VM
36/37	E/W	22	SERVICE AREA 1	AM, HD, TP,
38/39	E/W	56	SERVICE AREA 3	AR, AM, TP,
40/41	E/W	90	SERVICE AREA 5	AM, BBB, TP
42/43	E/W	126	SERVICE AREA 7	AM, DD, POP, TP
44/45	E/W	146	SERVICE AREA 8	AM, HD, TP
46	E/W	42	MICHIGAN CITY	TP, VM
47/48	E/W	41	7 MI E OF FT. WAYNE	TP, VM

Route shields shown: I-70, I-74, I-90, 94, US-30

INDIANA SERVICE STATIONS WITH RV DUMP FACILITIES

A. Gary

Name of Business:	Flying J Travel Plaza
Location:	I-80 & 94, Exit 9A (Grant Street).
Hours of Operation:	24 hours per day.
RV Information:	No charge for use of RV Dump. Waterfill, propane and diesel fuel available.
Station Type:	Truck stop (Conoco)

B. Haubstadt

Name of Business:	Lakeview Truck Plaza
Location:	I-64, Exit 25B (1 mile north on US-41)
Hours of Operation:	24 hours per day.
RV Information:	$5.00 charge for use of RV Dump. Waterfill

and diesel fuel available. No propane.

Station Type: Truck stop (Citgo)

C. Indianapolis
Name of Business: Flying J Travel Plaza
Location: I-465, Exit 4 (Harding Street, IN-37).
Hours of Operation: 24 hours per day.
RV Information: No charge for use of RV Dump. Waterfill, propane and diesel fuel available.
Station Type: Truck stop (Conoco)

D. Jasper
Name of Business: HRJ Automotive Service
Location: I-64, Exit 57 (12 miles north on US-231).
Hours of Operation: 24 hours per day.
RV Information: No charge for use of RV Dump. Waterfill and diesel fuel available. No propane.
Station Type: Truck stop (Unocal 76).

E. Knightstown
Name of Business: Gas America
Location: I-70, Exit 115 (IN-109).
Hours of Operation: 24 hours per day.
RV Information: No charge for use of RV Dump if remaining overnight at campground on property. Propane and diesel fuel available. No waterfill.
Station Type: Truck stop (Independent).

F. Leavenworth
Name of Business: Louisville West Stop 92
Location: I-64, Exit 92 (IN-66).
Hours of Operation: 24 hours per day.
RV Information: $5.00 charge for use of RV Dump. Waterfill and diesel fuel available. No propane.
Station Type: Truck stop (BP)

G. Silver Lake
Name of Business: McClure Oil
Location: IN-15, 2 miles north of Silver Lake.
Hours of Operation: 24 hours per day.
RV Information: No charge for use of RV Dump. Propane and diesel fuel available. No waterfill.
Station Type: Truck stop (Marathon).

IOWA
"Hawkeye State"

Capital: Des Moines	Largest City: Des Moines
Population: 2,913,387	Area: 55,941 sq. mi.
Highest Point: 1,670 ft.	Lowest Point: 480 ft.

Date of Statehood: December 28, 1846

GENERAL INFORMATION

Additional Information On Services

- **Rest Area Hours.** Rest Areas are open 24 hours per day, seven days per week.
- **Welcome Center Hours.** Welcome centers are staffed from 8 A.M. to 7 P.M., May through September.
- **Shelters.** All rest areas have sheltered tables.
- **Truck Parking.** All rest areas have truck parking, but parking at areas 12, 13, 26, 27, 28 and 29 is limited.
- **Tourist Information.** For tourist information call 1-800-345-IOWA.

Rest Area Usage Rules

- **Overnight Parking.** No overnight parking.
- **Camping.** Camping is not permitted.
- **Stay Limit.** Parking limited to 5 hours

Driving In Iowa

- **Emergencies.** For highway emergencies call 1-800-525-5555 to reach Iowa State Patrol.
- **Open Container.** Open containers of alcoholic beverages in the vehicle are not permitted.
- **Seat Belts.** Seat belts are required for all front seat occupants. Children 4 and under must be in a child restraint system.
- **Helmets.** Helmets not required for motorcyclists.
- **Road Conditions.** Dial 1-515-288-1047.

IOWA REST AREAS

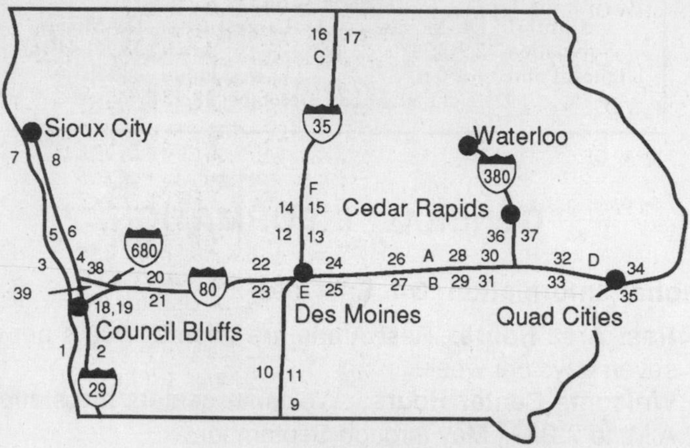

29	1/2	N/S	37	FG, TP, WR
	10 MI S OF COUNCIL BLUFFS			
	3/4	N/S	78	FG, TP, WR
	4 MI N OF MISSOURI VALLEY			
	5/6	N/S	108	FG, TP, WR
	6 MI S OF ONAWA			
	7	S	139	FG, TP, WR
	10 MI S OF SIOUX CITY			
	8	N	139	FG, TP, WR
	10 MI S OF SIOUX CITY			
35	9	N	6	FG, TP, WR
	6 MI N OF MISSOURI LINE			
	10/11	N/S	31	FG, TP, WR
	2 MI S OF OSCEOLA			
	12/13	N/S	93	FG, TP, WR
	8 MI N OF DESMOINES			
	14/15	N/S	119	FG, TP, WR
	6 MI N OF AMES			
	16	S	195	FG, TP, WR
	2 MI N OF CLEAR LAKE			
	17	N	195	FG, TP, WR
	2 MI N OF CLEAR LAKE			
80	18	W	19	FG, TP, WR, VM
	3 MI SW OF NEOLA			
	19	E	19	FG, TP, WR, VM
	3 MI SW OF NEOLA			
	20/21	E/W	80	FG, TP, WR
	4 MI E OF ADAIR			
	22	W	118	FG, TP, WR, VM
	3 MI W OF DES MIONES			
	23	E	118	FG, TP, WR, VM
	3 MI W OF DES MIONES			
	24/25	E/W	147	FG, TP, WR
	10 MI E OF DES MIONES			

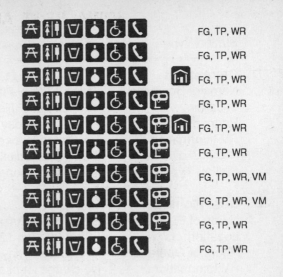

Location	Facilities
26/27 E/W 180 16 MI E OF NEWTON	FG, TP, WR
28 W 206 36 MI W OF IOWA CITY	FG, TP, WR
29 E 206 36 MI W OF IOWA CITY	FG, TP, WR
30/31 E/W 234 8 MI W OF IOWA CITY	FG, TP, WR
32 W 269 27 MI W OF DAVENPORT	FG, TP, WR
33 E 269 27 MI W OF DAVENPORT	FG, TP, WR
34 W 299 7 MI W OF ILLINOIS LINE	FG, TP, WR, VM
35 E 299 7 MI W OF ILLINOIS LINE	FG, TP, WR, VM
(380) 36/37 N/S 5 MI S OF CEDAR RAPIDS	FG, TP, WR
(680) 38/39 E/W 4 MI E OF I-29	FG, TP, WR

IOWA SERVICE STATIONS WITH RV DUMP FACILITIES

A. Brooklyn
Name of Business: Coastal Mart
Location: I-80, Exit 201 (IA-21).
Hours of Operation: 24 hours per day.
RV Information: No charge for use of RV Dump ($2.00 if not remaining at campground on property). Waterfill and diesel fuel available. No propane.
Station Type: Truck stop (Coastal).

B. Brooklyn
Name of Business: Brooklyn 80 Amoco
Location: I-80, Exit 197 (County Road V-18).
Hours of Operation: 24 hours per day.
RV Information: $1.00 charge for use of RV Dump. Waterfill, propane and diesel fuel available.
Station Type: Truck stop (Amoco).

C. Clear Lake
Name of Business: Coastal Mart
Location: I-35, Exit 194 (US-18 East)
Hours of Operation: 24 hours per day.
RV Information: No charge for use of RV Dump. Waterfill, and

diesel fuel available. No propane.
Station Type: Truck stop (Coastal).

D. Davenport
Name of Business: Flying J Travel Plaza
Location: I-80, Exit 292 (Northwest Blvd.).
Hours of Operation: 24 hours per day.
RV Information: No charge for use of RV Dump. Waterfill, propane and diesel fuel available.
Station Type: Truck stop (Conoco).

E. Des Moines
Name of Business: Bar B Travel Plaza
Location: I-35 & 80, Exit 126 (Douglas Avenue).
Hours of Operation: 24 hours per day.
RV Information: No charge for use of RV Dump. Waterfill and diesel fuel available. No propane.
Station Type: Truck stop (Independent).

F. Williams
Name of Business: Boondock's USA Truck Stop
Location: I-35, Exit 144.
Hours of Operation: 24 hours per day.
RV Information: No charge for use of RV Dump. Waterfill and diesel fuel available. No propane.
Station Type: Truck stop (Phillips 66).

KANSAS

"Sunflower State"

Capital: Topeka
Population: 2,477,574
Highest Point: 4,039 ft.

Largest City: Wichita
Area: 81,787 sq. mi.
Lowest Point: 680 ft.

Date of Statehood: January 29, 1861

GENERAL INFORMATION

Additional Information On Services

- **Rest Area Hours.** Rest Areas are open 24 hours per day, seven days per week.
- **Welcome Center Hours.** Welcome centers are staffed from 7 A.M. to 7 P.M. seven days per week between May 15 and September 15. The remainder of the year, centers are staffed daily from 9 A.M. to 5 P.M.
- **Tollway Service Plazas.** Areas 1,2,3,30,31 and 36 are service plazas along the Kansas Turnpike.
- **Tourist Information.** For tourist information call 1-800-2-KANSAS.

Rest Area Usage Rules

- **Overnight Parking.** Overnight parking is allowed for one night only.
- **Camping.** Camping is not permitted.
- **Stay Limit.** Parking limited to one night.

Driving In Kansas

- **Emergencies.** For highway emergencies along the Kansas Turnpike dial 1-800-827-PIKE, or *KTA on a cellular phone. Otherwise, call 911 (may not be operable in all counties) or dial the local police or local number for the highway patrol.
- **Open Container.** Open containers of alcoholic beverages in the passenger compartment of the vehicle are not permitted.
- **Seat Belts.** Seat belts are required for all front seat occupants. Children under 4 must be in a child restraint system. Children 4 through 14 must be in a seat belt.
- **Helmets.** Motorcycle operators and passengers18 and under must wear helmets.
- **Road Conditions.** Dial 1-913-296-6800.

Kansas ████████████████████

KANSAS REST AREAS

Route	Marker	N/S or E/W	Mile	Location	Services
35	1	N/S	26	BELLE PLAINE SERVICE PLAZA	CS, HD, TP
	2	N/S	65	TOWANDA SERVICE PLAZA	CS, HD, TP
	3	N/S	97	MATFIELD GREEN SERVICE PL	CS, HD, TP
	4/5	N/S		7 MI SW OF OTTAWA	TP, VM, WR
70	6/7	E/W		7 MI E OF COLORADO LINE	TP, WR
	8/9	E/W		5 MI SW OF COLBY	TP, WR
	10/11	E/W		3 MI NE OF OAKLEY	TP, WR
	12/13	E/W		3 MI E OF GRAINFIELD	TP, WR
	14/15	E/W		4 MI E OF WAKEENEY	TP, WR
	18/19	E/W		2 MI SE OF RUSSELL	TP, WR
	20/21	E/W		2 MI W OF US-156 JCT	HM, TP, WR
	22/23	E/W		2 MI NW OF SOLOMON	HM, TP, WR
	24/25	E/W		2 MI W OF JUNCTION CITY	HM, TP, WR
	26/27	E/W		4 MI W OF RTE 177 JCT	HM, SC, TP, WR
	28/29	E/W		25 MI W OF TOPEKA	HM, SC, TP, WRWR
	30	E/W	183	TOPEKA SERVICE PLAZA	CS, HD, TP
	31	E/W	209	LAWRENCE SERVICE PLAZA	CS, HD, TP
135	32/33	N/S		7 MI S OF NEWTON	TP, VM, WR
	34/35	N/S		8 MI N OF MC PHERSON	TP, WR
335	36	N/S	132	EMPORIA SERVICE PLAZA	CS, McD, TP
24	37	E/W		.5 MI W OF NICODEMUS	HM
	38	E/W		3 MI E OF CLAY CENTER	
36	39	E/W		2 MI S OF AXTELL	
	40	E/W		1 MI E OF TROY	HM
40	41	E/W		W EDGE OF WESKAN	HM
	42	E/W		E OF WALLACE	HM
50	43	E/W		4.5 MI W OF INGALLS	

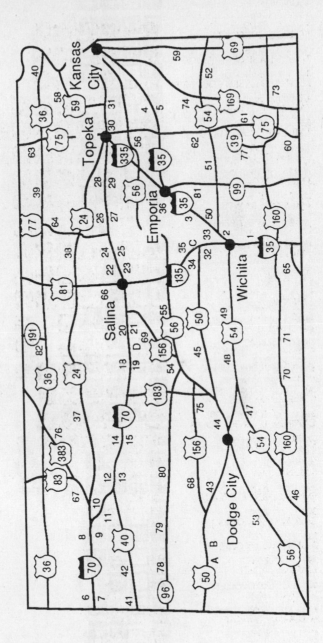

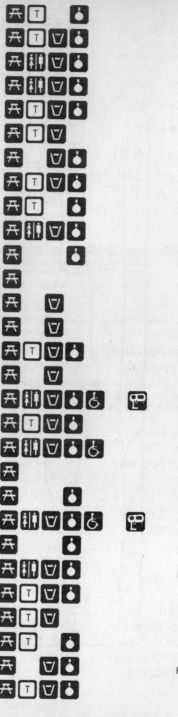

44 E/W 7 MI E OF DODGE CITY		HM
45 E/W STAFFORD		
(54) 46 E/W 11 MI NE OF LIBERAL		
47 E/W 1 MI E OF BLOOM		
48 E/W 1 MI E OF GREENSBURG		
49 E/W 13 MI E OF PRATT		
50 E/W 2 MI W OF ROSALIA		
51 E/W 2 MI W OF K-105 JCT		HM
52 E/W 1.5 MI E OF MORAN		
(56) 53 E/W US-83 JCT		
54 E/W 2 MI E OF GREAT BEND		HM
55 E/W 4 MI W OF LYONS		
56 E/W US 59 JCT		
(59) 58 N/S 1 MI W OF ATCHISON		HM
(69) 59 N/S 2.5 MI S OF PLEASONTON		HM
(75) 60 N/S N OF US-166 JCT		
61 N/S 2.5 MI NE OF NEODESHA		
62 N/S 5 MI NJ OF YATES CENTER		
63 N/S 3 MI W OF FAIRVIEW		
(77) 64 N/S E OF BLUE RAPIDS		HM
(81) 65 N/S 2 MI S OF CALDWELL		HM
66 N/S 8 MI N OF SALINA		
(83) 67 N/S 5 MI W OF REXFORD		HM
(156) 68 E/W K-140 JCT		HM
69 E/W K-23 WEST JCT		
(160) 70 E/W 2 MI S OF COLDWATER		
71 E/W W OF MEDICINE LODGE		
73 E/W 11 MI W OF PARSONS		HM
(169) 74 N/S W OF COLONY		

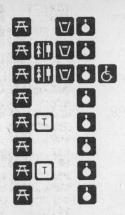

(183)	75 N/S 5 MI N OF US-56 JCT	
(383)	76 N/S NORTON RESERVOIR	
(39)	77 N/S 2 MI N OF FREDONIA	
(96)	78 E/W 4 MI E OF TRIBUNE	
	79 E/W 6 MI E OF LEOTI	
	80 E/W 2 MI E OF DIGHTON	
(99)	81 N/S 1 MI N OF HAMILTON	
(191)	82 N/S 2 MI N OF US-36	HM

KANSAS SERVICE STATIONS WITH RV DUMP FACILITIES

A. Deerfield

Name of Business: Country Corner West
Location: US-50 West & Main Street.
Hours of Operation: 24 hours per day.
RV Information: No charge for use of RV Dump. Waterfill and diesel fuel available. Can bottle exchange propane only--can not refill bottles.
Station Type: Truck stop (Farmland).

B. Garden City

Name of Business: Country Corner
Location: US-50 Business & US-83 (2 blocks West of junction).
Hours of Operation: 24 hours per day.
RV Information: No charge for use of RV Dump. Waterfill and diesel fuel available. Can bottle exchange propane only--can not refill bottles.
Station Type: Truck stop (Farmland).

C. Hesston

Name of Business: Save-A-Trip #18
Location: I-135, Exit 40 (Lincoln Avenue)
Hours of Operation: 24 hours per day.
RV Information: $2.00 charge for use of RV Dump. Waterfill and diesel fuel available. No propane. Campground on property.

Kansas ████████████████████ 77

Station Type: Truck stop (Phillips 66).

D. Wilson
Name of Business: The Waterin' Hole
Location: I-70, Exit 206 (KS-232 South).
Hours of Operation: 24 hours per day.
RV Information: No charge for use of RV Dump. Waterfill,
         propane and diesel fuel available.
Station Type: Truck stop (Texaco).

KENTUCKY

"Bluegrass State"

Capital:	Frankfort	Largest City:	Louisville
Population:	3,685,296	Area:	39,650 sq. mi.
Highest Point:	4,145 ft.	Lowest Point:	257 ft.

Date of Statehood: June 1, 1792

GENERAL INFORMATION

Additional Information On Services

- **Rest Area Hours.** Rest Areas are open 24 hours per day, seven days per week.
- **Welcome Center Hours.** Welcome centers are staffed from 8 A.M. to 8 P.M. seven days per week between April 1 and September 30. The remainder of the year, centers are staffed daily from 8 A.M. to 6 P.M.
- **Tourist Information.** For tourist information call 1-800-225-TRIP.

Rest Area Usage Rules

- **Overnight Parking.** No overnight parking.
- **Camping.** Camping is not permitted.
- **Stay Limit.** Parking limited to 4 hours.

Driving In Kentucky

- **Emergencies.** For highway emergencies call 1-800-222-5555 or dial the number for the local police.
- **Open Container.** No open container law, but it is an offense to consume alcoholic beverages on the highway.
- **Seat Belts.** All children less than 40 inches tall must be in a child restraint seat.
- **Helmets.** Motorcycle operators and passengers must wear helmets and eye protection.
- **Road Conditions.** Dial 1-502-564-4556.

KENTUCKY REST AREAS

24	1 W 1 MI E OF STATE LINE	🏕	🚻	🥤	🍼	♿	📞	🏠	TP, VM
	2 E US-45 JCT	🏕	🚻	🥤	🍼	♿	📞	🏠	TP, VM
64	3/4 E/W 20 MI E OF LOUISVILLE	🏕	🚻	🥤	🍼	♿	📞		TP, VM
	5/6 E/W 16 MI W OF LEXINGTON	🏕	🚻	🥤	🍼	♿	📞		TP, VM
	7 E 2 MI E OF WINCHESTER	🏕	🚻	🥤	🍼	♿	📞		TP, VM
	8 W 3 MI W OF MT STERLING	🏕	🚻	🥤	🍼	♿	📞		TP, VM
	9/10 E/W 3 MI E OF RTE 32	🏕	🚻	🥤	🍼	♿	📞		TP, VM
	11/12 E/W 17 MI W OF STATE LINE	🏕	🚻	🥤	🍼	♿	📞	🏠	TP, VM
65	13 N TENNESSEE LINE	🏕	🚻	🥤	🍼	♿	📞	🏠	TP, VM
	14/15 N/S N OF BOWLING GREEN	🏕	🚻	🥤	🍼	♿	📞		TP, VM
	16 S 2 MI N OF CAVE CITY		🚻	🥤	🍼	♿	📞		TP, VM
	17/18 N/S 10 MI S OF ELIZABETHTOWN	🏕	🚻	🥤	🍼	♿	📞		TP, VM
71	19/20 N/S 20 MI N OF LOUISVILLE	🏕	🚻	🥤	🍼	♿	📞		TP, VM
75	21 N TENNESSEE LINE	🏕	🚻	🥤	🍼	♿	📞	🏠	TP, VM
	22/23 N/S 5 MI S OF RICHMOND	🏕	🚻	🥤	🍼	♿	📞		TP, VM
	24/25 N/S 2 MI N OF GEORGETOWN	🏕	🚻	🥤	🍼	♿	📞		TP, VM
	26/27 N/S FLORENCE	🏕	🚻	🥤	🍼	♿	📞	🏠	TP, VM
402	28/29 E/W RTE 11 JCT	🏕	🚻	🥤	🍼	♿	📞		TP, VM

A. Lebanon Junction

Name of Business:	Davis Brothers Travel Plaza
Location:	I-65, Exit 105 (Preston Highway, KY-61).
Hours of Operation:	24 hours per day.
RV Information:	No charge for use of RV Dump. Waterfill and diesel fuel available. No propane.
Station Type:	Truck stop (Shell).

B. Walton

Name of Business:	Flying J Travel Plaza
Location:	I-75, Exit 171 (Walton-Verona Rd.).
Hours of Operation:	24 hours per day.
RV Information:	No charge for use of RV Dump. Waterfill, propane and diesel fuel available.
Station Type:	Truck stop (Conoco).

LOUISIANA

"Pelican State"

Capital: Baton Rouge   Largest City: New Orleans
Population: 4,219,973   Area: 50,820 sq. mi.
Highest Point: 535 ft.   Lowest Point: -5 ft.
Date of Statehood: April 30, 1812

GENERAL INFORMATION

Additional Information On Services

- **Rest Area Hours.** Rest Areas are open 24 hours per day, seven days per week.
- **Welcome Center Hours.** Welcome centers are staffed from 8 A.M. to 5:30 P.M. seven days per week year round.
- **Tourist Information.** For tourist information call 1-800-33-GUMBO.

Rest Area Usage Rules

- **Overnight Parking.** No overnight parking.
- **Camping.** Camping is not permitted.
- **Stay Limit.** No published limit.

Driving In Louisiana

- **Emergencies.** For highway emergencies call 911 (may not be operable in all counties) or call State Police at 1-504-295-8500.
- **Open Container.** Open containers of alcoholic beverages in the vehicle are not permitted.
- **Seat Belts.** Seat belts are required for all occupants. Children 5 and under must be in a child restraint system.
- **Helmets.** Motorcycle operators and passengers must wear helmets.
- **Road Conditions.** Dial 1-504-295-8500.

LOUISIANA REST AREAS

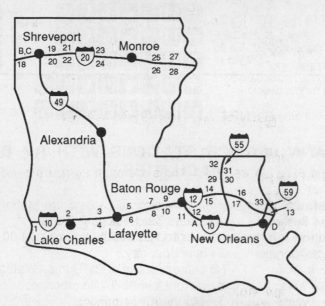

10	1 E 1 5 MI E OF TEXAS LINE	🅿 🚻 🗑 🍼 ♿ 📞 🏕 🏠	FG, GT, TP
	2 W 15 9 MI E OF SULPHUR	🅿 🚻 🗑 🍼 ♿ 📞 🏕	FG, GT, TP
	3/4 E/W 67 5 MI E OF JENNINGS	🅿 🚻 🗑 🍼 ♿ 📞 🏕	FG, GT, TP
	5/6 E/W 106 2 MI E OF LAFAYETTE	🅿 🚻 🗑 🍼 ♿ 📞 🏕	FG, GT, TP
	7/8 E/W 127 6 MI W OF ATCHAFALAYA RIVER	🅿 🚻 🗑 🍼 ♿ 📞 🏕	FG, GT, TP
	9/10 E/W 137 2 MI W OF 77	🅿 🚻 🗑 🍼 ♿ 📞 🏕	FG, GT, TP
	11/12 E/W 182 1 MI E OF GONZALES	🅿 🚻 🗑 🍼 ♿ 📞 🏕	FG, GT, TP
	13 W 270 MISSISSIPPI LINE	🅿 🚻 🗑 🍼 ♿ 📞 🏕 🏠	FG, GT, TP
12	14/15 E/W 27 2 MI E OF HOLDEN	🅿 🚻 🗑 🍼 ♿ 📞 🏕	FG, GT, TP
	16/17 E/W 60 21 MI E OF HAMMOND	🅿 🚻 🗑 🍼 ♿ 📞 🏕	FG, GT, TP
20	18 E 3 5 MI E OF TEXAS LINE	🅿 🚻 🗑 🍼 ♿ 📞 🏕 🏠	FG, GT, TP
	19/20 E/W 36 1 MI E OF FILLMORE	🅿 🚻 🗑 🍼 ♿ 📞 🏕	FG, GT, TP
	21/22 E/W 58 2 MI E OF ADA	🅿 🚻 🗑 🍼 ♿ 📞 🏕	FG, GT, TP
	23/24 E/W 96 10 MI E OF RUSTON	🅿 🚻 🗑 🍼 ♿ 📞 🏕	FG, GT, TP
	25/26 E/W 151 3 MI W OF DELHI	🅿 🚻 🗑 🍼 ♿ 📞 🏕	FG, GT, TP

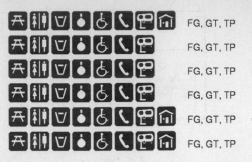

27 W 184 5 MI W OF MISSISSIPPI LINE		FG, GT, TP
28 E 184 5 MI W OF MISSISSIPPI LINE		FG, GT, TP
55 29/30 N/S 34 5 MI N OF HAMMOND		FG, GT, TP
31 N 54 2 MI N OF FLUKER		FG, GT, TP
32 S 65 3 MI N OF KENTWOOD		FG, GT, TP
59 33 S 1 10 MI S OF MISSISSIPPI LINE		FG, GT, TP

LOUISIANA SERVICE STATIONS WITH RV DUMP FACILITIES

A. Gonzales

Name of Business: USA Auto Truck Plaza
Location: I-10, Exit 177 (LA-30).
Hours of Operation: 24 hours per day.
RV Information: No charge for use of RV Dump. Waterfill and diesel fuel available. No propane.
Station Type: Truck stop (Chevron).

B. Greenwood

Name of Business: Kelly's 76 Truck Terminal
Location: I-20, Exit 5 (Greenwood Rd., US-79 & 80).
Hours of Operation: 24 hours per day.
RV Information: No charge for use of RV Dump ($5.00 if fuel not purchased). Waterfill and diesel fuel available. No propane. Campground.
Station Type: Truck stop (Unocal 76).

C. Greenwood

Name of Business: Flying J Travel Plaza
Location: I-20, Exit 3 (Carthage).
Hours of Operation: 24 hours per day.
RV Information: No charge for use of RV Dump. Waterfill, propane and diesel fuel available.
Station Type: Truck stop (Conoco).

D. New Orleans

Name of Business: Mardi Gras Truck Stop
Location: I-10, Exit 236B or 237. I-610, Elysian Field
Hours of Operation: 24 hours per day.
RV Information: No charge for use of RV Dump. Waterfill and diesel fuel available. No propane.
Station Type: Truck stop (Texaco).

MAINE

"Pine Tree State"

Capital:	Augusta	Largest City:	Portland
Population:	1,227,928	Area:	30,920 sq. mi.
Highest Point:	5,268 ft.	Lowest Point:	Sea Level

Date of Statehood: March 15, 1820

GENERAL INFORMATION

Additional Information On Services

- **Rest Area Hours.** Rest Areas are open 24 hours per day, seven days per week.
- **Welcome Center Hours.** Welcome centers are staffed from 9 A.M. to 5 P.M. seven days per week. Area 13 has a manned information center during summer months.
- **Tourist Information.** For tourist information call 1-800-533-9595.

Rest Area Usage Rules

- **Overnight Parking.** No overnight parking.
- **Camping.** Camping is not permitted.
- **Stay Limit.** No published limit.

Driving In Maine

- **Emergencies.** For highway emergencies call 1-800-482-0730 for the state police.
- **Open Container.** Open containers of alcoholic beverages in the passenger compartment of the vehicle are not permitted.
- **Seat Belts.** Seat belts are required for all occupants under 19. Children 4 and under must be in a child restraint system.
- **Helmets.** Helmets are not required for motorcyclists.
- **Road Conditions.** Dial 1-207-28-3427 for 24 hour road conditions from mid November through April 1st..

MAINE REST AREAS

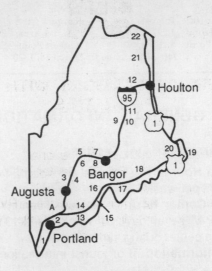

95 1 N 3 MI N NEW HAMPSHIRE LINE	⛱	🚻	🗑	🚰	♿	☎		🏠	FG, TP, VM
2 N YARMOUTH, I-95 & US-1 JCT	⛱	🚻	🗑	🚰	♿	☎		🏠	TP, VM
3/4 N/S 1 MI N OF RTE 27 JCT	⛱	🚻	🗑	🚰	♿	☎			FG, TP, VM
5/6 N/S 3 MI S OF PITTSFIELD	⛱	🚻	🗑	🚰	♿	☎			FG, TP
7/8 N/S 2 MI E OF RTE 69 JCT	⛱	🚻	🗑	🚰	♿	☎		🏠	FG, VM
9/10 N/S 1 MI S OF RTE 157 JCT	⛱	🚻	🗑	🚰	♿	☎			FG, TP
11 N 3 MI N OF RTE 157 JCT	⛱		🗑						FG
12 S HOULTON	⛱	🚻	🗑	🚰	♿	☎		🏠	FG, TP
1 13 E 1 MI E OF W BATH	⛱	🚻	🗑	🚰	♿	☎			
14 W 1 MI W OF W BATH	⛱		🗑						FG
15 E/W NEWCASTLE	⛱	🚻	🗑						FG
16 E/W GLEN COVE	⛱	T	🗑						FG
17 E/W VERONA	⛱	T	🗑						FG
18 E/W SULLIVAN	⛱	T	🗑						FG
19 N/S 5 MI N OF ROBBINSTON	⛱	T	🗑						FG

20 N/S CALAIS		
21 N/S 4 MI S OF CARIBOU		FG
22 N/S 2 MI E OF MADAWASKA		FG

MAINE SERVICE STATIONS WITH RV DUMP FACILITIES

A. Fairfield

Name of Business:	Truckers International
Location:	I-95, Exit 35 (Center Rd., ME-139).
Hours of Operation:	24 hours per day.
RV Information:	$2.00 charge for use of RV Dump. Waterfill and diesel fuel available. No propane.
Station Type:	Truck stop (Mobil).

MARYLAND
"Old Line State"

Capital:	Annapolis	Largest City:	Baltimore
Population:	4,781,468	Area:	9,891 sq. mi.
Highest Point:	3,360 ft.	Lowest Point:	Sea Level
	Date of Statehood:	April 28, 1788	

GENERAL INFORMATION

Additional Information On Services

- **Rest Area Hours.** Rest Areas are open 24 hours per day, seven days per week. However, the parking lot at area 10 closes at dusk; area 11 is open 7 A.M. to dusk; area 13 is open 8 A.M. to 8 P.M.
- **Welcome Center Hours.** Welcome centers are staffed from 9 A.M. to 5 P.M. Center at area 8 is staffed from 8 A.M. to 6 P.M. weekdays and 8 A.M. to 8 P.M. weekends and summer.
- **Tourist Information.** For tourist information call 1-800-543-1036.

Rest Area Usage Rules

- **Overnight Parking.** No overnight parking.
- **Camping.** Camping is not permitted.
- **Stay Limit.** Parking limited to 3 hours.

Driving In Maryland

- **Emergencies.** For highway emergencies call the Maryland State Police on C.B. channel 9 or dial 1-800-525-5555.
- **Open Container.** Open containers of alcoholic beverages in the vehicle are not permitted.
- **Seat Belts.** Seat belts are required for the driver and front seat passenger next to the door. Children 3 and under must be in a child restraint system. Children 3 through 5 must be in a child restraint system or seat belt.
- **Helmets.** Motorcycle operators and passengers must wear helmets and eye protection.
- **Road Conditions.** Dial 1-410-333-1122.

MARYLAND REST AREAS

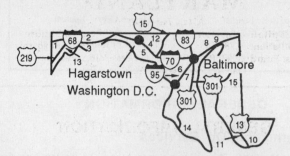

68	1 E 6 6 MI E OF W VIRGINIA LINE	⛱	🚻	🗑	💧	♿	☎		🏠	PW, TP, VM, VP
	2/3 E/W 70 8 MI W HANCOCK	⛱	🚻	🗑	💧	♿	☎		🏠	AS, VM, VP
70	4/5 E/W 39 15 MI W OF FREDERICK	⛱	🚻	🗑	💧	♿	☎	🖼	🏠	FG, PA, PW, TP, VM
95	6/7 N/S 37 20 MI S OF BALTIMORE	⛱	🚻	🗑	💧	♿	☎	🖼	🏠	TP, VM
	8 N/S 81 24 MI N OF BALTIMORE	⛱	🚻	🗑	💧	♿	☎		🏠	BBB, EX, RR, MF, SB, SH, TP
	9 N/S 95 38 MI N OF BALTIMORE	⛱	🚻	🗑	💧	♿	☎		🏠	BK, EX, MF, TB POP, TC, TX, TP
13	10 N 1 1 MI N OF VIRGINIA LINE	⛱	🚻	🗑	💧	♿	☎		🏠	PW, TP, VM
	11 S 18 MI N OF VIRGINIA LINE	⛱	🚻	🗑	💧	♿	☎		🏠	PW
15	12 S 1 MI S OF PENNSYLVANIA LINE	⛱	🚻	🗑	💧	♿	☎		🏠	PW, TP, VM
219	13 N/S 2 MI S OF I-68	⛱	🚻	🗑	💧	♿	☎			VM, VP
301	14 N 2 2 MI N VIRGINIA	⛱	🚻	🗑	💧	♿	☎		🏠	
	15 N/S 26 MI S OF DELAWARE LINE	⛱	🚻	🗑	💧	♿	☎			HM, PA, TP, VM

MASSACHUSETTS

"Bay State"

Capital: Boston	Largest City: Boston
Population: 6,016,425	Area: 7,826 sq. mi.
Highest Point: 3,491 ft.	Lowest Point: Sea Level

Date of Statehood: February 6, 1788

GENERAL INFORMATION

Additional Information On Services

- **Rest Area Hours.** Rest Areas are open 24 hours per day, seven days per week.
- **Welcome Center Hours.** Welcome centers are staffed from 9 A.M. to 5 P.M. seven days per week. Those on I-90 are staffed from 8 A.M. to 6 P.M. May 15th through October 15th and 8 A.M. to 4:30 P.M. October 16th through May 14th. Many of the others are closed in winter.
- **Tollway Service Plazas.** Areas 2 through 7 and 9 through 13 are tollway service plazas along the Massachusetts Turnpike.
- **Farmer's Market.** There is a farmer's market at areas 3, 9, 10, and 12 from May through October.
- **Tourist Information.** For tourist information call 1-617-727-3201.

Rest Area Usage Rules

- **Overnight Parking.** No overnight parking.
- **Camping.** Camping is not permitted.
- **Stay Limit.** Parking is restricted to occupied vehicles only. Unattended vehicles will be towed after 30 minutes.

Driving In Massachusetts

- **Emergencies.** For highway emergencies call the state police at 1-617-566-4500.
- **Open Container.** Open containers of alcoholic beverages in the passenger compartment of the vehicle are not permitted.
- **Seat Belts.** Children 5 and under must be in a child restraint system. Children 5 through 12 must be in a child restraint system or seat belt.
- **Helmets.** Motorcycle operators and passengers must wear helmets.
- **Road Conditions.** Dial 1-617-566-4500.

MASSACHUSETTS REST AREAS

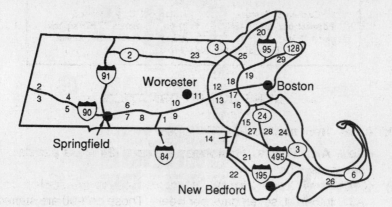

	#	Dir	Mile	Amenities		Services
84 / **90**	1	N	1	IN STURBRIDGE		TP
	2	W	8	LEE SERVICE PLAZA		MO, PW, TP, VM
	3	E	8	LEE SERVICE PLAZA		BK, MO, PW, TC, TP
	4	W	29	BLANDFORD SERVICE PLAZA		BK, MO, PW, TP
	5	W	29	BLANDFORD SERVICE PLAZA		MO, PW, TP, VM
	6	W	55	LUDLOW SERVICE PLAZA		MO, RR, TP
	7	E	55	LUDLOW SERVICE AREA		MF, MO, PW, RR, TC, TP
	8	E		7 MI E OF PALMER		TP
	9	E	80	CHARLTON SERVICE PLAZA		MA, MF, MO, PW, RR, TC, TP
	10	W	83	CHARLTON SERVICE PLAZA		BK, MA, MF, MO, PW, TC, TP
	11	W	105	WESTBOROUGH SERVICE PLAZ		MO, SB, PW, TP
	12	W	114	FRAMINGHAM SERVICE PLAZA		BK, MO, POP, PW, TC, TP
	13	E	117	NATICK SERVICE PLAZA		BK, MO, PW, TC, TP
95	14	S	10	N ATTLEBORO		TP
	15	N	10	MANSFIELD		TP
	16	S	28	WESTWOOD		TP
	17	S	32	DEDHAM		TP
	18	S	38	NEWTON		TP

Exit	Dir	Town	Mile	Facilities	
19	N	LEXINGTON	46	🏕 🚻 🚮 ⛽ ♿ 📞	TP
20	S	SALISBURY	89	🏕 🚻 🚮 ⛽ ♿ 📞	TP
(195) 21	W	SEEKONK	2	🏕 ⛽ 📞	
22	E	SWANSEA	6	🏕 ⛽	TP
(2) 23	W	HARVARD	111	🏕 ⛽	TP
(3) 24	N/S	PLYMOUTH		🏕 🚻 🚮 ⛽ ♿ 📞 🏠	TP
25	N	BILLERICA	74	🏕 📞	TP
(6) 26	E	BARNSTABLE	70	🏕 🚻 🚮 ⛽ ♿ 📞	TP
(24) 27/28	N/S	BRIDGEWATER	23	🏕 🚻 🚮 ⛽ ♿ 📞	TP
(128) 29	N	BEVERLY	9	🏕 🚻 🚮 ♿ 📞	TP

MICHIGAN

"Wolverine State"

Capital: Lansing **Largest City:** Detroit
Population: 9,258,344 **Area:** 56,817 sq. mi.
Highest Point: 1,980 ft. **Lowest Point:** 572 ft.
Date of Statehood: January 26, 1837

GENERAL INFORMATION

Additional Information On Services

- **Rest Area Hours.** Rest Areas are open 24 hours per day, seven days per week.
- **Welcome Center Hours.** Welcome centers are staffed from 9 A.M. to 5 P.M., EST, with the exception of centers at areas 57, 58 and 73, which are staffed from 8 A.M. to 4 P.M., CST. All welcome centers have expanded hours between June 1 and Labor Day.
- **Tourist Information.** For tourist information call 1-800-5432-YES.

Rest Area Usage Rules

- **Overnight Parking.** No overnight parking.
- **Camping.** Camping is not permitted.
- **Stay Limit.** Parking limited to 4 hours.

Driving In Michigan

- **Emergencies.** For highway emergencies call 1-800-525-5555 for the highway patrol.
- **Open Container.** Open containers of alcoholic beverages in the passenger compartment of the vehicle are not permitted.
- **Seat Belts.** Seat belts are required for all front seat occupants. Children 4 and under must be in a child restraint system if in the front. Children 1 through 4 must be in a child restraint system or seat belt if in the back.
- **Helmets.** Motorcycle operators and passengers must wear helmets.
- **Road Conditions.** Dial the local authorities. Also, between November 15 and April 15 road condition information is available from the welcome centers.

MICHIGAN REST AREAS

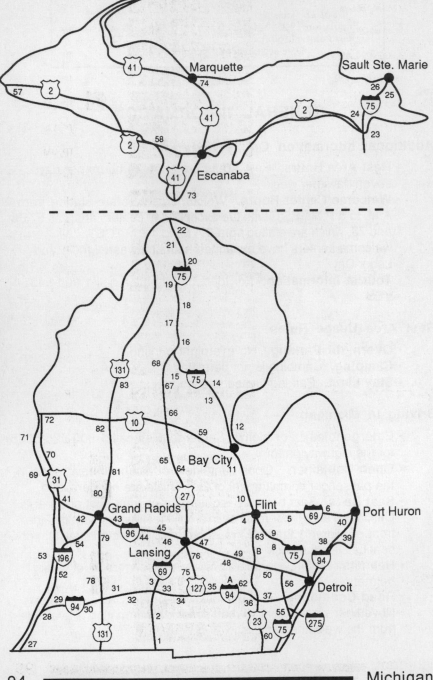

Michigan

Route	No.	Dir	MP	Location	Facilities	Lodging	Services
69	1	N	6	6 MI S OF COLDWATER		🏠	TP
	2	N	28	3 MI N OF M-60			TP
	3	S	40	2 MI N OF I-94			TP
	4	N	126	7 MI W OF I-75			TP
	5	E	161	8 MI E OF LAPEER			TP
	6	W	174	2 MI W OF CAPAC			TP
75	7	N	10	4 MI S OF MONROE		🏠	TP, VM
	8	S	95	4 MI NW OF CLARKSTON			TP, VM
	9	N	96	6 MI N OF CLARKSTON			TP, VM
	10	S	129	2 MI S OF RTE 57			TP, VM
	11	S	158	2 MI S OF RTE 84			TP
	12	N	175	16 MI NW OF BAY CITY			TP
	13		201	1 MI SE OF RTE 33			TP
	14	N	210	3 MI S OF WEST BRANCH			TP
	15	S	235	4 MI S OF RTE 18			TP
	16	N	252	3 MI S OF GRAYLING			TP, VM
	17	S	262	8 MI N OF GRAYLING			TP, VM
	18	N	277	4 MI S OF GAYLORD			TP
	19	S	287	5 MI N OF GAYLORD			TP
	20	N	317	8 MI N OF INDIAN RIVER			TP
	21	S	328	11 MI S OF MAKINAW CITY			TP
	22	N	338	AT MACKINAW CITY		🏠	TP
	23	N	344	N END OF MACKINAC BRIDGE		🏠	TP
	24	S	345	1 MI N OF MACKINAC BRIDGE			TP
	25	N	389	5 MI S OF SAULT STE MARIE			TP
	26	S	394	IN SAULT STE MARIE		🏠	TP
94	27	E	0	INDIANA LINE		🏠	TP, VM
	28	E	36	2 MI E OF I-196			TP
	29	W	42	1 MI E OF WATERVLIET			TP

#	Dir	Mile	Location	Facilities	Notes
30	E	72	2 MI W OF US-131	🏕️ 🚻 🗑️ 🍼 ♿ 📞	TP
31	W	85	11 MI E OF US-131	🏕️ 🚻 🗑️ 🍼 ♿ 📞	TP, VM
32	E	96	2 MI W OF RTE 66	🏕️ 🚻 🗑️ 🍼 ♿ 📞	TP
33	W	113	2 MI E OF MARSHALL	🏕️ 🚻 🗑️ 🍼 ♿ 📞	TP
34	E	135	3 MI W OF JACKSON	🏕️ 🚻 🗑️ 🍼 ♿ 📞	TP
35	W	150	10 MI E OF JACKSON	🏕️ 🚻 🗑️ 🍼 ♿ 📞	TP
36	E	168	3 MI W OF ANN ARBOR	🏕️ 🚻 🗑️ 🍼 ♿ 📞	TP
37	W	188	5 MI E OF YPSILANTI	🏕️ 🚻 🗑️ 🍼 ♿ 📞	TP
38	W	251	4 MI N OF NEW BALTIMORE	🏕️ 🚻 🗑️ 🍼 ♿ 📞	TP
39	E	255	5 MI E OF RICHMOND	🏕️ 🚻 🗑️ 🍼 ♿ 📞	TP
40	W	274	AT PORT HURON	🏕️ 🚻 🗑️ 🍼 ♿ 📞 🏠	TP
41	W	8	3 MI SE OF FRUITPORT	🏕️ 🚻 🗑️ 🍼 ♿ 📞	TP
42	E	25	5 MI W OF RTE 37	🏕️ 🚻 🗑️ 🍼 ♿ 📞	TP
43	W	46	3 MI E OF RTE 11	🏕️ 🚻 🗑️ 🍼 ♿ 📞	TP, VM
44	E	63	4 MI W OF RTE 66	🏕️ 🚻 🗑️ 🍼 ♿ 📞	TP
45	W	79	2 MI E OF PORTLAND	🏕️ 🚻 🗑️ 🍼 ♿ 📞	TP
46	E	87	2 MI E OF RTE 100	🏕️ 🚻 🗑️ 🍼 ♿ 📞	TP
47	W	111	6 MI E OF US 127	🏕️ 🚻 🗑️ 🍼 ♿ 📞	TP, VM
48	E	135	2 MI SW OF HOWELL	🏕️ 🚻 🗑️ 🍼 ♿ 📞	TP
49	W	141	3 MI E OF HOWELL	🏕️ 🚻 🗑️ 🍼 ♿ 📞	TP
50	E	160	3 MI W OF I-696	🏕️ 🚻 🗑️ 🍼 ♿ 📞	TP
52	N	28	5 MI N OF SOUTH HAVEN	🏕️ 🚻 🗑️ 🍼 ♿ 📞	TP
53	S	43	4 MI S OF HOLLAND	🏕️ 🚻 🗑️ 🍼 ♿ 📞	TP
54	N	58	6 MI E OF ZEELAND	🏕️ 🚻 🗑️ 🍼 ♿ 📞	TP
55	S	4	1 MI S OF CARLETON	🏕️ 🚻 🗑️ 🍼 ♿ 📞	TP
56	N	23	2 MI N OF US-12	🏕️ 🚻 🗑️ 🍼 ♿ 📞	TP
57	E		WISCONSIN LINE	🏕️ 🚻 🗑️ 🍼 ♿ 📞 🏠	
58	E/W		IRON MOUNTAIN	🏕️ 🚻 🗑️ 🍼 ♿ 📞 🏠	
59	W		MIDLAND	🏕️ 🚻 🗑️ 🍼 ♿ 📞	

Route markers:
- I-96 (rows 41–50)
- I-196 (rows 52–54)
- I-275 (rows 55–56)
- US-2 (row 57)
- US-10 (row 59)

Route	Site	Direction	No.	Location	Facilities	Lodging	VM
23	60	N	7	8 MI S OF DUNDEE	picnic, restrooms, trash, water, handicap, phone	🏠	VM
	62	S	47	3 MI N OF RTE 14	picnic, restrooms, trash, water, handicap, phone		VM
	63	N	81	3 MI N OF FENTON	picnic, restrooms, trash, water, handicap, phone		
27	64	N		4 MI S OF ALMA	picnic, restrooms, trash, water, handicap, phone		VM
	65	S		3 MI N OF ALMA	picnic, restrooms, trash, water, handicap, phone		
	66	N/S		2 MI N OF CLARE	picnic, restrooms, trash, water, handicap, phone	🏠	VM
	67	N		7 MI S OF RTE 55	picnic, restrooms, trash, water, handicap, phone		
	68	S		8 MI N OF RTE 55	picnic, restrooms, trash, water, handicap, phone		
31	69	S		5 MI S OF WHITEHALL	picnic, restrooms, trash, water, handicap, phone		
	70	N		6 MI S OF RTE 20	picnic, restrooms, trash, water, handicap, phone		
	71	S		8 MI N OF RTE 20	picnic, restrooms, trash, water, handicap, phone		
	72	N		6 MI S OF LUDINGTON	picnic, restrooms, trash, water, handicap, phone		
41	73	N		WISCONSIN LINE	picnic, restrooms, trash, water, handicap, phone	🏠	
	74	N		SE OF MARQUETTE	picnic, restrooms, trash, water, handicap, phone	🏠	
127	75	S		9 MI N OF JACKSON	picnic, restrooms, trash, water, handicap, phone		
	76	N		1 MI S OF I-96	picnic, restrooms, trash, water, handicap, phone		
131	78	S	42	5 MI N OF KALAMAZOO	picnic, restrooms, trash, water, handicap, phone		
	79	N	77	8 MI S OF GRAND RAPIDS	picnic, restrooms, trash, water, handicap, phone		VM
	80	S	99	1 MI N OF ROCKFORD	picnic, restrooms, trash, water, handicap, phone		VM
	81	N	122	2 MI N OF RTE 46	picnic, restrooms, trash, water, handicap, phone		
	82	S	136	3 MI S OF BIG RAPIDS	picnic, restrooms, trash, water, handicap, phone		
	83	N	174	4 MI S OF CADILLAC	picnic, restrooms, trash, water, handicap, phone		

MICHIGAN SERVICE STATIONS WITH RV DUMP FACILITIES

A. Dexter

Name of Business:	Wolverine Truck Plaza
Location:	I-94, Exit 167 (Baker Rd.).
Hours of Operation:	24 hours per day.
RV Information:	No charge for use of RV Dump. Waterfill and

diesel fuel available. No propane.
Station Type: Truck stop (Unocal 76).

B. Hartland
Name of Business: Oasis Truck Stop
Location: US-23, Exit 67 (Highland Rd., MI-59).
Hours of Operation: 24 hours per day. (RV Dump open 8:30 A.M.
                       to 5:30 P.M.)
RV Information: No charge for use of RV Dump. Diesel fuel
                       available. No waterfill or propane.
Station Type: Truck stop (Amoco).

MINNESOTA

"Gopher State

Capital: St. Paul
Population: 4,375,099
Highest Point: 2,301 ft.

Largest City: Minneapolis
Area: 79,289 sq. mi.
Lowest Point: 602 ft.

Date of Statehood: May 11, 1858

GENERAL INFORMATION

Additional Information On Services

- **Rest Area Hours.** Rest Areas are open 24 hours per day, seven days per week.
- **Welcome Center Hours.** Welcome centers are staffed during daylight hours year round.
- **Winter Closures.** Rest areas 41, 47, 48, 50, 51,and 54 are closed from November through May.
- **Advertising.** Areas 1, 4, 6, 10, 11, 12, 22, 23, 24, 25, 32, 34 and 35 participate in "Info Stop," a public advertising program.
- **Tourist Information.** For tourist information, call 1-800-657-3700 or 296-5029 in the Twin Cities.

Rest Area Usage Rules

- **Overnight Parking.** No overnight parking.
- **Camping.** Camping or sleeping outside of vehicle is not permitted.
- **Stay Limit.** Parking limited to 6 hours.

Driving In Minnesota

- **Emergencies.** For highway emergencies call 911 (may not be operable in all counties) or dial the local police or local number for the highway patrol.
- **Open Container.** No open container law, but it is an offense to consume alcoholic beverages on the highway.
- **Seat Belts.** Seat belts are required for all front seat occupants. Children 4 and under must be in a child restraint system. Children 4 through 11 must be in a child restraint system or seat belt.
- **Helmets.** Helmets not required for motorcyclists.
- **Road Conditions.** In the Twin Cities, call 612-296-3076. Elsewhere in Minnesota, dial 1-800-542-0220. Outside of Minnesota, call 1-800-544-4751.

MINNESOTA REST AREAS

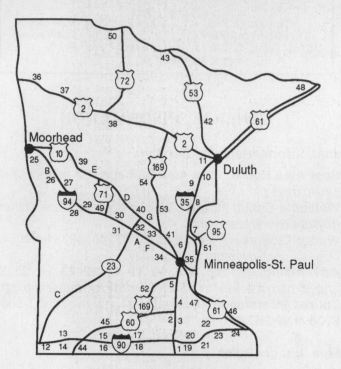

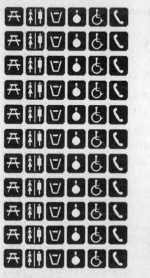

35 1 N 1 .5 MI N OF IOWA LINE	🏠	PW, TP, TR, VM
2/3 N/S 35 7 MI S OF OWATONNA		PA, PW, TR, TP, VM
4 N 68 9 MI N OF FARIBAULT		PA, PW, TR, TP, VM
5 S 75 S OF ELKO		PA, PW, TR, TP, VM
6 S 131 AT FOREST LAKE		PW, TP, VM
7 N 153 1.5 MI N OF HARRIS		PW, TP, TR, VM
8 N 5 MI N OF SANDSTONE		PW, TP, VM
9 S 2 MI N OF WILLOW RIVER		PW, TP, VM
10 N 226 1 MI S OF MAHTOWA		PA, PW, TP, TR, VM, VP
11 N/S W LIMITS OF DULUTH	🏠	PW, SC, TP, VM
90 12 E 1 1 MI W SOUTH DAKOTA LINE	🏠	PW, TP, TR, VM

Route	No.	Dir.	Mile	Location	Facilities
	13/14	E/W	24	3 MI W OF ADRIAN	PA, PW, TP
	15/16	E/W	69/72	2 MI W OF JACKSON	PA, PW, TP,VM
	17/18	E/W	119	1 MI W OF BLUE EARTH	PA, PW, TP, TR, VM, VP
	19	E	163	4 MI E OF ALBERT LEA	PA, PW, TP, TR, VM, VP
	20	W	171	5 MI W OF AUSTIN	PA, PW, TP, TR, VM
	21	E	202	3 MI S OF HIGHFOREST	PA, PW, TP,VM
	22	W	220	3 MI E OF US-52 JCT	PW, TP, VM
	23	E	244	14 MI E OF ST. CHARLES	PA, PW, TP, TR, VM, VP
	24	E/W	276	WISCONSIN LINE	PW, TP, TR, VM, VP
94	25	E	1	LIMITS OF MOORHEAD	PA, PW, TP,VM
	26	E	60	8 MI E OF FERGUS FALLS	PW, VM, TP, TR, VP
	27	W	69	18 MI E OF FERGUS FALLS	PW, TP, VM
	28	E	99	2 MI W OF ALEXANDRIA	PW, PA, TP,VM
	29	W	105	2 MI E OF ALEXANDRIA	PW, TP, TR,VM
	30/31	E/W	152	3 MI E OF ALBANY	PA, PW, TP, TR, VM
	32	W	177	1 MI W OF RTE 24 JCT	PA, PW, TP, TR, VM
	33	E	187	9 MI E OF RTE 24 JCT	PA, PW, TP, TR, VM, VP
	34	E	215	2 MI W OF I-494 JCT	PA, PW, TP, VM, VP
	35	W	258	3 MI W OF WISCONSIN LINE	HM, PA, PW, TP, TR, VM,VP
2	36	E/W	12	9 MI E OF EAST GRAND FORKS	TP, VM
	37	E/W	59	1 MI E OF US-59 JCT	PW, TP, VM
	38	E/W	131	CASS LAKE	BL, F, PW, TP
10	39	E/W	55	1 MI SE OF FRAZEE	TP, TR, VM
	40	N/S		ST. CLOUD	PA, PW, TP, TR, VM, VP
	41	E/W		6 MI NW OF ANOKA	VM
53	42	N/S		9 MI S OF EVELETH	PW, TP, TR,VM
	43	N/S		IN INTERNATIONAL FALLS	VM
60	44	E/W		WORTHINGTON	PA, PW, TP, TR, VM
	45	E/W		5 MI E OF ST JAMES	TP, VM

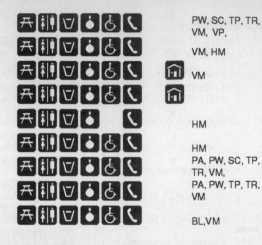

(61) 46 N/S AT BAPTISM RIVER			PW, SC, TP, TR, VM, VP,
47 N/S 77 5 MI N OF LAKE CITY			VM, HM
48 N/S 446 GRAND PORTAGE			VM
(71) 49 N/S 48 AT SAUK CENTER			
(72) 50 N/S 130 IN BAUDETTE			HM
(95) 51 N/S 101 1 MI N OF US-96 JCT			HM
(169) 52 N/S MINNESOTA VALLEY			PA, PW, SC, TP, TR, VM,
53 N/S 11 MI N OF MILICA			PA, PW, TP, TR, VM
54 N/S 233 1 MI S OF GARRISON			BL, VM

MINNESOTA SERVICE STATIONS WITH RV DUMP FACILITIES

A. Clearwater

Name of Business: Clearwater Travel Plaza
Location: I-94, Exit 178 (County Road 24).
Hours of Operation: 24 hours per day.
RV Information: $5.00 charge for use of RV Dump. Waterfill, propane and diesel fuel available.
Station Type: Truck stop (Amoco).

B. Fergus Falls

Name of Business: Interstate Texaco
Location: I-94, Exit 50 (US-59).
Hours of Operation: 24 hours per day.
RV Information: No charge for use of RV Dump ($2.00 if fuel not purchased). Waterfill, propane and diesel fuel available.
Station Type: Truck stop (Texaco).

C. Marshall

Name of Business: Ampride
Location: US-59 & MN-23 Bypass.
Hours of Operation: 24 hours per day.
RV Information: No charge for use of RV Dump. Waterfill, propane and diesel fuel available.
Station Type: Truck stop (Farmland)

D. Motley

Name of Business:	El Ray Truck Stop
Location:	US-10, MN-210 & MN-64 junction.
Hours of Operation:	24 hours per day.
RV Information:	No charge for use of RV Dump. Waterfill, propane and diesel fuel available.
Station Type:	Truck stop (Unocal 76).

E. Perham

Name of Business:	Perham Oasis
Location:	US-10 & MN-78.
Hours of Operation:	24 hours per day.
RV Information:	No charge for use of RV Dump ($5.00 if less than $40.00 of fuel purchased). Waterfill and diesel fuel available. No propane.
Station Type:	Truck stop (Conoco).

F. Rogers

Name of Business:	Twin City West Auto Truck Plaza
Location:	I-94, Exit 207 (MN-101).
Hours of Operation:	24 hours per day.
RV Information:	No charge for use of RV Dump. Waterfill and diesel fuel available. No propane.
Station Type:	Truck stop (Unocal 76).

G. Saint Cloud

Name of Business:	Holiday Station
Location:	I-94, Exit 171 (County Road 75).
Hours of Operation:	24 hours per day.
RV Information:	No charge for use of RV Dump. Waterfill, propane and diesel fuel available.
Station Type:	Truck stop (Holiday).

Minnesota

MISSISSIPPI

"Magnolia State"

Capital: Jackson	**Largest City:** Jackson
Population: 2,520,638	**Area:** 47,296 sq. mi.
Highest Point: 806 ft.	**Lowest Point:** Sea Level

Date of Statehood: December 10, 1817

GENERAL INFORMATION

Additional Information On Services

- **Rest Area Hours.** Rest areas are open 24 hours per day, seven days per week.
- **Welcome Center Hours.** Welcome centers are staffed from 8 A.M. to 5 P.M.
- **Tourist Information.** For tourist information call 1-800-647-2290.

Rest Area Usage Rules

- **Overnight Parking.** Overnight parking is permitted.
- **Camping.** Camping is not permitted.
- **Stay Limit.** No published limit.

Driving In Mississippi

- **Emergencies.** For highway emergencies call 1-800-843-5352 in Mississippi or dial 1-601-987-1212.
- **Open Container.** No open container law, but it is an offense to consume alcoholic beverages on the highway.
- **Seat Belts.** Seat belts are required for all front seat occupants. Children 2 and under must be in a child restraint system. Children 2 through 4 must be in a child restraint system or seat belt.
- **Helmets.** Motorcycle operators and passengers must wear helmets and eye protection.
- **Road Conditions.** Dial 1-601-987-1212.

MISSISSIPPI REST AREAS

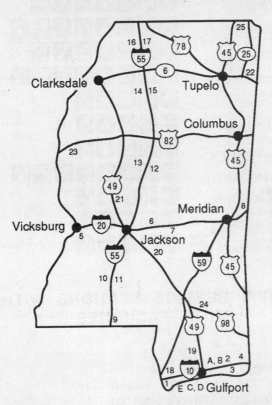

 1   E/W
LOUISIANA LINE

     2/3   E/W
4 MI W OF PASCAGOULA

     4   W
2 MI W OF ALABAMA LINE

(20)   **5**   E
LOUISANA LINE

     6   W
2 MI W OF MORTON

     7   E
2 MI E OF FOREST

     8   W
8 MI W OF ALABAMA LINE

(55)   **9**   N
3 MI N OF LOUISIANA LINE

     10/11   N/S
6 MI S OF HAZLEHURST

     12   N
10 MI S OF VAIDEN

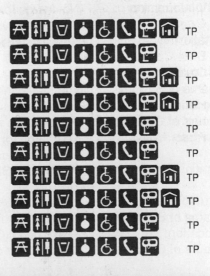

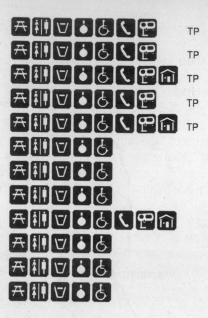

	Location		Facilities	
	13 S 2 MI S OF VAIDEN			TP
	14/15 N/S 4 MI S OF BATESVILLE			TP
	16 S 1 MI S OF HERNANDO			TP
	17 N 3 MI S OF HERNANDO			TP
(59)	18 N 3 MI N OF LOUISIANA LINE			TP
(49)	19 N/S 1 MI N OF WIGGINS			
	20 N/S 3 MI N OF SANITORIUM			
	21 N/S .5 MI S OF POCAHANTAS			
(78)	22 W 3 MI W OF ALABAMA LINE			
(82)	23 E/W 2 MI E OF LELAND			
(98)	24 E/W 4 MI E OF NEW AUGUSTA			
(25)	25 N/S 1 MI S OF TENNESSEE LINE			

MISSISSIPPI SERVICE STATIONS WITH RV DUMP FACILITIES

A. Biloxi

Name of Business:	West Beach Shell
Location:	US-90 & Veterans Blvd.
Hours of Operation:	24 hours per day.
RV Information:	No charge for use of RV Dump. Waterfill and diesel fuel available. No propane.
Station Type:	Service station with mini-mart (Shell).

B. Biloxi

Name of Business:	Interstate Shell
Location:	I-10, Exit 44 (Cedar Lake Rd.).
Hours of Operation:	5:30 A.M. to midnight.
RV Information:	No charge for use of RV Dump. Diesel fuel available. No waterfill or propane.
Station Type:	Truck stop (Shell).

C. Gulfport

Name of Business:	Flying J Travel Plaza
Location:	I-10, Exit 30 (Canal Rd.).
Hours of Operation:	24 hours per day.

RV Information:	No charge for use of RV Dump. Waterfill, propane and diesel fuel available.
Station Type:	Truck stop (Conoco).

D. Gulfport

Name of Business:	Highway 94 Shell
Location:	I-10, Exit 34B (US-49 & Cresote Rd.).
Hours of Operation:	24 hours per day.
RV Information:	No charge for use of RV Dump. Waterfill and diesel fuel available. No propane.
Station Type:	Truck stop (Shell).

E. Pass Christian

Name of Business:	Mississippi Fuel Center
Location:	I-10, Exit 24 (Menge Ave.)
Hours of Operation:	24 hours per day.
RV Information:	No charge for use of RV Dump. Waterfill, propane and diesel fuel available.
Station Type:	Truck stop (Amoco).

GENERAL INFORMATION

Additional Information On Services

- **Rest Area Hours.** Rest Areas are open 24 hours per day, seven days per week.
- **Welcome Center Hours.** Welcome centers are open from 8 A.M. to 5 P.M. year-round; closed Sunday.
- **Tourist Information.** For tourist information call 1-314-751-4133.

Rest Area Usage Rules

- **Overnight Parking.** Overnight parking is permitted.
- **Camping.** Camping or sleeping outside of vehicles is not permitted. Erection of tents or other shelters is not permitted.
- **Stay Limit.** No published limit.

Driving In Missouri

- **Emergencies.** For highway emergencies call 1-800-525-5555.
- **Open Container.** No open container law, but it is an offense to consume alcoholic beverages on the highway.
- **Seat Belts.** Seat belts are required for all front seat occupants. Children 4 and under must be in a child restraint system if in front and a child restraint system or seat belt if in back.
- **Helmets.** Motorcycle operators and passengers must wear helmets and eye protection.
- **Road Conditions.** Dial 1-314-751-3313.

MISSOURI REST AREAS

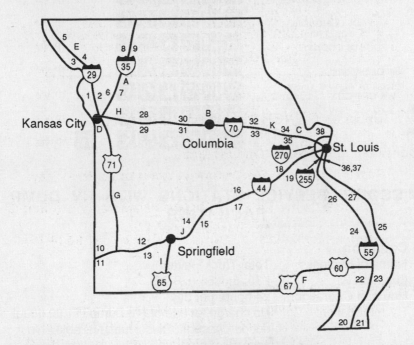

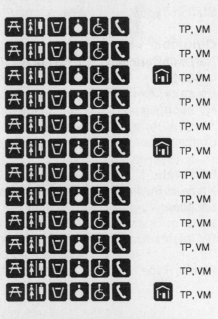

🛣️ 29	1/2 N/S 26 3 MI S OF RTE 116 JCT	🏕️	🚻	🗑️	🍼	♿	📞		TP, VM
	3/4 N/S 82 3 MI SE OF MOUND CITY	🏕️	🚻	🗑️	🍼	♿	📞		TP, VM
	5 S 109 1 MI S OF US-136 JCT	🏕️	🚻	🗑️	🍼	♿	📞	🏠	TP, VM
🛣️ 35	6/7 N/S 34 5 MI S OF RTE 116 JCT	🏕️	🚻	🗑️	🍼	♿	📞		TP, VM
	8/9 N/S 81 11 MI S OF US-136 JCT	🏕️	🚻	🗑️	🍼	♿	📞		TP, VM
🛣️ 44	10/11 E/W 3 2 MI E OF OKLAHOMA LINE	🏕️	🚻	🗑️	🍼	♿	📞	🏠	TP, VM
	12/13 E/W 51 6 MI SW OF HALLTOWN	🏕️	🚻	🗑️	🍼	♿	📞		TP, VM
	14/15 E/W 109 2 MI SW OF CONWAY	🏕️	🚻	🗑️	🍼	♿	📞		TP, VM
	16/17 E/W 177 7 MI W OF ROLLA	🏕️	🚻	🗑️	🍼	♿	📞		TP, VM
	18/19 E/W 235 3 MI SW OF SAINT CLAIR	🏕️	🚻	🗑️	🍼	♿	📞		TP, VM
🛣️ 55	20/21 N/S 2 5 MI S OF RTE-164	🏕️	🚻	🗑️	🍼	♿	📞		TP, VM
	22/23 N/S 41 1 MI N OF MARSTON	🏕️	🚻	🗑️	🍼	♿	📞	🏠	TP, VM

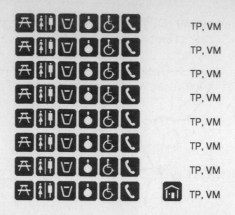

24/25 N/S 110 3 MI N OF FRUITLAND			TP, VM
26/27 N/S 159 2 MI N OF BLOOMSDALE			TP, VM
28/29 E/W 57 1 MI W OF CONCORDIA			TP, VM
30/31 E/W 104 S EDGE OF BOONVILE			TP, VM
32/33 E/W 168 W OF DANVILLE			TP, VM
34/35 E/W 198 WRIGHT CITY			TP, VM
36/37 E/W 3 3 MI E OF I-55 JCT			TP, VM
38 E/W 34 1 MI W OF ILLINOIS LINE			TP, VM

MISSOURI SERVICE STATIONS WITH RV DUMP FACILITIES

A. Cameron

Name of Business:	Total Truck Haven
Location:	I-35, Exit 54 (US-36).
Hours of Operation:	24 hours per day.
RV Information:	No charge for use of RV Dump ($1.00 if fuel not purchased). Diesel fuel available. No waterfill or propane.
Station Type:	Truck stop (Total).

B. Columbia

Name of Business:	Midway Auto/Truck Plaza
Location:	I-70, Exit 121 (UA-40).
Hours of Operation:	24 hours per day.
RV Information:	No charge for use of RV Dump. Waterfill and diesel fuel available. No propane.
Station Type:	Truck stop (Independent).

C. Foristell

Name of Business:	St. Louis West 70 Truck Plaza
Location:	I-70, Exit 203 (County Road W).
Hours of Operation:	24 hours per day.
RV Information:	No charge for use of RV Dump. Waterfill, propane and diesel fuel available.
Station Type:	Truck stop (Mobil).

D. Kansas City
Name of Business: Conoco Fuel Stop
Location: I-435, Exit 57 (Front St.).
Hours of Operation: 24 hours per day.
RV Information: No charge for use of RV Dump. Waterfill, propane and diesel fuel available.
Station Type: Truck stop (Conoco).

E. Mound City
Name of Business: Squaw Creek Truck Plaza
Location: I-29, Exit 79 (MO-159).
Hours of Operation: 24 hours per day.
RV Information: No charge for use of RV Dump. Waterfill and diesel fuel available. No propane.
Station Type: Truck stop (Phillips 66).

F. Neelyville
Name of Business: State LIne Truck Stop
Location: US-67 South (MO/AR state line).
Hours of Operation: 24 hours per day.
RV Information: No charge for use of RV Dump. Waterfill and diesel fuel available. No propane.
Station Type: Truck stop (Conoco).

G. Nevada
Name of Business: Nevada Fuel Mart
Location: US-71, Camp Clark Exit.
Hours of Operation: 24 hours per day.
RV Information: No charge for use of RV Dump. Diesel fuel available. No waterfill or propane.
Station Type: Truck stop (Phillips 66).

H. Oak Grove
Name of Business: Kansas City East 76 Auto/Truck Stop
Location: I-70, Exit 28 (County Road H).
Hours of Operation: 24 hours per day.
RV Information: No charge for use of RV Dump. Waterfill and diesel fuel available. No propane.
Station Type: Truck stop (Unocal 76).

I. Ozark
Name of Business: Tony's Convenience Center
Location: US-65, CC & J Exit.

Hours of Operation:	24 hours per day.
RV Information:	No charge for use of RV Dump. Waterfill, propane and diesel fuel available.
Station Type:	Truck stop (Texaco).

J. Strafford

Name of Business:	Git-N-G0
Location:	I-44, Exit 88 (MO-125).
Hours of Operation:	24 hours per day.
RV Information:	No charge for use of RV Dump. Waterfill and diesel fuel available. No propane.
Station Type:	Truck stop (Phillips 66).

K. Warrenton

Name of Business:	Flying J Travel Plaza
Location:	I-70, Exit 188 (MO-B).
Hours of Operation:	24 hours per day.
RV Information:	No charge for use of RV Dump. Waterfill, propane and diesel fuel available.
Station Type:	Truck stop (Conoco).

MONTANA

"Treasure State"

Capital: Helena	Largest City: Billings
Population: 799,065	Area: 145,392 sq. mi.
Highest Point: 12,799 ft.	Lowest Point: 1,820 ft.

Date of Statehood: November 8, 1889

GENERAL INFORMATION

Additional Information On Services

- **Rest Area Hours.** All rest areas closed Nov. 15 through April 15, except 1, 2, 10, 11, 12, 13, 17, 18, 21, 22, 25, 26, 35, 36, and 39.
- **Tourist Information.** For tourist information call 1-800-548-3390.

Rest Area Usage Rules

- **Overnight Parking.** Overnight parking is permitted, but not encouraged.
- **Camping.** Camping or sleeping outside of vehicle is not permitted.
- **Stay Limit.** No published limit.

Driving In Montana

- **Emergencies.** For highway emergencies call the highway patrol at 1-800-525-5555.
- **Open Container.** Governed by local ordnance. In some cities, open containers of alcoholic beverages in the passenger compartment of the vehicle are not permitted.
- **Seat Belts.** Seat belts are required for all occupants. Children 4 and under or less than 40 pounds must be in a child restraint system.
- **Helmets.** Motorcycle operators and passengers 18 and under must wear helmets.
- **Road Conditions.** Dial 1-800-332-6171

MONTANA REST AREAS

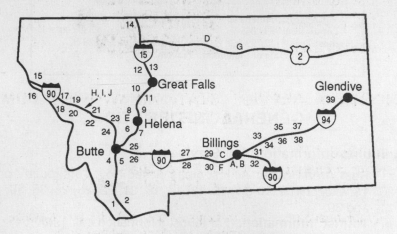

15 1/2 N/S 10 MI N OF DELL	🏕 🚻 ▽ 🍼 ♿ 📞	TP
3 S 10 MI S OF DILLON	🏕 🚻 ▽ 🍼 ♿	TP
4/5 N/S 8 MI N OF DIVIDE	🏕 🚻 ▽ 🍼 ♿	TP
6/7 N/S 2 MI N OF JEFFERSON CITY	🏕 🚻 ▽ 🍼 ♿	TP
8/9 N/S 3 MI S OF WOLF CREEK	🏕 🚻 ▽ 🍼 ♿	TP
10/11 N/S 6 MI N OF CRAIG	🏕 🚻 ▽ 🍼 ♿ 📞	TP
12/13 N/S 8 MI N OF DUTTON	🏕 🚻 ▽ 🍼 ♿ 📞	TP
14 S 1 MI S OF CANADA LINE	🏕 🚻 ▽ 🍼 ♿ 📺	TP
90 15/16 E/W 5 MI E OF IDAHO LINE	🏕 🚻 ▽ 🍼 ♿	TP
17/18 E/W 12 MI E OF SUPERIOR	🏕 🚻 ▽ 🍼 ♿ 📞	TP
19/20 E/W 5 MI W OF ALBERTON	🏕 🚻 ▽ 🍼 ♿	TP
21/22 E/W 11 MI W OF DRUMMOND	🏕 🚻 ▽ 🍼 ♿ 📞	TP
23/24 E/W 4 MI W OF GARRISON	🏕 🚻 ▽ 🍼 ♿ 📞	TP
25/26 E/W 10 MI E OF BUTTE	🏕 🚻 ▽ 🍼 ♿	TP
27/28 E/W 12 MI E OF BIG TIMBER	🏕 🚻 ▽ 🍼 ♿ 📞	TP
29/30 E/W 8 MI E OF COLUMBUS	🏕 🚻 ▽ 🍼 ♿ 📞	TP
31/32 E/W 21 MI E OF BILLINGS	🏕 🚻 ▽ 🍼 ♿	TP

33/34 E/W 8 MI W OF CUSTER	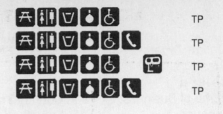		TP
35/36 E/W 12 MI E OF BIG HORN			TP
37/38 E/W 14 MI E OF FORSYTH			TP
39 E 16 MI E OF TERRY			TP

MONTANA SERVICE STATIONS WITH RV DUMP FACILITIES

A. Billings

Name of Business: Flying J Travel Plaza
Location: I-90, Exit 455 (Johnson Rd.).
Hours of Operation: 24 hours per day.
RV Information: No charge for use of RV Dump. Waterfill, propane and diesel fuel available.
Station Type: Truck stop (Conoco).

B. Billings

Name of Business: Sinclair West Parkway
Location: I-90, Exit 446 (Laurel rd.).
Hours of Operation: 24 hours per day.
RV Information: No charge for use of RV Dump. Waterfill and diesel fuel available. No propane.
Station Type: Truck stop (Sinclair).

C. Columbus

Name of Business: Town Pump
Location: I-90, Exit 455 (MT-78)
Hours of Operation: 24 hours per day.
RV Information: No charge for use of RV Dump ($5.00 if fuel not purchased). Diesel fuel available. No waterfill or propane.
Station Type: Truck stop (EXXON).

D. Havre

Name of Business: CENEX Supply
Location: US-2, (First St.).
Hours of Operation: 24 hours per day (service station open 7 A.M. to 10 P.M.).
RV Information: No charge for use of RV Dump. Diesel fuel available. Waterfill not available in winter

months. Propane is available only during service station hours..

Station Type: Truck stop (CENEX).

E. Helena

Name of Business: High Country Travel Plaza
Location: I-15, Exit 192 (US-12 E & 287 NE).
Hours of Operation: 24 hours per day.
RV Information: No charge for use of RV Dump. Waterfill, propane and diesel fuel available.
Station Type: Truck stop (Conoco).

F. Laurel

Name of Business: Pelican Truck Plaza
Location: I-90, Exit 437 (MT-2, Frontage Rd. S.)
Hours of Operation: 24 hours per day.
RV Information: No charge for use of RV Dump ($4.00 if fuel not purchased). Waterfill, propane and diesel fuel available.
Station Type: Truck stop (Sinclair).

G. Malta

Name of Business: West Side Self Service
Location: US-2W & Hwy. 242
Hours of Operation: 5 A.M. to midnight.
RV Information: No charge for use of RV Dump. Waterfill, propane and diesel fuel available.
Station Type: Truck stop (Conoco).

H. Missoula

Name of Business: Muralt's Truck Plaza
Location: I-90, Exit 96 (US-93).
Hours of Operation: 24 hours per day.
RV Information: No charge for use of RV Dump ($3.00 if fuel not purchased). Waterfill, propane and diesel fuel available.
Station Type: Truck stop (Conoco).

I. Missoula

Name of Business: Crossroads Truck Center
Location: I-90, Exit 96 (US-93).
Hours of Operation: 24 hours per day.
RV Information: $1.00 charge for use of RV Dump ($2.00 if

fuel not purchased). Waterfill, propane and diesel fuel available.

Station Type: Truck stop (Sinclair).

J. Missoula

Name of Business: CENEX Supply and Marketing
Location: I-90, Exit 101 (Reserve St.).
Hours of Operation: 24 hours per day.
RV Information: No charge for use of RV Dump. Waterfill, propane and diesel fuel available.
Station Type: Service station with mini-mart (CENEX).

NEBRASKA

"Cornhusker State"

Capital: Lincoln	Largest City: Omaha
Population: 1,578,385	Area: 77,227 sq. mi.
Highest Point: 5,426 ft.	Lowest Point: 840 ft.

Date of Statehood: March 1, 1867

GENERAL INFORMATION

Additional Information On Services

- **Rest Area Hours.** Rest Areas are open 24 hours per day, seven days per week.
- **Welcome Center Hours.** Welcome centers in the Mountain Time Zone are staffed from 8 A.M. to 4 P.M. seven days per week between Memorial Day and Labor Day. Welcome centers in the Central Time Zone are staffed from 9 A.M. to 5 P.M. seven days per week between Memorial Day and Labor Day. In addition to the hours listed above, welcome centers at rest areas 7,8, and 27 are staffed sporadically between March 1 and Memorial Day and between Labor Day and October 31. The time zone line runs vertically between North Platte and Ogallala.
- **Historical Plaques.** Most rest areas have historical plaques. Additionally, rest area 3 has an observation area and "Golden Link" in I-80 roadway commemorating the completion of Interstate 80 in Nebraska.
- **Sculptures.** Sculpture displays are available at several of the rest areas and are listed below by rest area, sculpture title and artist:

  Rest Area 4. "Roadway Confluence" by Hans Van de Bovenkamp.

  Rest Area 8. "Up/Over" by Linda Howard.

  Rest Area 11. "Nebraskan Gateway" by Anthony Padovano.

  Rest Area 15. "Nebraska Wind Sculpture" by George Baker.

  Rest Area 20. "Erma's Desire" by John Raimondi.

  Rest Area 21. "Crossing the Plains" by Bradford Graves.

  Rest Area 24. "Arrival" by Paul Von Ringelheim.

  Rest Area 26. "Memorial to the American Bandshell" by Richard Field.

- **Tourist Information.** For tourist information call 1-800-228-4307.

Rest Area Usage Rules

- **Overnight Parking.** No overnight parking.
- **Camping.** Camping or sleeping outside of vehicle is not permitted.
- **Stay Limit.** Maximum length of stay is limited to 5 hours.

Driving In Nebraska

- **Emergencies.** For highway emergencies call 1-800-525-5555. For statewide Crime Stoppers, call 1-800-422-1494. Marijuana Hot Line on 1-800-742-9333.
- **Open Container.** No open container law, but it is an offense to consume alcoholic beverages on the highway.
- **Seat Belts.** Children 4 and under or 40 pounds and under must be in a child restraint system. Children 4 and 5 must be in a child restraint system or seat belt. Children under 4 but weighing more than 40 pounds may be secured with a seat belt.
- **Helmets.** Motorcycle operators and passengers must wear helmets.
- **Road Conditions.**
  Omaha. 1-402-553-5000
  Lincoln. 1-402-471-4533
  Norfolk. 1-402-370-3464
  Grand Island. 1-308-384-3555
  North Platte. 1-308-535-8052
  ScottsBluff. 1-308-632-1351

NEBRASKA REST AREAS

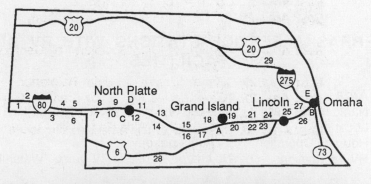

Route	No.	Dir.	Location	Exit	Facilities	Notes
80	1	E	KIMBALL	10	picnic, restroom, water, trash, handicap, phone, shelter	PA, TP
	2	W	KIMBALL	25	picnic, restroom, water, trash, handicap, phone, shelter	PA, TP
	3	E	SIDNEY	51	picnic, restroom, water, trash, handicap, phone, shelter	PA,TP
	4	W	SIDNEY	61	picnic, restroom, water, trash, handicap, phone, shelter	PA, TP, SC
	5/6	E/W	CHAPPELL	82/88	picnic, restroom, water, trash, handicap, phone, shelter	TP
	7	E	OGALLALA	124	picnic, restroom, water, trash, handicap, phone, shelter	PA, TP
	8	W	OGALLALA	133	picnic, restroom, water, trash, handicap, phone, shelter	PA,TP, SC
	9/10	E/W	SUTHERLAND	160	picnic, restroom, water, trash, handicap, phone, shelter	PA (EB), TP, HM (EB)
	11/12	E/W	BRADY	194	picnic, restroom, water, trash, handicap, phone, shelter	PA,TP, F (WB), SC (WB)
	13/14	E/W	COZAD	227	picnic, restroom, water, trash, handicap, phone, shelter	PA,TP
	15/16	E/W	KEARNEY	269	picnic, restroom, water, trash, handicap, phone, shelter	PA,TP, F, SC (WB)
	17	E	GIBBON	285	picnic, restroom, water, trash, handicap, phone, shelter	PA,TP
	18	W	ALDA	305	picnic, restroom, water, trash, handicap, phone, shelter	PA,TP, F
	19/20	E/W	GRAND ISLAND	315	picnic, restroom, water, trash, handicap, phone, shelter	PA (EB),TP, F (EB), SC (EB)
	21/22	E/W	YORK	350	picnic, restroom, water, trash, handicap, phone, shelter	PA,TP, SC (WB)
	23	W	GOEHNER	375	picnic, restroom, water, trash, handicap, phone, shelter	PA,TP
	24	E	BLUE RIVER	381	picnic, restroom, water, trash, handicap, phone, shelter	PA,TP, SC
	25	W	LINCOLN	405	picnic, restroom, water, trash, handicap, phone, shelter	PA,TP
	26	E	PLATTE RIVER	425	picnic, restroom, water, trash, handicap, phone, shelter	PA,TP, SC
	27	W	MELIA HILL	431	picnic, restroom, water, trash, handicap, phone, shelter	PA,TP
6	28	E/W	2.5 MI E OF MC COOK		picnic, restroom, water, trash, handicap	TP
275	29	E/W	3 MI W OF RTE 15 JCT		picnic, restroom, water, trash, handicap	TP

NEBRASKA SERVICE STATIONS WITH RV DUMP FACILITIES

A. Alda

Name of Business:	Grand Island West 76 Auto/Truck Plaza
Location:	I-80, Exit 305 (Alda Rd.).
Hours of Operation:	24 hours per day.
RV Information:	No charge for use of RV Dump. Waterfill and

diesel fuel available. No propane.

Station Type: Truck stop (Unocal 76).

B. Gretna

Name of Business: Flying J Travel Plaza
Location: I-80, Exit 432 (NE-31).
Hours of Operation: 24 hours per day.
RV Information: No charge for use of RV Dump. Waterfill, propane and diesel fuel available.
Station Type: Truck stop (Conoco).

C. Hershey

Name of Business: Tomahawk Truck Stop
Location: I-80, Exit 164 (Hershey Rd.).
Hours of Operation: 24 hours per day.
RV Information: No charge for use of RV Dump. Waterfill, propane and diesel fuel available.
Station Type: Truck stop (Texaco).

D. North Platte

Name of Business: Coastal Mart
Location: I-80, Exit 177 (Jeffers Rd., US-83).
Hours of Operation: 6 A.M. to midnight.
RV Information: No charge for use of RV Dump. Waterfill available. No propane or diesel fuel.
Station Type: Service station with mini-mart (Coastal).

E. Omaha

Name of Business: Sapp Brothers Plaza
Location: I-80, Exit 440 (NE-50).
Hours of Operation: 24 hours per day.
RV Information: No charge for use of RV Dump. Waterfill, propane and diesel fuel available.
Station Type: Truck stop (Texaco).

NEVADA

"Silver State"

Capital: Carson City	**Largest City:** Las Vegas
Population: 1,201,833	**Area:** 108,889 sq. mi.
Highest Point: 13,143 ft.	**Lowest Point:** 470 ft.

Date of Statehood: October 31, 1864

GENERAL INFORMATION

Additional Information On Services

- **Rest Area Hours.** Rest Areas are open 24 hours per day, seven days per week. Area 9 is closed December through April.
- **Welcome Center Hours.** Welcome centers are staffed from 8 A.M. to 5 P.M. seven days per week.
- **Tourist Information.** For tourist information call 1-800-638-2328.

Rest Area Usage Rules

- **Overnight Parking.** Overnight parking is permitted.
- **Camping.** Camping is permitted.
- **Stay Limit.** Areas 14 and 16 have a 24 hour limit. The other areas have an 18 hour limit.

Driving In Nevada

- **Emergencies.** For highway emergencies dial 0 and ask for ZENITH 1-2000 for the highway patrol.
- **Open Container.** Open containers of alcoholic beverages in the passenger compartment of the vehicle are not permitted.
- **Seat Belts.** Seat belts are required for all occupants. Children 5 and under or less than 40 pounds must be in a child restraint system.
- **Helmets.** Motorcycle operators and passengers must wear helmets.
- **Road Conditions.** Dial 1-702-793-1313 for northern Nevada and 1-702-486-3116 from southern Nevada.

NEVADA REST AREAS

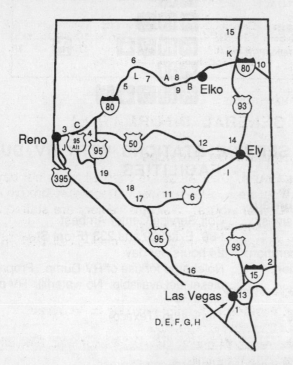

15	1 JEAN	N			🚻	🗑	🍼	♿	📞		🏠	
	2 MESQUITE	S		⛱	🚻	🗑	🍼	♿	📞		🏠	
80	3 WADSWORTH	W	42	⛱	🚻	🗑	🍼	♿	📞			TP
	4 US-95 JCT, TRINITY	E	83	⛱	🚻	🗑	🍼	♿	📞			
	5 COSGRAVE	E	158	⛱	🚻	🗑	🍼		📞	📺		TP
	6 BUTTON POINT	W	188	⛱	🚻	🗑	🍼	♿	📞			TP
	7 VALMY	E	217	⛱	🚻	🗑	🍼		📞	📺		TP
	8/9 BEOWAWE	E/W	255	⛱	🚻	🗑	🍼	♿		📺		TP
	10 WENDOVER	W		⛱	🚻						🏠	
6	11 9 MI E OF TONOPAH	E/W		⛱	🚻							
50	12 HICKISON SUMMIT	E/W		⛱	🚻							
93	13 2 MI N OF BOULDER CITY	N/S		⛱	🚻	🗑	🍼	♿	📞		🏠	

14 E/W 3 MI N OF ELY	⛺ 🚻 🗑 ⚫	📟	TP
15 N/S 5 MI N OF CONTACT	⛺ 🚻		
95 16 N/S LATHROP WELLS	⛺ 🚻 🗑		
17 N/S 13 MI NW OF TONAPAH	⛺ 🚻 🗑 ⚫	📟	TP
18 N/S LUNING	⛺ 🚻		
19 N/S NW EDGE OF HAWTHORNE	⛺ 🚻 🗑 ⚫ ♿		

NEVADA SERVICE STATIONS WITH RV DUMP FACILITIES

A. Battle Mountain

Name of Business:	Colt Service Center Ambest
Location:	I-80, Exits 229 and 233 (Front St.).
Hours of Operation:	24 hours per day.
RV Information:	No charge for use of RV Dump. Propane and diesel fuel available. No waterfill. RV park on property.
Station Type:	Truck stop (Texaco).

B. Carlin

Name of Business:	Fuel America Express
Location:	I-80, Exit 280 (10th St.).
Hours of Operation:	24 hours per day.
RV Information:	No charge for use of RV Dump ($5.00 if fuel not purchased). Waterfill and diesel fuel available. No propane.
Station Type:	Truck stop (Phillips 66).

C. Fernley

Name of Business:	Truck Inn
Location:	I-80, Exit 48 (Truck Way).
Hours of Operation:	24 hours per day.
RV Information:	No charge for use of RV Dump. Waterfill, propane and diesel fuel available.
Station Type:	Truck stop (Chevron).

D. Las Vegas

Name of Business:	Blue Diamond Center
Location:	I-15, Exit 33.

Hours of Operation: 24 hours per day.
RV Information: $3.00 charge for use of RV Dump. Waterfill, propane and diesel fuel available.
Station Type: Truck stop (Unocal 76).

E. Las Vegas
Name of Business: Bus Stop
Location: I-15, Exit 37 (Tropicana, west to Polaris, right to Naples).
Hours of Operation: 6 A.M. to 9 P.M.
RV Information: No charge for use of RV Dump. Waterfill and propane available. Diesel fuel only.
Station Type: Truck stop.

F. Las Vegas
Name of Business: King 8 Truck Plaza
Location: I-15, Exit 37 (Tropicana West).
Hours of Operation: 24 hours per day.
RV Information: No charge for use of RV Dump ($5.00 if fuel not purchased. Waterfill, propane and diesel fuel available.
Station Type: Truck stop (Independent).

G. North Las Vegas
Name of Business: Flying J Travel Plaza
Location: I-15, Exit 46 (Cheyenne Ave.).
Hours of Operation: 24 hours per day.
RV Information: No charge for use of RV Dump. Waterfill, propane and diesel fuel available.
Station Type: Truck stop (Conoco).

H. North Las Vegas
Name of Business: Magic Wand Truck Stop
Location: I-15, Exit 46 (Cheyenne West, north on Losee).
Hours of Operation: 24 hours per day.
RV Information: No charge for use of RV Dump. Waterfill and diesel fuel available. No propane.
Station Type: Truck stop (Independent).

I. Preston
Name of Business: Lane's Preston Truck Center
Location: NV-318, 7 miles S. of US-6.

Hours of Operation: 7 A.M. to 9 P.M.
RV Information: $2.00 charge for use of RV Dump. Waterfill, propane and diesel fuel available.
Station Type: Truck stop (Phillips 66).

J. Verdi

Name of Business: Boomtown Casino Truck Stop
Location: I-80, Exit 4 (Garson Rd.).
Hours of Operation: 24 hours per day.
RV Information: $5.00 charge for use of RV Dump. Waterfill, propane and diesel fuel available. RV park on property; RV dump at park.
Station Type: Truck stop (EXXON).

K. Wells

Name of Business: Flying J Travel Plaza
Location: I-80, Exit 352 (Hwy. 93).
Hours of Operation: 24 hours per day.
RV Information: No charge for use of RV Dump. Waterfill, propane and diesel fuel available.
Station Type: Truck stop (Conoco).

L. Winnemucca

Name of Business: Flying J Travel Plaza
Location: I-80, Exit 176 (Winnemucca Blvd.).
Hours of Operation: 24 hours per day.
RV Information: No charge for use of RV Dump. Waterfill, propane and diesel fuel available.
Station Type: Truck stop (Independent).

NEW HAMPSHIRE

"Granite State"

Capital: Concord	**Largest City:** Manchester
Population: 1,105,000	**Area:** 9,027 sq. mi.
Highest Point: 6,288 ft.	**Lowest Point:** Sea Level
Date of Statehood: June 21, 1788	

GENERAL INFORMATION

Additional Information On Services

- **Rest Area Hours.** Rest Areas 5,6, and 12 are open 24 hours per day, seven days per week, year round. Areas 1-4, 7, 8, 11 and 18 are open from 7 A.M. to 11 P.M., year round. Areas 14, 15, 16, 17, and 19 are open only from Memorial Day through Columbus Day.
- **Welcome Center Hours.** Welcome centers are privately run and are staffed from approximately 8 A.M. to 5 P.M. year round.
- **Tourist Information.** For tourist information call 1-603-271-2343. Additionally, New Hampshire has numerous toll free "800" numbers that provide recorded information on various activities. For recorded information on New Hampshire events and attractions, call 1-800-258-3608.

Rest Area Usage Rules

- **Overnight Parking.** Overnight parking is notpermitted.
- **Camping.** Camping is not permitted.
- **Stay Limit.** Stays in excess of four hours permitted only when emergency conditions exist.

Driving In New Hampshire

- **Emergencies.** For highway emergencies call 1-800-525-5555.
- **Open Container.** Open containers of alcoholic beverages in the passenger compartment of the vehicle are not permitted.
- **Seat Belts.** Seat belts or child restraint systems are required for all children 12 and under.
- **Helmets.** Motorcycle operators and passengers 18 and under must wear helmets.
- **Road Conditions.** Dial 1-603-485-5767 or 1-603-485-9526.

NEW HAMPSHIRE REST AREAS

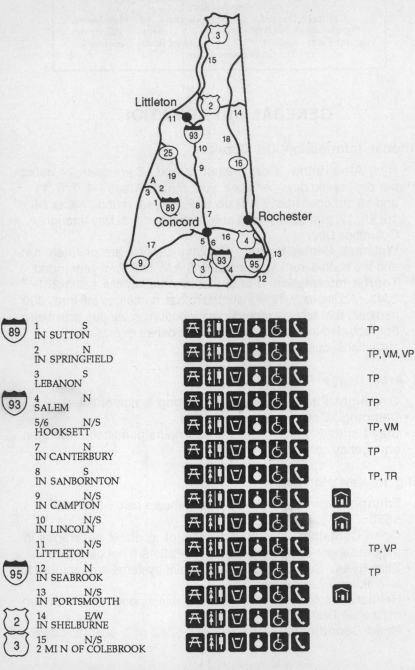

#			Facilities		Notes
(89) 1	S	IN SUTTON	🏕️🚻🗑️⛽♿📞		TP
2	N	IN SPRINGFIELD	🏕️🚻🗑️⛽♿📞		TP, VM, VP
3	S	LEBANON	🏕️🚻🗑️⛽♿📞		TP
(93) 4	N	SALEM	🏕️🚻🗑️⛽♿📞		TP
5/6	N/S	HOOKSETT	🏕️🚻🗑️⛽♿📞		TP, VM
7	N	IN CANTERBURY	🏕️🚻🗑️⛽♿📞		TP
8	S	IN SANBORNTON	🏕️🚻🗑️⛽♿📞		TP, TR
9	N/S	IN CAMPTON	🏕️🚻🗑️⛽♿📞	🏠	
10	N/S	IN LINCOLN	🏕️🚻🗑️⛽📞	🏠	
11	N/S	LITTLETON	🏕️🚻🗑️⛽♿📞		TP, VP
(95) 12	N	IN SEABROOK	🏕️🚻🗑️⛽♿📞		TP
13	N/S	IN PORTSMOUTH	🏕️🚻🗑️⛽♿📞	🏠	
(2) 14	E/W	IN SHELBURNE	🏕️🚻🗑️⛽♿📞		
(3) 15	N/S	2 MI N OF COLEBROOK	🏕️🚻🗑️⛽♿📞		

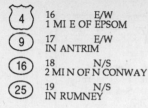

	16 E/W 1 MI E OF EPSOM	
4	16 E/W 1 MI E OF EPSOM	
9	17 E/W IN ANTRIM	
16	18 N/S 2 MI N OF N CONWAY	
25	19 N/S IN RUMNEY	

NEW HAMPSHIRE SERVICE STATIONS WITH RV DUMP FACILITIES

A. Lebanon

Name of Business: Exit 18 Truck Stop
Location: I-89, Exit 18 (NH-120).
Hours of Operation: 24 hours per day.
RV Information: No charge for use of RV Dump ($5.00 if fuel not purchased). Waterfill, propane and diesel fuel available.
Station Type: Truck stop (Coastal).

NEW JERSEY
"Garden State"

Capital: Trenton   **Largest City:** Newark
Population: 7,730,188   **Area:** 7,521 sq. mi.
Highest Point: 1,803 ft.   **Lowest Point:** Sea Level
Date of Statehood: December 18, 1787

GENERAL INFORMATION

Additional Information On Services

- **Rest Area Hours.** Rest Areas are open 24 hours per day, seven days per week.
- **Welcome Center Hours.** Welcome centers are staffed from 9 A.M. to 5 P.M. (hours may vary).
- **Toll Road Service Plazas.** Areas 13 through 35 are toll road service plazas along the Garden State Parkway, the New Jersey/Atlantic City Expressway and the New Jersey Turnpike.
- **Fresh Farm Market.** Farley Service Plaza (#22) has a fresh farm market with fresh fruits and vegetables from May through September.
- **State Police.** There is a State Police station at Farley Service Plaza (#22).
- **Truck Prohibition.** Trucks are not permitted north of mile marker 105 on the Garden State Parkway.
- **Airport Shuttle.** There is a shuttle service to Newark Airport from Montvale Service Plaza (#21).
- **Tourist Information.** For tourist information call 1-800-537-7397.

Rest Area Usage Rules

- **Overnight Parking.** Overnight parking is permitted, but limited and not encouraged.
- **Camping.** Camping is not permitted.
- **Stay Limit.** No published limit.

Driving In New Jersey

- **Emergencies.** For highway emergencies call 911 (may not be operable in all counties) or dial the highway patrol at 609-882-2000.
- **Open Container.** Open containers of alcoholic beverages in

the passenger compartment of the vehicle are not permitted.
- **Seat Belts.** Seat belts are required for all front seat occupants. Children under 4 and under 40 pounds must be in a child restraint system.
- **Helmets.** Motorcycle operators and passengers must wear helmets.
- **Road Conditions.** Dial 1-609-882-2000.

NEW JERSEY REST AREAS

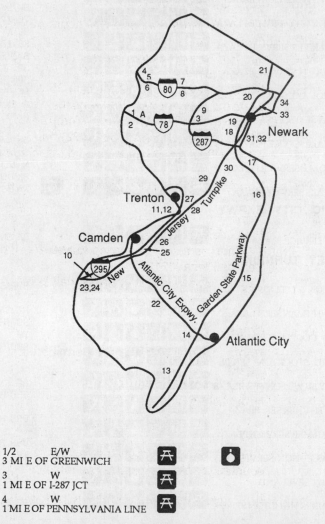

(78)	1/2 3 MI E OF GREENWICH	E/W	🏕	🚻	
	3 1 MI E OF I-287 JCT	W	🏕		VP
(80)	4 1 MI E OF PENNSYLVANIA LINE	W	🏕		VP

			Amenities	Notes
5	W	2 MI E OF COLUMBIA		VP
6	E	3 MI E OF COLUMBIA		PW, TP, VM,VP
7/8	E/W	5 MI W OF NETCONG		TP
9	N	3 MI N OF BERNARDSVILLE		PW, TP, VM
10	N	2 MI N OF DELAWARE LINE		PW, TP, VM
11/12	N/S	4 MI S OF BORDENTOWN		PW, TP, VM

(Routes 287 and 295 shields shown at entries 9 and 10.)

GARDEN STATE PARKWAY

			Notes
13	N/S 18	OCEANVIEW SERVICE PLAZA	MO, RR, TP
14	N/S 41	ATLANTIC CITY SERVICE PLAZA	BK, MF, MO, TC, TP
15	N/S 76	FORKED RIVER SERVICE PLAZA	BK, MF, MO, SB, TB, TC,TP
16	N/S 100	MONMOUTH SERVICE PLAZA	BK,MF,MO,NA, SB,TB,TC,TP
17	N/S 124	CHEESEQUAKE SERVICE PLAZA	BBB, BK, MF, MO, TC
18	N/S 133	RAHWAY SERVICE PLAZA	S: EX, SH N: EX, TX
19	N/S 142	VAUX HALL SERVICE PLAZA	McD, MO
20	N/S 153	BROOKDALE SERVICE PLAZA	S: MCD, MO N: MO
21	N/S 171	MONTVALE SERVICE PLAZA	BK,DD,MF,MO, NA,SB,TB,TC

NJ/ATLANTIC CITY EXPWY.

			Notes
22	E/W 21	FARLEY SERVICE PLAZA	BK, SN, TP

NEW JERSEY TURNPIKE

			Notes
23/24	N/S 5	C. BARTON & J. FENWICK	BBB, SN, TP
25	S 30	WALT WHITMAN SER. PLAZA	RR, SN, TP
26	N 39	JAMES F. COOPER SER PLAZA	BBB, RR, SN, TP
27	S 59	RICHARD STOCKTON SER PL	BBB, RR, SN, TP
28	S 59	WOODROW WILSON SER PLAZA	RR, SN, TP
29	S 72	MOLLY PITCHER SER. PLAZA	BBB, RR, SN, TP
30	N 79	JOYCE KILMER SERVICE PLAZA	BBB, RR, SN, TP
31	S 93	THOMAS EDISON SERVICE PL	BBB, RR, SN, TP
32	N 93	GROVER CLEVELAND	RR, SN, TP
34	S 111	ALEXANDER HALILTON SER. PL	RR, SN, TP

NEW JERSEY SERVICE STATIONS WITH RV DUMP FACILITIES

A. Bloomsbury

Name of Business:	Garden State Truck Plaza
Location:	I-78, Exit 7 (NJ-173).
Hours of Operation:	24 hours per day.
RV Information:	No charge for use of RV Dump ($7.00 if fuel not purchased). Waterfill, propane and diesel fuel available.
Station Type:	Truck stop (Independent).

NEW MEXICO

"Land of Enchantment"

Capital: Santa Fe	Largest City: Albuquerque
Population: 1,515,069	Area: 121,412 sq. mi.
Highest Point: 13,461 ft.	Lowest Point: 2,817 ft.

Date of Statehood: January 6, 1912

GENERAL INFORMATION

Additional Information On Services

- **Rest Area Hours.** Rest Areas are open 24 hours per day, seven days per week.
- **Welcome Center Hours.** Welcome centers are open from 8 A.M. to 5 P.M. year-round.
- **Tourist Information.** For tourist information call 1-800-545-2040.

Rest Area Usage Rules

- **Overnight Parking.** Overnight parking permitted.
- **Camping.** Camping or sleeping outside of vehicle is not permitted.
- **Stay Limit.** Parking limited to 24 hours.

Driving In New Mexico

- **Emergencies.** For highway emergencies call 911 (may not be operable in all counties) or dial the highway patrol at 1-505-827-9000.
- **Open Container.** Open containers of alcoholic beverages in the passenger compartment of the vehicle are not permitted.
- **Seat Belts.** Seat belts are required for all front seat occupants and all children under 11. Children 1 and under must be in a child restraint system. Children 1 through 5 must be in a child restraint system in front and a child restraint system or seat belt in the rear.
- **Helmets.** Motorcycle operators and passengers under 18 must wear helmets.
- **Road Conditions.** Dial 1-800-432-4269 in New Mexico and 1-505-827-6300 out of state.

NEW MEXICO REST AREAS

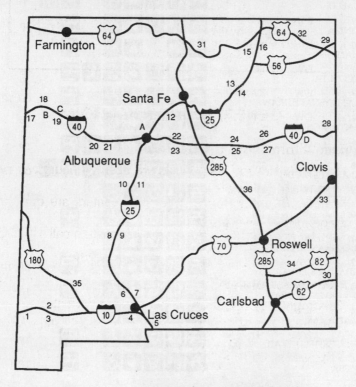

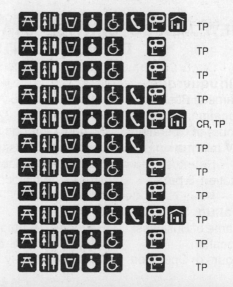

(10)	1	E/W	20	🧺	🚻	🗑	💧	♿	☎	🚐	🏠	TP
	LORDSBURG											
	2	E	53	🧺	🚻	🗑	💧	♿		🚐		TP
	YUCCA											
	3	W	61	🧺	🚻	🗑	💧	♿		🚐		TP
	GAGE											
	4	E	135	🧺	🚻	🗑	💧	♿	☎	🚐		TP
	LAS CRUCES											
	5	W	164	🧺	🚻	🗑	💧	♿	☎	🚐	🏠	CR, TP
	TEXAS LINE											
(25)	6/7	N/S	23	🧺	🚻	🗑	💧	♿	☎			TP
	FT SELDEN											
	8/9	N/S	114	🧺	🚻	🗑	💧	♿		🚐		TP
	FT CRAIG											
	10/11	N/S	167	🧺	🚻	🗑	💧	♿		🚐		TP
	WALKING SANDS											
	12	N	268	🧺	🚻	🗑	💧	♿	☎	🚐	🏠	TP
	LA BAJADA											
	13/14	N/S	376	🧺	🚻	🗑	💧	♿		🚐		TP
	FT UNION											
	15/16	N/S	435	🧺	🚻	🗑	💧	♿		🚐		TP
	THAXTON											

New Mexico ▬▬▬▬▬▬▬▬▬▬▬▬ 135

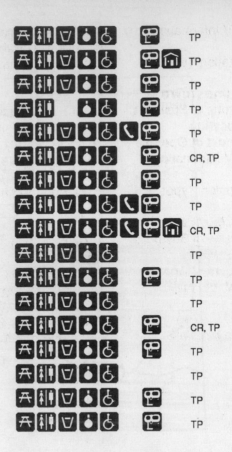

Route	Exit	Dir	Mile	Location	Facilities
40	17	E	3	MANUELITO	TP
	18	W		GALLUP	TP
	19	E	40	CINIZA	TP
	20	E	95	MALPAIS	TP
	21	E/W	102	ACOMITA	TP
	22/23	E/W	207	RATTLYSNAKE DRAW	CR, TP
	24/25	E/W	251	ANTON CHICO	TP
	26/27	E/W	301	PAJARITO	TP
	28	W	373	LLANO ESTACDO	CR, TP
56	29	W	85	RABBIT EAR	TP
62	30	W	108	1 MI E OF HOBBS	TP
64	31	W	191	RIO GRANDE GORGE	TP
	32	E/W	341	GRANDE SIERRA	CR, TP
70	33	E/W	431	BLACKWATER DRAW	TP
82	34	E/W	43	MALJAMAR	TP
180	35	E/W	141	BUTTERFIELD TRAIL	TP
285	36	N/S	151	MESA	TP

NEW MEXICO SERVICE STATIONS WITH RV DUMP FACILITIES

A. Albuquerque
Name of Business: Albuquerque 76 Auto/Truck Plaza
Location: I-40 & I-25, Exit 227A (Candileria).
Hours of Operation: 24 hours per day.
RV Information: No charge for use of RV Dump. Waterfill and diesel fuel available. No propane.
Station Type: Truck stop (Unocal 76).

B. Gallup
Name of Business: Baggett's 76 Auto/Truck Plaza
Location: I-40, Exit 16 (US-66 W).
Hours of Operation: 24 hours per day.

| RV Information: | No charge for use of RV Dump. Waterfill and diesel fuel available. No propane. |
| Station Type: | Truck stop (Unocal 76). |

C. Jamestown

Name of Business:	Giant Travel Center
Location:	I-40, Exit 39 (17 miles east of Gallup).
Hours of Operation:	24 hours per day.
RV Information:	No charge for use of RV Dump. Waterfill, propane and diesel fuel available.
Station Type:	Truck stop (Giant).

D. Tucumcari

Name of Business:	Tucumcari Truck Terminal
Location:	I-40, Exit 329.
Hours of Operation:	24 hours per day.
RV Information:	No charge for use of RV Dump ($5.00 if fuel not purchased). Waterfill and diesel fuel available. No propane.
Station Type:	Truck stop (Shell).

NEW YORK

"Empire State"

Capital: Albany	Largest City: New York City
Population: 17,990,455	Area: 47,831 sq. mi.
Highest Point: 5,344 ft.	Lowest Point: Sea Level
Date of Statehood: July 26, 1786	

GENERAL INFORMATION

Additional Information On Services

- **Rest Area Hours.** Rest Areas are open 24 hours per day, seven days per week.
- **Welcome Center Hours.** Welcome centers at areas 13, 20 and 29 are open all year. Others are seasonal. When open, centers operate 7 days per week, 8 hours per day.
- **Travel Plazas.** Areas 11 through 18, 20, 35, 36, 39 through 45, 47 through 50, 53 through 56 and 59 through 61 are travel plazas along the New York State Thruway system. All plazas have ATM machines and TDD dialing for the deaf.
- **Tourist Information.** For tourist information call 1-800-CALL NYS or 1-518-474-4116.

Rest Area Usage Rules

- **Overnight Parking.** No overnight parking.
- **Camping.** Camping is not permitted.
- **Stay Limit.** Parking limited to 3 hours.

Driving In New York

- **Emergencies.** For highway emergencies call 911 (may not be operable in all counties) or dial the local police or local number for the highway patrol. To aid in the apprehension of individuals driving while intoxicated, call 1-800-Curb-DWI.
- **Open Container.** No open container law, but open containers are prohibited on the New York state thruway system.
- **Seat Belts.** Seat belts are required for all front seat occupants and all children aged 4 through 10 riding in the back seat. Children 4 and under must be in a child restraint system.
- **Helmets.** Motorcycle operators and passengers must wear helmets.
- **Road Conditions.** Dial 1-800-THRUWAY for thruway system road conditions and 1-800-THE ROAD otherwise.

NEW YORK REST AREAS

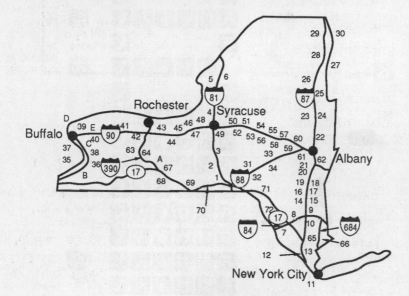

Exit	Dir	Mile	Location	Facilities	Services
16	S	96	ULSTER	picnic, restroom, water, fuel, handicap, phone	MO, NA, RR, TC, TP
17	N	99	9 MI N OF KINGSTON	picnic, phone	TP
18	N	103	MALDEN	picnic, restroom, water, fuel, handicap, phone, lodging	CV, MO, McD, TP, VM
19	S	103	11 MI S OF CATSKILL	picnic, phone	TP
20	S	127	NEW BALTIMORE	restroom, water, fuel, handicap, phone, lodging	BBB, MO, MF, RR, TC, TP
21	S	139	3 MI S OF ALBANY	picnic, phone	TP
22	N		14 MI N OF ALBANY	picnic, restroom, water, fuel, handicap, phone	TP
23/24	N/S		GLEN FALLS	picnic, restroom, water, fuel, handicap, phone	TP
25	N		6 MI N OF POTTERSVILLE	picnic, restroom, water, fuel, handicap, phone	TP
26	N		NORTH HUDSON	picnic, restroom, water, fuel, handicap, phone	TP
27	N		46 MI S OF PLATTSBURGH	picnic, restroom, water, fuel, handicap, phone	TP
28	S		33 MI S OF PLATTSBURGH	picnic, restroom, water, fuel, handicap, phone	TP
29	S		7 MI N OF PLATTSBURGH	picnic, restroom, water, fuel, handicap, phone, lodging	TP
30	N		7 MI N OF PLATTSBURGH	picnic, restroom, water, fuel, handicap, phone	TP
31/32	E/W		13 MI W OF ONEONTA (88)	picnic, restroom, water, fuel, handicap, phone	TP
33/34	E/W		14 MI E OF ONEONTA	picnic, restroom, water, fuel, handicap, phone	TP
35/36	E/W	447	ANGOLA (90)	restroom, water, fuel, handicap, phone, lodging	DN, McD, MO, TP
37/38	E/W	443	7 MI W OF HAMBURG	picnic, phone	TP
39	W	412	CLARENCE	restroom, water, fuel, handicap, phone, lodging	BK, NA, SN, TP
40	E	397	PEMBROKE	restroom, water, fuel, handicap, phone, lodging	BK, POP, TC, SN, TP
41	W	376	ONTARIO	picnic, restroom, water, fuel, handicap, phone	MO, McD, TP
42	E	366	SCOTTSVILLE	restroom, water, fuel, handicap, phone, lodging	BK, DD, MO, TC, TP
43	W	350	SENECA	restroom, water, fuel, handicap, phone, lodging	BK, MO, SB, TP
44	E	337	CLIFTON SPRINGS	restroom, water, fuel, handicap, phone	RR, SB, TC, SN, TP
45	W	324	JUNIUS PONDS	restroom, water, fuel, handicap, phone	DD, RR, SN, TC, TP
46	W	318	15 MI W OF WEEDSPORT	picnic, phone	TP
47	E	310	PORT BYRON	picnic, restroom, water, fuel, handicap, phone	MO, McD, MI, TP
48	W	292	WARNERS	picnic, restroom, water, fuel, handicap, phone, lodging	MO, McD, MI, TP
49	E	280	DEWITT	picnic, restroom, water, fuel, handicap, phone	BJ, McD, SN, TP

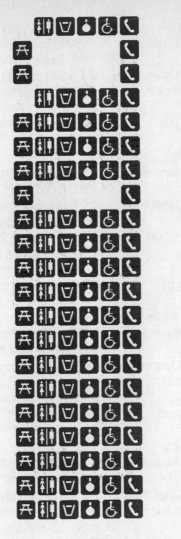

Exit	Dir.	MP	Location	Amenities
50	W	266	CHITTENANGO	DD, SB, SN, TC, TP
51	W	256	3 MI W OF VERONA	TP
52	E	250	3 MI E OF VERONA	TP
53	E	244	ONEIDA	BK, SB, SN, TC, TP
54	W	227	SCHUYLER	BR, McD, SN, TP
55	E	210	INDIAN CASTLE	BK, DD, MF, SN, TC, TP
56	W	210	IROQUOIS	BBB, MF, RR, SN, TP
57/58	E/W	184	10 MI E OF CANAJOHARIE	TP
59	E	172	MOHAWK	BR, McD, SN, TP
60	W	168	PATTERSONVILLE	BBB, MF, RR, SN, TC, TP
61	E	153	GUILDERLAND	McD, MS, SN, TP
62	W		12 MI S OF ALBANY	TP
63/64	N/S		MOUNT MORRIS (390)	TP
65	S		2 MI S OF KATONAH (684)	TP
66	N		12 MI N OF KATONAH	TP
67	W		3 MI W OF BATH (17)	TP
68	E		11 MI E OF BATH	TP
69	W		2 MI E OF LOWMAN	TP
70	E		11 MI W OF OWEGO	TP
71	W		10 MI E OF HANCOCK	TP
72	E		2 MI E OF ROSCOE	TP

NEW YORK SERVICE STATIONS WITH RV DUMP FACILITIES

A. Donsville

Name of Business:	Travel Port
Location:	I-390, Exit 5 (Commerce Dr.).
Hours of Operation:	24 hours per day.
RV Information:	No charge for use of RV Dump. Waterfill, propane and diesel fuel available.
Station Type:	Truck stop (Mobil).

B. Fredonia

Name of Business:	Get-N-Go Mini-Mart
Location:	I-90, Exit 59 (NY-60).
Hours of Operation:	24 hours per day.
RV Information:	$5.00 charge for use of RV Dump. Waterfill, propane and diesel fuel available.
Station Type:	Service station with mini-mart (Keystone).

C. Hamburg

Name of Business:	Exit 57 Truck Plaza
Location:	I-90, Exit 57 (NY-75 N)
Hours of Operation:	24 hours per day (from Sunday, 10 A.M. to Saturday 12 noon).
RV Information:	$15.00 charge for use of RV Dump, includes chemical added to tanks. Waterfill and diesel fuel available. No propane.
Station Type:	Truck stop (Atlantic).

D. Niagara Falls

Name of Business:	Junior's Fuel Plaza
Location:	I-190, Exit 22 (US-62 N).
Hours of Operation:	24 hours per day.
RV Information:	$12.00 charge for use of RV Dump. Waterfill and diesel fuel available. No propane.
Station Type:	Truck stop (BP).

E. Pembroke

Name of Business:	Buffalo I-90 East 76 Auto/Truck Center
Location:	I-90, Exit 48A (NY-77).
Hours of Operation:	24 hours per day.
RV Information:	No charge for use of RV Dump. Waterfill, propane and diesel fuel available.
Station Type:	Truck stop (Unocal 76).

NORTH CAROLINA

"Tar Heel State"

Capital: Raleigh	**Largest City:** Charlotte
Population: 6,628,637	**Area:** 48,798 sq. mi.
Highest Point: 6,684 ft.	**Lowest Point:** Sea Level

Date of Statehood: November 21, 1789

GENERAL INFORMATION

Additional Information On Services

- **Rest Area Hours.** Rest Areas are open 24 hours per day, seven days per week.
- **Welcome Center Hours.** Welcome centers are staffed from 8 A.M. to 5 P.M.
- **Boat Dock.** A boat dock is available at area 43.
- **Tourist Information.** For tourist information call 1-800-VISIT-NC.

Rest Area Usage Rules

- **Overnight Parking.** No overnight parking.
- **Camping.** Camping or erection of tents, booths or structures of any kind is not permitted.
- **Stay Limit.** Parking limited to 4 hours.

Driving In North Carolina

- **Emergencies.** For highway emergencies call 1-800-622-7956 to reach the Highway Patrol. With a cellular phone, dial *HP.
- **Open Container.** Open containers of alcoholic beverages in the passenger compartment of the vehicle are not permitted.
- **Seat Belts.** Seat belts are required for all front seat occupants. This law will soon be expanded to include all vehicle occupants. Children 3 and under must be in a child restraint system. Children 3 through 6 must be in a child restraint system or seat belt.
- **Helmets.** Motorcycle operators and passengers must wear helmets.
- **Road Conditions.** Dial 1-800-622-7956.

NORTH CAROLINA REST AREAS

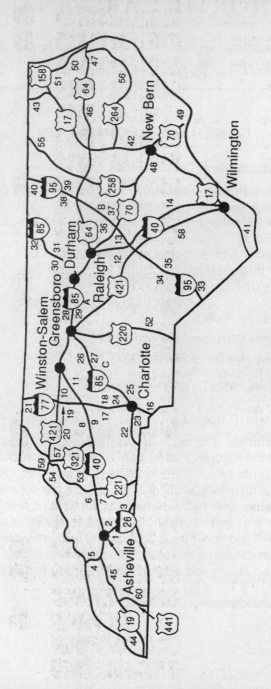

Route	Exit	Direction	Location	Facilities	Lodging	Codes
26	1/2	E/W	12 MI SE OF ASHEVILLE	🏕🚻♿📞		FG, TP, VM
	3	W	3 MI N SOUTH CAROLINA LINE	🏕🚻♿📞	🏠	FG, TP, VM
40	4/5	E/W	10 MI E OF TENNESSEE LINE	🏕🚻♿📞	🏠	FG, TP, VM
	6/7	E/W	1 MI E OF MARION	🏕🚻♿📞		FG, TP, VM
	8/9	E/W	10 MI E OF HICKORY	🏕🚻♿📞		FG, TP, VM
	10/11	E/W	18 MI W OF WINSTON-SALEM	🏕🚻♿📞		FG, TP, VM
	12/13	E/W	1 MI N OF US-301	🏕🚻♿📞		FG, TP, VM
	14	E/W	RTE 24 JCT	🏕🚻♿📞		FG, TP, VM
77	16	N	2 MI N SOUTH CAROLINA LINE	🏕🚻♿📞	🏠	FG, TP, VM
	17/18	N/S	12 MI S OF STATESVILLE	🏕🚻♿📞		FG, TP, VM
	19	S	1 MI S OF RTE 901	🏕🚻♿📞		FG, TP, VM
	20	N	2 MI N OF RTE 901	🏕🚻♿📞		FG, TP, VM
	21	S	VIRGINIA LINE	🏕🚻♿📞	🏠	FG, TP, VM
85	22/23	N/S	2 MI N OF SC LINE	🏕🚻♿📞	🏠	FG, TP, VM
	24/25	N/S	1 MI N OF CONCORD	🏕🚻♿📞		FG, TP, VM
	26/27	N/S	3 MI N OF THOMASVILLE	🏕🚻♿📞		FG, TP, VM
	28/29	N/S	3 MI SW OF BURLINGTON	🏕🚻♿📞		FG, TP, VM
	30/31	N/S	6 MI S OF OXFORD	🏕🚻♿📞		FG, TP, VM
	32	S	2 MI S OF VIRGINIA LINE	🏕🚻♿📞	🏠	FG, TP, VM
95	33	N	5 MI N SOUTH CAROLINA LINE	🏕🚻♿📞	🏠	FG, TP, VM
	34/35	N/S	1 MI S OF RTE 53	🏕🚻♿📞		FG, TP, VM
	36/37	N/S	5 MI NE OF SMITHFIELD	🏕🚻♿📞		FG, TP, VM
	38/39	N/S	1 MI N OF RTE 43	🏕🚻♿📞		FG, TP, VM
	40	S	1 MI S OF VIRGINIA LINE	🏕🚻♿📞	🏠	FG, TP
17	41	N/S	RTE 130 ON SHALLOTTE BYPASS	🏕🚻♿📞	🏠	FG, TP
	42	N/S	11 MI N OF NEW BERN	🚻♿📞		FG, TP
	43	N/S	1 MI S VIRGINIA LINE	🏕🚻♿📞	🏠	FG, TP
19	44	N/S	ANDREWS BYPASS	🏕🚻♿📞		FG, TP
	45	N/S	I MI NE OF BLUE RIDGE PKWY	🏕🚻♿📞		FG, TP

North Carolina 145

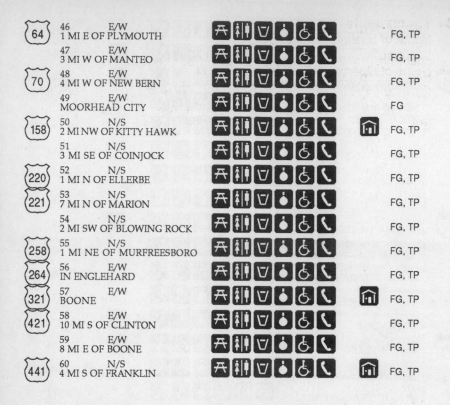

(64)	46 E/W 1 MI E OF PLYMOUTH		FG, TP
	47 E/W 3 MI W OF MANTEO		FG, TP
(70)	48 E/W 4 MI W OF NEW BERN		FG, TP
	49 E/W MOORHEAD CITY		FG
(158)	50 N/S 2 MI NW OF KITTY HAWK		FG, TP
	51 N/S 3 MI SE OF COINJOCK		FG, TP
(220)	52 N/S 1 MI N OF ELLERBE		FG, TP
(221)	53 N/S 7 MI N OF MARION		FG, TP
	54 N/S 2 MI SW OF BLOWING ROCK		FG, TP
(258)	55 N/S 1 MI NE OF MURFREESBORO		FG, TP
(264)	56 E/W IN ENGLEHARD		FG, TP
(321)	57 E/W BOONE		FG, TP
(421)	58 E/W 10 MI S OF CLINTON		FG, TP
	59 E/W 8 MI E OF BOONE		FG, TP
(441)	60 N/S 4 MI S OF FRANKLIN		FG, TP

NORTH CAROLINA SERVICE STATIONS WITH RV DUMP FACILITIES

A. Graham/Haw River

Name of Business: Flying J Travel Plaza
Location: I-40 & 85, Exit 150 (Jimmy Kerr Rd.).
Hours of Operation: 24 hours per day.
RV Information: No charge for use of RV Dump. Waterfill, propane and diesel fuel available.
Station Type: Truck stop (Conoco).

B. Kenly

Name of Business: Truckstops of America
Location: I-95, Exit 106 (Truckstop Rd.)
Hours of Operation: 24 hours per day.
RV Information: No charge for use of RV Dump. Waterfill and diesel fuel available. No propane.
Station Type: Truck stop (Texaco).

C. Thomasville

Name of Business:	Gas Mart
Location:	US-29 & 70 and Business 85.
Hours of Operation:	7 A.M. to 10 P.M.
RV Information:	$3.00 charge for use of RV Dump. Waterfill and diesel fuel available. No propane.
Station Type:	Truck stop (Independent).

NORTH DAKOTA

"Sioux State and Flickertail State"

Capital: Bismarck   **Largest City:** Fargo
Population: 638,800   **Area:** 70,665 sq. mi.
Highest Point: 3,506 ft.   **Lowest Point:** 750 ft.
Date of Statehood: November 2, 1889

GENERAL INFORMATION

Additional Information On Services

- **Rest Area Hours.** Rest Areas are open 24 hours per day, seven days per week.
- **Welcome Center Hours.** Welcome centers are staffed from 9 A.M. to 5 P.M.
- **Tourist Information.** For tourist information call in state, 1-800-472-2100; out of state, 1-800-437-2077; from Canada, 1-800-537-8879.

Rest Area Usage Rules

- **Overnight Parking.** No overnight parking.
- **Camping.** Camping is not permitted.
- **Stay Limit.** No published limit.

Driving In North Dakota

- **Emergencies.** For highway emergencies call 1-800-472-2121 for the highway patrol.
- **Open Container.** Open containers of alcoholic beverages in the passenger compartment of the vehicle are not permitted.
- **Seat Belts.** Children 3 and under must be in a child restraint system. Children 3 through 10 must be in a child restraint system or seat belt.
- **Helmets.** Motorcycle operators and passengers under 18 must wear helmets.
- **Road Conditions.** Dial 1-800-472-2686.

NORTH DAKOTA REST AREAS

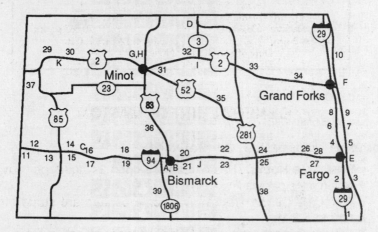

	Location		Mile
29 1	N	2	
2 MI N OF BORDER			TP
2/3	N/S	40	
7 MI S OF RTE 46			TP
4/5	N/S	72	
1.5 MI NW OF HARWOOD			TP
6/7	N/S	98	
1 MI W OF KELSO			TP
8/9	N/S	120	
2 MI N OF BUXTON			TP
10	N	178	
3 MI N OF RTE 17			TP
94 11	E	12	
10 MI E OF BEACH			TP
12	W	15	
13 MI E OF BEACH			TP
13	W	33	
7 MI E OF MEDORA			TP
14/15	E/W	71	
6 MI E OF DICKINSON			TP
16/17	E/W	94	
9 MI E OF RICHARDTON			TP
18/19	E/W	120	
8 MI W OF NEW SALEM			TP
20/21	E/W	168	
8 MI E OF BISMARCK			TP
22/23	E/W	222	
8 MI W OF MEDINA			TP
24/25	E/W	254	
4 MI W OF JAMESTOWN			TP
26	W	304	
2 MI E OF ORISKA			TP
27	E	328	
4 MI W OF CASSELTON			TP

28 W 337 2 MI W OF MAPLETON	🚻 🚮 🚰 ♿ 📞 📺	TP
(2) 29 E/W 31 5 MI W OF WILISTON	🚻 🚮 🚰 ♿ 📞	
30 E/W 72 17 MI W OF STANLEY	🚻 🚮 🚰 ♿ 📞 📺	
31 E/W 162 6 MI SW OF GRANVILLE	🚻 🚮 🚰 ♿ 📞	
32 E/W 219 8 MI E OF RUGBY	🚻 🚮 🚰 ♿ 📞 📺	
33 E/W 277 8 MI SE OF DEVILS LAKE	🚻 🚮 🚰 ♿ 📞	
34 E/W 330 3 MI N OF LARIMORE	🚻 🚮 🚰 ♿ 📞	
(52) 35 E/W 208 1 MI W OF SYKESTON	🚻 🚮 🚰 ♿ 📞	
(83) 36 N/S 121 4 MI SE OF WASHBURN	🚻 🚮 🚰 ♿	
(85) 37 N/S 176 7 MI S OF US-2 JCT	🚻 🚮 🚰 ♿ 📞	
(281) 38 N/S 39 9 MI N OF EDGELEY	🚻 🚮 🚰 ♿ 📞	
(1806) 39 N/S 43 1 MI S OF FORT RICE	🚻 🚮 🚰 ♿ 📞	

NORTH DAKOTA SERVICE STATIONS WITH RV DUMP FACILITIES

A. Bismarck

Name of Business:	CENEX Convenience Store
Location:	I-94, Exit 161 (Centennial Rd.).
Hours of Operation:	24 hours per day.
RV Information:	No charge for use of RV Dump. Waterfill, propane and diesel fuel available.
Station Type:	Truck stop (CENEX).

B. Bismarck

Name of Business:	Truck Plaza 35
Location:	I-94, Exit 157 (Tyler Pkwy.).
Hours of Operation:	24 hours per day.
RV Information:	No charge for use of RV Dump. Waterfill, propane and diesel fuel available.
Station Type:	Truck stop (Conoco).

C. Dickinson

Name of Business:	The General Store
Location:	I-94, Exit 61 (ND-22).
Hours of Operation:	24 hours per day.

RV Information: No charge for use of RV Dump. Waterfill and diesel fuel available. No propane.
Station Type: Truck stop (CENEX).

D. Dunseith
Name of Business: Dale's Truck Stop
Location: US-281 and ND-3 & 5.
Hours of Operation: 24 hours per day.
RV Information: $1.00 charge for use of RV Dump. Waterfill and diesel fuel available. No propane.
Station Type: Truck stop Conoco).

E. Fargo
Name of Business: Flying J Travel Plaza
Location: I-29, Exit 62 (32nd Ave.).
Hours of Operation: 24 hours per day.
RV Information: No charge for use of RV Dump. Propane and diesel fuel available. No waterfill.
Station Type: Truck stop (Conoco).

F. Grand Forks
Name of Business: StaMart Truck Plaza #13
Location: I-29, Exit 141 (US-2).
Hours of Operation: 24 hours per day.
RV Information: No charge for use of RV Dump. Waterfill and diesel fuel available. No propane.
Station Type: Truck stop (Independent).

G. Minot
Name of Business: Behm's Truck Stop
Location: US-2 & 52 W.
Hours of Operation: 24 hours per day.
RV Information: No charge for use of RV Dump ($2.00 if fuel not purchased). Propane and diesel fuel available. No waterfill.
Station Type: Truck stop (Conoco).

H. Minot
Name of Business: Econo Stop
Location: US-2 & 52 Bypass East.
Hours of Operation: 24 hours per day.
RV Information: No charge for use of RV Dump. Waterfill, propane and diesel fuel available.

North Dakota ████████████████

Station Type: Truck stop (Sinclair).

I. Rugby
Name of Business: Truckers Inn/Hub
Location: US-2 & ND-3.
Hours of Operation: 24 hours per day.
RV Information: No charge for use of RV Dump. Waterfill, propane and diesel fuel available.
Station Type: Truck stop (Sinclair).

J. Sterling
Name of Business: Tops CENEX Truck Stop
Location: I-94, Exit 182 (US-83 S).
Hours of Operation: 24 hours per day.
RV Information: No charge for use of RV Dump. Waterfill and diesel fuel available. No propane.
Station Type: Truck stop (CENEX).

K. Williston
Name of Business: OK Conoco North
Location: US-2 & 85 North.
Hours of Operation: 24 hours per day.
RV Information: No charge for use of RV Dump. Waterfill and diesel fuel available. No propane.
Station Type: Truck stop (Conoco).

OHIO

"Buckeye State"

Capital: Columbus   Largest City: Cleveland
Population: 10,847,115   Area: 40,975 sq. mi.
Highest Point: 1,550 ft.   Lowest Point: 433 ft.
Date of Statehood: March 1, 1803

GENERAL INFORMATION

Additional Information On Services

- **Rest Area Hours.** Rest Areas are open 24 hours per day, seven days per week.
- **Welcome Center Hours.** Welcome centers are staffed from 8 A.M. to 6 P.M.
- **Travel Plazas.** Areas 34, 35, and 46 through 59 are travel plazas along the Ohio Turnpike.
- **Travel Trailer Facilities.** Travel trailer facilities are provided at 6 service service plazas on the Ohio Turnpike: 46, 50, 51, 54, 55, and 59. The charge at areas 50 and 51 is $2.00 per night, since electrical outlets and wastewater drains are available. There is no charge for the others and electrical outlets and wastewater drains are not provided. All facilities are open for occupancy from 4 P.M. to 10 A.M. the following day and are rented on a first come, first served basis.
- **Truck Parking.** Areas 1 and 2 have expanded truck parking of approximately 50 spaces each. All others have approximately 10 spaces each.
- **Tourist Information.** For tourist information call 1-800-BUCKEYE.

Rest Area Usage Rules

- **Overnight Parking.** No overnight parking.
- **Camping.** Camping is not permitted.
- **Stay Limit.** Parking limited to 3 hours.

Driving In Ohio

- **Emergencies.** For highway emergencies call 1-800-425-5555.
- **Open Container.** Open containers of alcoholic beverages in the passenger compartment of the vehicle are not permitted.
- **Seat Belts.** Seat belts are required for all front seat occupants.

Children 4 and under or 40 pounds or less must be in a child restraint system.
- **Helmets.** Motorcycle operators and passengers under 18 or who have been driving for less than one year must wear helmets.
- **Road Conditions.** Dial 1-614-466-2660.

OHIO REST AREAS

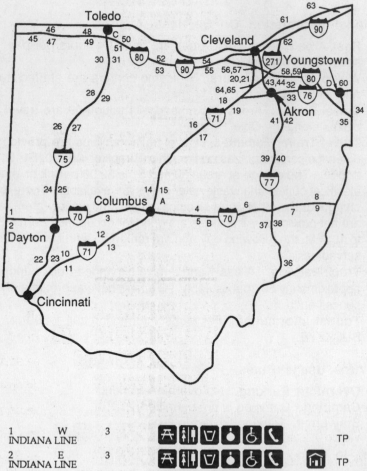

🛣️ 70	1 W INDIANA LINE	3	🪑 🚻 🗑️ 🍼 ♿ 📞				TP
	2 E INDIANA LINE	3	🪑 🚻 🗑️ 🍼 ♿ 📞	🏠			TP
	3 E BRIGHTON	69	🪑 🚻 🗑️ 🍼 ♿ 📞				TP
	4/5 E/W HEBRON	130	🪑 🚻 🗑️ 🍼 ♿ 📞				TP
	6 W ZANESVILLE	160	🪑 🚻 🗑️ 🍼 ♿ 📞				TP

Interstate	Exit	Dir	Mile	Amenities	Services
	7 OLD WASHINGTON	E	188	🏕️ 🚻 🗑️ 🍼 ♿ 📞	TP
	8/9 MORRISTOWN	E/W	210	🏕️ 🚻 🗑️ 🍼 ♿ 📞 🏠	TP
71	10/11 LEBANON	N/S	35	🏕️ 🚻 🗑️ 🍼 ♿ 📞 🏠	TP
	12/13 JEFFERSONVILLE	N/S	67	🏕️ 🚻 🗑️ 🍼 ♿ 📞	TP
	14/15 DELAWARE	N/S	119	🏕️ 🚻 🗑️ 🍼 ♿ 📞	TP
	16/17 ASHLAND	N/S	180	🏕️ 🚻 🗑️ 🍼 ♿ 📞	TP
	18/19 W. SALEM	N/S	197	🏕️ 🚻 🗑️ 🍼 ♿ 📞	TP
	20/21 BRUNSWICK	N/S	224	🏕️ 🚻 🗑️ 🍼 ♿ 📞	TP
75	22/23 MONROE	N/S	27	🏕️ 🚻 🗑️ 🍼 ♿ 📞 🏠	TP
	24/25 PIQUA	N/S	81	🏕️ 🚻 🗑️ 🍼 ♿ 📞	TP
	26/27 LIMA	N/S	116	🏕️ 🚻 🗑️ 🍼 ♿ 📞	TP
	28/29 FINDLAY	N/S	155	🏕️ 🚻 🗑️ 🍼 ♿ 📞	TP
	30/31 BOWLING GREEN	N/S	178	🏕️ 🚻 🗑️ 🍼 ♿ 📞 🏠	TP
76	32/33 RAVENNA	E/W	45	🏕️ 🚻 🗑️ 🍼 ♿ 📞	TP
	34/35 GLACIER HLS/MAHONING	E/W	237	🏕️ 🚻 🗑️ 🍼 ♿ 📞	BP, McD, TP
77	36 1.5 MI N OF MARIETTA	N	10	🏕️ 🚻 🗑️ 🍼 ♿ 📞 🏠	TP
	37/38 BYESVILLE	N/S	37	🏕️ 🚻 🗑️ 🍼 ♿ 📞	TP
	39/40 NEW PHILADELPHIA	N/S	85	🏕️ 🚻 🗑️ 🍼 ♿ 📞	TP
	41/42 CANTON	N/S	115	🏕️ 🚻 🗑️ 🍼 ♿ 📞	TP
	43/44 PENNISULA	N/S	141	🏕️ 🚻 🗑️ 🍼 ♿ 📞	TP
80	45 6 MI E OF GATE 2	E	19	🏕️ 🚻 🗑️ 🍼 ♿ 📞 🏠	TP
	46 INDIAN MEADOWS	W	21	🏕️ 🚻 🗑️ 🍼 ♿ 📞 📺	BP, HD, TP
	47 TIFFIN RIVER	E	21	🏕️ 🚻 🗑️ 🍼 ♿ 📞	BP, HD, TP
	48/49 FALLEN TIMBER/OAK OPENING	E/W	49	🏕️ 🚻 🗑️ 🍼 ♿ 📞	BP, GS, TP
	50/51 WYANDOT/ BLUE HERON	E/W	77	🏕️ 🚻 🗑️ 🍼 ♿ 📞 📺	BP, HD, TP
	52/53 COM PERRY/ERIE ISLANDS	N/S	100	🏕️ 🚻 🗑️ 🍼 ♿ 📞	BP, RAX, TP
	54/55 VERMILLION VLY/MIDDLE RG	E/W	140	🏕️ 🚻 🗑️ 🍼 ♿ 📞 📺	BBB, BK, BP, TP
	56/57 TOWPATH/GREAT LAKES	E/W	170	🏕️ 🚻 🗑️ 🍼 ♿ 📞	BP, McD, TP
	58 PORTAGE	W	197	🏕️ 🚻 🗑️ 🍼 ♿ 📞	BP, DD, POP, TP

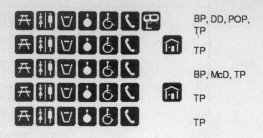

59 E 197 BRADY'S LEAP		BP, DD, POP, TP
60 W 237 PENNSYLVANIA LINE		TP
(90) 61/62 E/W 198 PAINESVILLE		BP, McD, TP
63 W 243 CONNEAUT		TP
(271) 64/65 E/W 8 RICHFIELD		TP

OHIO SERVICE STATIONS WITH RV DUMP FACILITIES

A. Berkshire

Name of Business: Flying J Travel Plaza
Location: I-71, Exit 131 (US-36).
Hours of Operation: 24 hours per day.
RV Information: No charge for use of RV Dump. Waterfill, propane and diesel fuel available.
Station Type: Truck stop (Conoco).

B. Buckeye Lake

Name of Business: Buckeye Lake Truck Stop
Location: I-70, Exit 129A (OH-79).
Hours of Operation: 24 hours per day.
RV Information: No charge for use of RV Dump. Waterfill, propane (bottle exchange only) and diesel fuel available.
Station Type: Truck stop (Englefield).

C. Perrysburg

Name of Business: Flying J Travel Plaza
Location: I-280, Exit 1B
Hours of Operation: 24 hours per day.
RV Information: No charge for use of RV Dump. Waterfill, propane and diesel fuel available.
Station Type: Truck stop (Conoco).

D. Youngstown

Name of Business: Youngstown 76 Auto/Truck Plaza
Location: I-80, Exit 223A (OH-46 S).
Hours of Operation: 24 hours per day.
RV Information: No charge for use of RV Dump. Waterfill and diesel fuel available. No propane.
Station Type: Truck stop (Unocal 76).

OKLAHOMA

"Sooner State"

Capital: Oklahoma City   **Largest City:** OklahomaCity
Population: 3,145,585   **Area:** 68,782 sq. mi.
Highest Point: 4,973 ft.   **Lowest Point:** 287 ft.
Date of Statehood: November 16, 1907

GENERAL INFORMATION

Additional Information On Services

- **Rest Area Hours.** Rest Areas are open 24 hours per day, seven days per week.
- **Welcome Center Hours.** Welcome centers are staffed 8 hours per day in the off season and 12 hours per day from May 1 through Labor Day.
- **Toll Road Service Plazas.** Areas 15 through 27 are toll road service plazas.
- **Tourist Information.** For tourist information call 1-800-652-6552.

Rest Area Usage Rules

- **Overnight Parking.** Overnight parking permitted.
- **Camping.** Camping is not permitted.
- **Stay Limit.** No published limit.

Driving In Oklahoma

- **Emergencies.** For highway emergencies call 1-405-425-2424 for the highway patrol.
- **Open Container.** Open containers of alcoholic beverages in the passenger compartment of the vehicle are not permitted.
- **Seat Belts.** Seat belts are required for all front seat occupants. Children 6 and under must be in a child restraint system or seat belt.
- **Helmets.** Motorcycle operators and passengers under 18 must wear helmets.
- **Road Conditions.** Dial 1-405-425-2385

OKLAHOMA REST AREAS

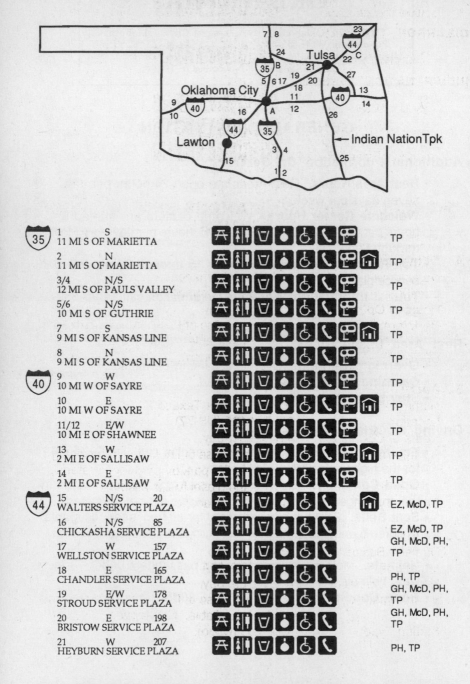

| 22 E/W 287 VINTA SERVICE PLAZA | 🍴🚻🚮🍼♿📞 | 🏠 | GH, McD, PH, TP |
| 23 W 313 MIAMI SERVICE PLAZA | 🍴🚻🚮🍼♿📞 | 🏠 | PH, TP |

CIMARRON TURNPIKE

| 24 E/W 36 LONE CHIMNEY SERVICE PLAZ | 🍴🚻🚮🍼♿📞 | McD, PH, TP |

INDIAN NATION TURNPIKE

25 N/S 17 ANTLERS SERVICE PLAZA	🍴🚻🚮🍼♿📞	EZ, McD, TP
26 N/S 94 EUFAULA SERVICE PLAZA	🍴🚻🚮🍼♿📞	EZ, McD, TP
27 E/W 25 MUSKOGEE SERVICE PLAZA	🍴🚻🚮🍼♿📞	EZ, McD, TP

OKLAHOMA SERVICE STATIONS WITH RV DUMP FACILITIES

A. Oklahoma City

Name of Business:	Truckstops of America
Location:	I-40, Exit 142 (Council Rd.).
Hours of Operation:	24 hours per day.
RV Information:	No charge for use of RV Dump. Waterfill and diesel fuel available. No propane.
Station Type:	Truck stop (Conoco).

B. Perry

Name of Business:	Sooner's Corner Texaco
Location:	I-35, Exit 185 (US-77).
Hours of Operation:	24 hours per day.
RV Information:	No charge for use of RV Dump if remaining overnight at RV park on property. Waterfill, propane and diesel fuel available.
Station Type:	Truck stop (Texaco).

C. Pryor

Name of Business:	Circle K Truxtop
Location:	US-69 & US-69A
Hours of Operation:	24 hours per day.
RV Information:	No charge for use of RV Dump. Waterfill and diesel fuel available. No propane.
Station Type:	Truck stop (Citgo).

OREGON

"Beaver State"

Capital: Salem	**Largest City:** Portland
Population: 2,842,321	**Area:** 96,184 sq. mi.
Highest Point: 11,235 ft.	**Lowest Point:** Sea Level

Date of Statehood: February 14, 1859

GENERAL INFORMATION

Additional Information On Services

- **Rest Area Hours.** Rest Areas open 24 hours per day, every day.
- **Welcome Center Hours.** Welcome centers staffed May thru Oct.
- **State Parks.** The following rest areas are state parks: 3, 21, 22, 38, 45, 46, 50, 53, 56, 60, 61, 62, 65 and 68.
- **Tourist Information.** For tourist information call 1-800-547-7842 from outside Oregon, 1-800-233-3306 from within Oregon and 378-3451 from Salem.

Rest Area Usage Rules

- **Overnight Parking.** Overnight parking is permitted.
- **Camping.** Camping or sleeping outside of vehicle is not permitted.
- **Stay Limit.** Parking limited to 12 hours within any 24 hour period.

Driving In Oregon

- **Emergencies.** For highway emergencies call 911 (may not be operable in all counties) or dial the local police or local number for the highway patrol (posted on rest area telephones). To report crime or accidents and fish and wildlife violations, call 1-800-452-7888. To report drunk drivers, call 1-800-24 DRUNK.
- **Open Container.** No open container law, but it is an offense to consume alcoholic beverages on the highway.
- **Seat Belts.** Seat belts are required for all occupants. Children 1 and under or less than 40 pounds must be in a child restraint system.
- **Helmets.** Motorcycle operators and passengers must wear helmets.
- **Road Conditions.** Dial 1-503-889-3999 or 1-503-976-PASS.

OREGON REST AREAS

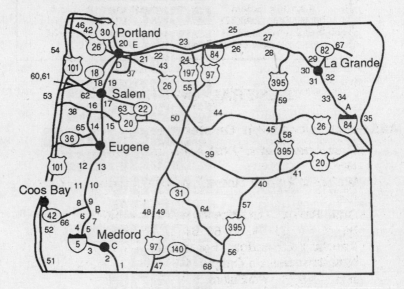

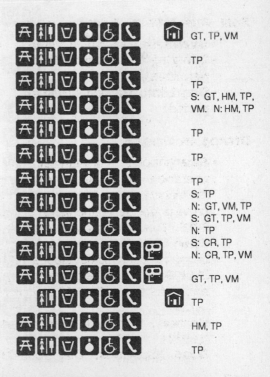

	Location			Facilities	Notes
(5)	1 N 10 10 MI N OF CA LINE			🪑🚻🗑🚰♿📞 🏠	GT, TP, VM
	2 S 22 7 MI S OF MEDFORD			🪑🚻🗑🚰♿📞	TP
	3 N/S 45 11 MI S OF GRANTS PASS			🪑🚻🗑🚰♿📞	TP
	4/5 N/S 62 5 MI N OF GRANTS PASS			🪑🚻🗑🚰♿📞	S: GT, HM, TP, VM. N: HM, TP
	6/7 N/S 82 25 MI N OF GRANTS PASS			🪑🚻🗑🚰♿📞	TP
	8/9 N/S 112 12 MI S OF ROSEBURG			🪑🚻🗑🚰♿📞	TP
	10/11 N/S 143 20 MI N OF ROSEBURG			🪑🚻🗑🚰♿📞	TP
	12/13 N/S 178 14 MI S OF EUGENE			🪑🚻🗑🚰♿📞	S: TP N: GT, VM, TP
	14/15 N/S 206 13 MI N OF EUGENE			🪑🚻🗑🚰♿📞	S: GT, TP, VM N: TP
	16/17 N/S 241 8 MI N OF ALBANY			🪑🚻🗑🚰♿📞📺	S: CR, TP N: CR, TP, VM
	18/19 N/S 282 14 MI S OF PORTLAND			🪑🚻🗑🚰♿📞📺	GT, TP, VM
	20 N/S INTERSTATE BRIDGE			🚻🗑🚰♿📞 🏠	TP
(84)	21 E 55 10 MI E OF CASCADE LOCKS			🪑🚻🗑🚰♿📞	HM, TP
	22 W 66 3 MI E OF HOOD RIVER (SP)			🪑🚻🗑🚰♿📞	TP

Route	Site	Dir.	Mile	Location	Notes
	23/24	E/W	73	11 MI W OF THE DALLES	HM, TP
	25/26	E/W	161	2 MI W OF BOARDMAN	E: GT, TP W: TP
	27/28	E/W	186	20 MI W OF PENDLETON	CR , HM, TP
	29/30	E/W	228	18 MI E OF PENDLETON	HM, TP
	31/32	E/W	268	9 MI SE OF LAGRANDE	HM, TP
	33/34	E/W	295	10 MI W OF BAKER	HM, TP
	35	E/W	336	38 MI W OF ONTARIO	HM, TP
	36	W	377	1 MI SE OF ONTARIO	GT, HM, TP, VM
205	37	W	8	2 MI W OF OREGON CITY	TP
20	38	E/W	32	22 MI W OF CORVALLIS	
	39	E/W	43	41 MI E OF BEND	CR
	40	E/W	114	18 MI W OF BURNS	
	41	E/W	156	24 MI E OF BURNS	
26	42	E/W	28	31 MI E OF SEASIDE	
	43	E/W	54	4 MI E OF RHODODENDRON	
	44	E/W	49	40 MI W OF PRINEVILLE	
	45	E/W	155	4 MI W OF JOHN DAY	
30	46	E/W	75	22 MI E OF ASTORIA	
97	47	N/S	283	8 MI S OF KLAMATH FALLS (SP)	GT, HM, VM
	48/49	N/S	206	5 MI S OF CHEMULT	
	50	N/S	113	25 MI N OF BEND	GT, HM
101	51	N/S	356	2 MI N OF BROOKING	GT, VM
	52	N/S	319	10 MI N OF GOLD BEACH	
	53	N/S	115	N OF LINCOLN CITY (SP)	GT
	54	N/S	71	5 MI S OF TILLAMOOK	
197	55	N/S	69	21 MI S OF MAUPIN	
395	56	N/S	126	17 MI N OF LAKEVIEW (SP)	
	57	N/S	60	82 MI N OF LAKEVIEW	
	58	N/S	11	10 MI S OF JOHN DAY	

162

	59 N/S 93 3 MI S OF LONG CREEK		
(18)	60/61 E/W 10 13 MI E OF LINCOLN CITY		HM
(22)	62 W 22 4 MI W OF SALEM (SP)		
	63 E/W 35 37 MI E OF SALEM		
(31)	64 N/S 69 63 MI N OF LAKEVIEW		
(36)	65 E/W 38 3 MI W OF GOLDSON (SP)		
(42)	66 E/W 59 24 MI W OF OF ROSEBURG		
(82)	67 E/W 39 25 MI NW OF ENTERPRISE		
(140)	68 E/W 83 12 MI W OF LAKEVIEW		

OREGON SERVICE STATIONS WITH RV DUMP FACILITIES

A. Baker

Name of Business:	Baker Truck Corral
Location:	I-84, Exit 304 (Campbell St.).
Hours of Operation:	24 hours per day.
RV Information:	No charge for use of RV Dump ($2.00 If fuel not purchased). Waterfill, propane and diesel fuel available.
Station Type:	Truck stop (Sinclair).

B. Canyonville

Name of Business:	Fat Harvey's Truck Stop
Location:	I-5, exit 99 (Jeffries Rd.).
Hours of Operation:	24 hours per day.
RV Information:	No charge for use of RV Dump ($2.00 if fuel not purchased). Waterfill, propane and diesel fuel available.
Station Type:	Truck stop (ARCO).

C. Phoenix/Medford

Name of Business:	Pear Tree Center
Location:	I-5, Exit 24 (Fern Valley Rd.).
Hours of Operation:	24 hours per day.
RV Information:	No charge for use of RV Dump ($4.00 if fuel not purchased). Waterfill, propane and diesel fuel available.

Station Type: Truck stop (Texaco).

D. Portland
Name of Business: Jubitz Truck Stop
Location: I-5, Exit 307 E (Vancouver Way).
Hours of Operation: 24 hours per day.
RV Information: No charge for use of RV Dump ($5.00 if fuel
                           not purchased). Waterfill, propane and diesel
                           fuel available.
Station Type: Truck stop (Independent).

E. Troutdale
Name of Business: Flying J Travel Plaza
Location: I-84, Exit 17 (Frontage Rd.).
Hours of Operation: 24 hours per day.
RV Information: No charge for use of RV Dump. Waterfill,
                           propane and diesel fuel available.
Station Type: Truck stop (Conoco).

PENNSYLVANIA

"Keystone State"

Capital: Harrisburg	**Largest City:** Philadelphia
Population: 11,881,643	**Area:** 44,966 sq. mi.
Highest Point: 3,213 ft.	**Lowest Point:** Sea Level

Date of Statehood: December 12, 1787

GENERAL INFORMATION

Additional Information On Services

- **Rest Area Hours.** Rest Areas are open 24 hours per day, seven days per week.
- **Welcome Center Hours.** Welcome centers are staffed from 8 A.M. to 5 P.M. seven days per week. Hours extent to 8 A.M. to 6 P.M. from May through September.
- **Toll Road Service Plazas.** Areas 1, 2 and 5 through 25 are service plazas along the Pennsylvania Turnpike and the Turnpike Extension.
- **Tourist Information.** For tourist information call 1-800-VISIT-PA.

Rest Area Usage Rules

- **Overnight Parking.** No overnight parking.
- **Camping.** Camping or sleeping outside of vehicle is not permitted.
- **Stay Limit.** Parking limited to 2 hours.

Driving In Pennsylvania

- **Emergencies.** For highway emergencies call 911 (may not be operable in all counties) or dial the local police or local number for the highway patrol.
- **Open Container.** Open containers of alcoholic beverages in the passenger compartment of the vehicle are not permitted.
- **Seat Belts.** Seat belts are required for all front seat occupants. Children 4 and under must be in a child restraint system in front. Children under 1 must be in a child restraint system in the rear and children 1 through 4 must be in a child restraint system or seat belt in the rear.
- **Helmets.** Motorcycle operators and passengers must wear helmets.

• **Road Conditions.** Dial 1-717-939-9551 for information concerning the Pennsylvania Turnpike. Otherwise, dial 1-814-355-7545.

PENNSYLVANIA REST AREAS

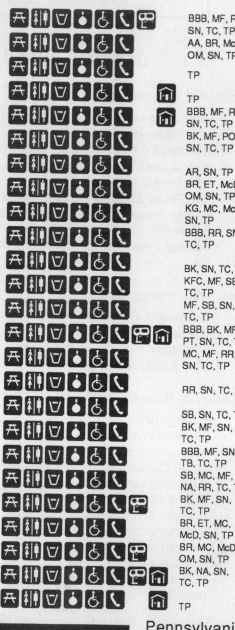

(9)

1   N/S   34
ALLENTOWN SERVICE PLAZA — BBB, MF, RR, SN, TC, TP

2   N/S   66
HICKORY RUN SERVICE PLAZA — AA, BR, McD, OM, SN, TP

(70)

3   E
4 MI S OF CRYSTAL SPRING — TP

4   W
MARYLAND LINE — TP

(76)

5   E   22
ZELIENOPLE SERVICE PLAZA — BBB, MF, RR, SN, TC, TP

6   W   31
BUTLER SERVICE PLAZA — BK, MF, POP, SN, TC, TP

7   E   49
OAKMONT SERVICE PLAZA — AR, SN, TP

8   E   75
HEMPFIELD SERVICE PLAZA — BR, ET, McD, OM, SN, TP

9   W   78
NEW STANTON SERVICE PLAZA — KG, MC, McD, SN, TP

10   E   112
SOMERSET SERVICE PLAZA — BBB, RR, SN, TC, TP

11   W   112
SOMERSET SERVICE PLAZA — BK, SN, TC, TP

12   W   147
MIDWAY SERVICE PLAZA — KFC, MF, SB, TC, TP

13   E   147
MIDWAY SERVICE PLAZA — MF, SB, SN, TC, TP

14   E/W   172
SIDELING HILL SERVICE PLAZA — BBB, BK, MF, PT, SN, TC, TP

15   W   202
BLUE MT SERVICE PLAZA — MC, MF, RR, SN, TC, TP

16   E   219
PLAINFIELD SERVICE PLAZA — RR, SN, TC, TP

17   E   250
HIGHSPIRE SERVICE PLAZA — SB, SN, TC, TP

18   W   258
LAWN SERVICE PLAZA — BK, MF, SN, TC, TP

19   E   290
BOWMANSVILLE SERVICE PLZA — BBB, MF, SN, TB, TC, TP

20   W   305
PETER J CAMIEL SERVICE PLAZA — SB, MC, MF, NA, RR, TC, TP

21   E   324
VALLEY FORGE SERVICE PLAZA — BK, MF, SN, TC, TP

22   E   328
KING OF PRUSSIA PLAZA — BR, ET, MC, McD, SN, TP

23   E   352
NESHAMINY SERVICE PLAZA — BR, MC, McD, OM, SN, TP

24   W   352
NESHAMINY SERVICE PLAZA — BK, NA, SN, TC, TP

(78)

25   W
1 MI W OF EASTON — TP

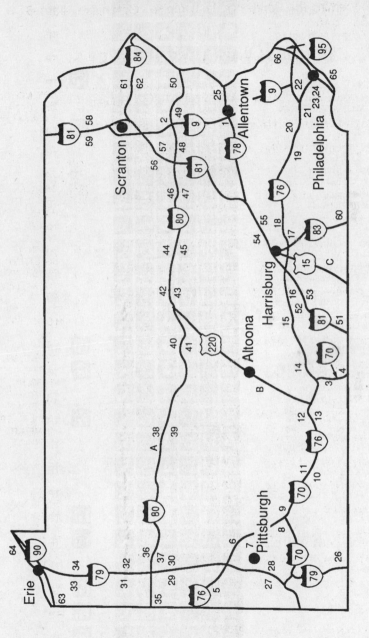

Route	Exit	Dir	Location	Amenities	Lodging	
79	26	N	4 MI N OF WVA LINE	🏕🚻🚰⛽♿☎	🏠	TP
	27/28	N/S	10 MI N OF CANONSBURG	🏕🚻🚰⛽♿☎		TP
	29/30	N/S	4 MI N OF ELLIOT MILLS	🏕🚻🚰⛽♿☎		TP
	31/32	N/S	2 MI N OF WILLIAMS CORNERS	🏕🚻🚰⛽♿☎		TP
	33	S	8 MI N OF MSIERTOWN	🏕🚻🚰⛽♿☎	🏠	TP
	34	N	8 MI N OF MSIERTOWN	🏕🚻🚰⛽♿☎		TP
80	35	E	OHIO LINE	🏕🚻🚰⛽♿☎	🏠	TP
	36/37	E/W	11 MI E OF I-79	🏕🚻🚰⛽♿☎		TP
	38/39	E/W	7 MI W OF FALL CREEK	🏕🚻🚰⛽♿☎		TP
	40/41	E/W	5 MI W OF RTE 144	🏕🚻🚰⛽♿☎		TP
	42/43	E/W	7 MI E OF CARROLL	🏕🚻🚰⛽♿☎		TP
	44/45	E/W	7 MI E OF MILTON	🏕🚻🚰⛽♿☎		TP
	46/47	E/W	5 MI E OF MIFFINVILLE	🏕🚻🚰⛽♿☎		TP
	48	E	2 MI W OF WHITE HAVEN	🏕🚻🚰⛽♿☎		TP
	49	E	1 MI E OF I-380	🏕🚻🚰⛽♿☎		TP
	50	W	NEW JERSEY LINE	🏕🚻🚰⛽♿☎	🏠	TP
81	51	N	3 MI N OF MARYLAND LINE	🏕🚻🚰⛽♿☎	🏠	TP
	52	S	11 MI SW OF CARLISLE	🏕🚻🚰⛽♿☎		TP
	53	N	11 MI SW OF CARLISLE	🏕🚻🚰⛽♿☎	🏠	TP
	54/55	N/S	16 MI NE OF HARRISBURG	🏕🚻🚰⛽♿☎		TP
	56/57	N/S	6 MI N OF I-80	🏕🚻🚰⛽♿☎		TP
	58	N	8 MI N OF CLARKS SUMMIT	🏕🚻🚰⛽♿☎		TP
	59	S	13 MI N OF CLARKS SUMMIT	🏕🚻🚰⛽♿☎	🏠	TP
83	60	N	3 MI N OF MARYLAND LINE	🚻🚰⛽♿☎	🏠	TP
84	61/62	E/W	1 MI W OF RTE 390	🏕🚻🚰⛽♿☎		TP
90	63	E	OHIO LINE	🏕🚻🚰⛽♿☎	🏠	TP
	64	W	NEW YORK LINE	🏕🚻🚰⛽♿☎	🏠	TP
95	65	N	DELAWARE LINE	🏕🚻🚰⛽♿☎	🏠	TP
	66	S	NEW JERSEY LINE	🏕🚻🚰⛽♿☎	🏠	TP

PENNSYLVANIA SERVICE STATIONS WITH RV DUMP FACILITIES

A. Brookville

Name of Business: Truckstops of America
Location: I-80, Exit 13 (PA-36 N.
Hours of Operation: 24 hours per day.
RV Information: No charge for use of RV Dump ($5.00 if fuel not purchased). Diesel fuel available. No waterfill or propane.
Station Type: Truck stop (BP).

B. East Freedom

Name of Business: Freedom Junction Auto/Truck Plaza
Location: US-220 and PA-36.
Hours of Operation: 24 hours per day.
RV Information: $3.00 charge for use of RV Dump. Waterfill, propane and diesel fuel available.
Station Type: Truck stop (Mobil).

C. Gettysburg

Name of Business: Spangler's Restaurant and Truck Stop
Location: US-15 and PA-394.
Hours of Operation: 6 A.M. to 10 P.M.
RV Information: $5.00 charge for use of RV Dump ($10.00 if fuel not purchased). Waterfill, propane and diesel fuel available.
Station Type: Truck stop (Texaco).

RHODE ISLAND

"Ocean State"

Capital: Providence	**Largest City:** Providence
Population: 1,003,464	**Area:** 1,049 sq. mi.
Highest Point: 812 ft.	**Lowest Point:** Sea Level

Date of Statehood: May 29, 1790

GENERAL INFORMATION

Additional Information On Services

- **Rest Area Hours.** Rest Area is open 24 hours per day, seven days per week.
- **Welcome Cemter Hours.** The welcome center is staffed from 8:30 A.M. to 6:30 P.M. May 15th through October 15th and from 8:30 A.M. to 4:30 P.M. October 15th through May 15th.
- **Tourist Information.** For tourist information call 1-800-556-2484 or 1-401-277-2601.

Rest Area Usage Rules

- **Overnight Parking.** Overnight parking is permitted, but not encouraged.
- **Camping.** Camping or sleeping outside of vehicle is not permitted.
- **Stay Limit.** No published limit.

Driving In Rhode Island

- **Emergencies.** For highway emergencies call 1-401-647-3311 for the highway patrol.
- **Open Container.** Open containers of alcoholic beverages in the passenger compartment of the vehicle are not permitted.
- **Seat Belts.** Children 4 and under or 40 pounds and under must be in a child restraint system.
- **Helmets.** Motorcycle operators and passengers must wear helmets and eye protection.
- **Road Conditions.** Dial 1-401-647-3311.

RHODE ISLAND REST AREAS

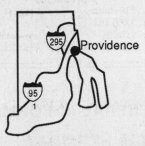

 1   N/S
BETWEEN EXITS 2 AND 3    TP

SOUTH CAROLINA

"Palmetto State"

Capital: Columbia	**Largest City:** Columbia
Population: 3,486,703	**Area:** 30,225 sq. mi.
Highest Point: 3,560 ft.	**Lowest Point:** Sea Level

Date of Statehood: May 23, 1788

GENERAL INFORMATION

Additional Information On Services

- **Rest Area Hours.** Rest Areas are open 24 hours per day, seven days per week.
- **Welcome Center Hours.** Welcome centers are staffed from 8 A.M. to 5:30 P.M. seven days per week.
- **Tourist Information.** For tourist information call 1-803-734-0235.

Rest Area Usage Rules

- **Overnight Parking.** No overnight parking.
- **Camping.** Camping or sleeping outside of vehicle is not permitted.
- **Stay Limit.** No published limit.

Driving In South Carolina

- **Emergencies.** For highway emergencies call 1-800-768-1501 for the highway patrol.
- **Open Container.** Open containers of alcoholic beverages in the passenger compartment of the vehicle are not permitted.
- **Seat Belts.** Seat belts are required for all front seat occupants. Children 6 and under must be properly restrained in either seat. This means children 1 and under must be in a child restraint system. Children 2 and over may be in a seat belt instead of a child restraint system if in the rear; children 4 and over may be in a seat belt in front.
- **Helmets.** Motorcycle operators and passengers 21 and under must wear helmets.
- **Road Conditions.** Dial 1-800-768-1501.

SOUTH CAROLINA REST AREAS

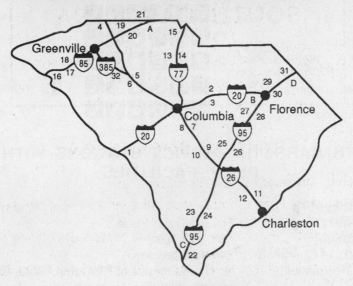

20	1 GEORGIA LINE	E	.5	⛱	🚻	⛟	🍼	♿	☎	🏠	TP, VM
	2/3 CAMDEN	E/W	92	⛱	🚻	⛟	🍼	♿	☎		TP, VM
26	4 NORTH CAROLINA LINE	E	2	⛱	🚻	⛟	🍼	♿	☎	🏠	TP, VM
	5/6 CLINTON	E/W	63	⛱	🚻	⛟	🍼	♿	☎		TP, VM
	7/8 COLUMBIA	E/W	123	⛱	🚻	⛟	🍼	♿	☎		TP, VM
	9/10 ORANGEBURG	E/W	151	⛱	🚻	⛟	🍼	♿	☎		TP, VM
	11/12 HANAHAN	E/W	203	⛱	🚻	⛟	🍼	♿	☎		TP, VM
77	13/14 2 MI N OF RTE 9	N/S	65	⛱	🚻	⛟	🍼	♿	☎		TP, VM
	15 2 MI S NORTH CAROLINA LINE	S	88	⛱	🚻	⛟		♿	☎	🏠	TP, VM
85	16 2 MI N OF GEORGIA LINE	N	2	⛱	🚻	⛟	🍼	♿	☎	🏠	TP, VM
	17 ANDERSON	N	18	⛱	🚻	⛟	🍼	♿	☎		TP, VM
	18 ANDERSON	S	23	⛱	🚻	⛟	🍼	♿	☎		TP, VM
	19/20 GAFNEY	N/S	89	⛱	🚻	⛟	🍼	♿	☎		TP, VM
	21 NORTH CAROLINA LINE	S	103	⛱	🚻	⛟	🍼	♿	☎	🏠	TP, VM
95	22 5 MI N OF GEORGIA LINE	N	5	⛱	🚻	⛟	🍼	♿	☎	🏠	TP, VM
	23/24 WATTERBORO	N/S	47	⛱	🚻	⛟	🍼	♿	☎		TP, VM

25 SANTEE	S	99		🏠	TP, VM
26 SANTEE	N	99			TP, VM
27/28 SHILOH	N/S	138			TP, VM
29/30 DARLINGTON	N/S	172			TP, VM
31 NORTH CAROLINA LINE	S	195		🏠	TP, VM
385 32 LAURENS	N/S	7			TP, VM

SOUTH CAROLINA SERVICE STATIONS WITH RV DUMP FACILITIES

A. Blacksburg

Name of Business:	Flying J Travel Plaza
Location:	I-85, Exit 102.
Hours of Operation:	24 hours per day.
RV Information:	No charge for use of RV Dump. Waterfill, propane and diesel fuel available.
Station Type:	Truck stop (Conoco).

B. Florence

Name of Business:	Petro Stopping Center # 58
Location:	I-95, Exit 169 (TV Rd.).
Hours of Operation:	24 hours per day.
RV Information:	No charge for use of RV Dump. Waterfill and diesel fuel available. No propane.
Station Type:	Truck stop (Texaco).

C. Hardeeville

Name of Business:	Joker Joe's El Cheapo #44
Location:	I-95, Exit 8 (Hwy. 88).
Hours of Operation:	24 hours per day.
RV Information:	$2.50 charge for use of RV Dump. Propane and diesel fuel available. No waterfill.
Station Type:	Truck stop (BP).

D. Latta

Name of Business:	Flying J Travel Plaza
Location:	I-95, Exit 181 (SC-38).
Hours of Operation:	24 hours per day.
RV Information:	No charge for use of RV Dump. Waterfill, propane and diesel fuel available.
Station Type:	Truck stop (Conoco).

SOUTH DAKOTA

"Coyote State"

Capital: Pierre	Largest City: Sioux Falls
Population: 696,004	Area: 75,955 sq. mi.
Highest Point: 7,242 ft.	Lowest Point: 962 ft.

Date of Statehood: November 2, 1889

GENERAL INFORMATION

Additional Information On Services

- **Rest Area Hours.** Rest Areas are open 24 hours per day, seven days per week.
- **Welcome Center Hours.** Welcome centers are staffed at least 8 hours per day from mid-May through mid-September.
- **Tourist Information.** For tourist information call 1-800-952-3625.

Rest Area Usage Rules

- **Overnight Parking.** No overnight parking.
- **Camping.** Camping is not permitted.
- **Stay Limit.** Parking limited to 4 hours.

Driving In South Dakota

- **Emergencies.** For highway emergencies call 1-605-773-3536 for the highway patrol.
- **Open Container.** Open containers of alcoholic beverages in the passenger compartment of the vehicle are not permitted.
- **Seat Belts.** Children under 2 must be in a child restraint system. Those under 5 must be in a child restraint system or seat belt.
- **Helmets.** Motorcycle operators and passengers under 18 must wear helmets.
- **Road Conditions.** Dial 1-605-773-3536.

SOUTH DAKOTA REST AREAS

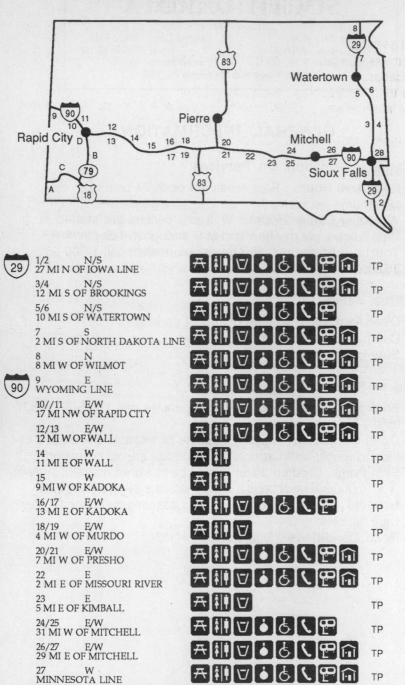

29 1/2   N/S
27 MI N OF IOWA LINE   TP

3/4   N/S
12 MI S OF BROOKINGS   TP

5/6   N/S
10 MI S OF WATERTOWN   TP

7   S
2 MI S OF NORTH DAKOTA LINE   TP

8   N
8 MI W OF WILMOT   TP

90 9   E
WYOMING LINE   TP

10//11   E/W
17 MI NW OF RAPID CITY   TP

12/13   E/W
12 MI W OF WALL   TP

14   W
11 MI E OF WALL   TP

15   W
9 MI W OF KADOKA   TP

16/17   E/W
13 MI E OF KADOKA   TP

18/19   E/W
4 MI W OF MURDO   TP

20/21   E/W
7 MI W OF PRESHO   TP

22   E
2 MI E OF MISSOURI RIVER   TP

23   E
5 MI E OF KIMBALL   TP

24/25   E/W
31 MI W OF MITCHELL   TP

26/27   E/W
29 MI E OF MITCHELL   TP

27   W
MINNESOTA LINE   TP

SOUTH DAKOTA SERVICE STATIONS WITH RV DUMP FACILITIES

A. Edgemont

Name of Business:	Nelson's One Stop
Location:	US-18 and SD-471.
Hours of Operation:	24 hours per day.
RV Information:	No charge for use of RV Dump. Waterfill and diesel fuel available. No propane.
Station Type:	Truck stop (Conoco).

B. Hermosa

Name of Business:	Battle Creek Station
Location:	SD-79 and SD-40 and SD-36.
Hours of Operation:	6 A.M. to 11 P.M. (to 9 P.M. in winter).
RV Information:	No charge for use of RV Dump. Waterfill, propane and diesel fuel available.
Station Type:	Truck stop (Texaco).

C. Hot Springs

Name of Business:	Pop-In Mart
Location:	US-18 and US-385.
Hours of Operation:	6 A.M. to 11 P.M. (to 10 P.M. in winter).
RV Information:	No charge for use of RV Dump. Waterfill and diesel fuel available. No propane.
Station Type:	Truck stop (Amoco).

D. Rapid City

Name of Business:	Conoco Travel Plaza
Location:	I-90, Exit 61 (St. Patrick St.).
Hours of Operation:	24 hours per day.
RV Information:	No charge for use of RV Dump. Waterfill, propane and diesel fuel available.
Station Type:	Truck stop (Conoco).

TENNESSEE

"Volunteer State"

Capital:	Nashville	Largest City:	Memphis
Population:	4,877,185	Area:	41,328 sq. mi.
Highest Point:	6,643 ft.	Lowest Point:	182 ft.

Date of Statehood: June 1, 1796

GENERAL INFORMATION

Additional Information On Services

- **Rest Area Hours.** Rest Areas are open 24 hours per day, seven days per week.
- **Welcome Center Hours.** Welcome centers are staffed at least 12 hours per day and are open 24 hours per day.
- **Tourist Information.** For tourist information call 1-800-836-6200.

Rest Area Usage Rules

- **Overnight Parking.** No overnight parking.
- **Camping.** Camping is not permitted.
- **Stay Limit.** 2 hour limit.

Driving In Tennessee

- **Emergencies.** For highway emergencies call 1-615-251-5240 for the highway patrol.
- **Open Container.** Open containers of alcoholic beverages in the passenger compartment of the vehicle are not permitted.
- **Seat Belts.** Seat belts are required for all front seat occupants. Children 3 and under must be in a child restraint system. Children 3 through 5 must be in a child restraint system or seat belt.
- **Helmets.** Motorcycle operators and passengers must wear helmets.
- **Road Conditions.** Dial 1-800-858-6349 in Tennessee and 1-615-741-2015 outside of Tennessee. Note: Tennessee requires lights on when raining.

TENNESSEE REST AREAS

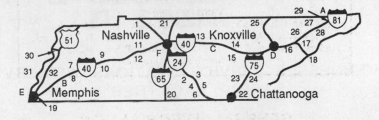

#				
24 1 S 1 1 MI S OF KENTUCKY LINE			PW, TP, VM
2/3 E/W 134 1 MI W OF US-64			PW, TP, VM, WR
4 E 160 1 MI E OF TN-28			PW, VM
5 W 160 1 MI E OF TN-28			PW, TP, VM
6 E 172 1 MI N OF GA STATE LINE			PW, TP, VM
40 7/8 E/W 73 5 MI E OF TN-138			PW, TP, VM
9/10 E/W 130 5 MI E OF TN-69			PW, TP, VM
11/12 E/W 170 3 MI W OF TN-46			PW, TP, VM
13 E/W 267 5 MI W OF TN-56			PW, TP, VM
14/15 E/W 338 9 MI E OF US-127			PW, TP, VM
16 E 420 I MI E OF TN-92			PW, TP, VM
17 W 425 1 MI E OF TN-113			PW, TP, VM
18 W 446 1 MI W OF HARTFORD			PW, VM
55 19 N 3 3 MI N OF MS STATE LINE			PW, TP, VM
65 20 N 3 3 MI N OF AL STATE LINE			PW, TP, VM
21 S 121 AT KY STATE LINE			PW, TP, VM
75 22 N 1 1 MI N OF GA STATE LINE			PW, TP, VM
23/24 N/S 45 3 MI S OF TN-30			PW, TP, VM
25 S 161 AT KY STATE LINE			PW, TP, VM
81 26 S 2 2 MI E OF I-40			PW, TP, VM
27/28 N/S 40 9 MI E OF TN-70			PW, TP, VM

29 S 75 AT VA STATE LINE		PW, TP, VM
30 E 9 9 MI E OF MO LINE		PW, TP, VM
31/32 N/S 5 MI N OF COVINGTON		PW, TP

TENNESSEE SERVICE STATIONS WITH RV DUMP FACILITIES

A. Bristol

Name of Business: Ponderosa Truck Stop
Location: I-81, Exit 74B (US-11).
Hours of Operation: 24 hours per day.
RV Information: $15.00 charge for use of RV Dump. Waterfill, propane and diesel fuel available.
Station Type: Truck stop (EXXON).

B. Brownsville

Name of Business: Fuel Mart
Location: I-40, Exit 66 (US-70).
Hours of Operation: 24 hours per day.
RV Information: No charge for use of RV Dump. Diesel fuel available. No waterfill or propane.
Station Type: Truck stop (Independent).

C. Cookeville

Name of Business: Middle Tennessee Auto Truck Plaza
Location: I-40, Exit 288 (TN-111 S).
Hours of Operation: 24 hours per day.
RV Information: No charge for use of RV Dump. Waterfill and diesel fuel available. No propane.
Station Type: Truck stop (Phillips 66).

D. Knoxville

Name of Business: Flying J Travel Plaza
Location: I-40 & 75, Exit 369 (Watt Rd.).
Hours of Operation: 24 hours per day.
RV Information: No charge for use of RV Dump. Waterfill, propane and diesel fuel available.
Station Type: Truck stop (Conoco).

E . Memphis

Name of Business:	St. Louis Truck Plaza
Location:	I-40, Exit 18 (US-64).
Hours of Operation:	24 hours per day.
RV Information:	No charge for use of RV Dump. Waterfill, propane and diesel fuel available.
Station Type:	Truck stop (Texaco).

F . Nashville

Name of Business:	Truckstops of America
Location:	I-65, Exit 85 (J. Robertson Pkwy.).
Hours of Operation:	24 hours per day.
RV Information:	No charge for use of RV Dump. Waterfill and diesel fuel available. No propane.
Station Type:	Truck stop (BP).

TEXAS

"Lone Star State"

Capital: Austin
Largest City: Houston
Population: 16,986,510
Area: 262,134 sq. mi.
Highest Point: 8,749 ft.
Lowest Point: Sea level
Date of Statehood: December 29, 1845

GENERAL INFORMATION

Additional Information On Services

- **Rest Area Hours.** Rest Areas are open 24 hours per day, seven days per week.
- **Welcome Center Hours.** Welcome centers are staffed from 8 A.M. to 5 P.M. seven days per week, with expanded hours in the summer.
- **Tourist Information.** For tourist information call 1-800-452-9292.

Rest Area Usage Rules

- **Overnight Parking.** Overnight parking is permitted.
- **Camping.** Camping is not permitted.
- **Stay Limit.** No published limit.

Driving In Texas

- **Emergencies.** For highway emergencies call 1-800-525-5555 for the highway patrol.
- **Open Container.** Open containers of alcoholic beverages in the passenger compartment of the vehicle are not permitted.
- **Seat Belts.** Seat belts are required for all front seat occupants. Children under 2 must be in a child restraint system. Children 2 through 4 must be in a child restraint system or seat belt.
- **Helmets.** Motorcycle operators and passengers must wear helmets.
- **Road Conditions.** Dial 1-800-452-9292.

Route	Exit	Dir	Location	Facilities	Notes
10	1	S	3 MI S OF NM STATE LINE	⛲🚻🗑🍼♿📞 🏠	TP
	2/3	E/W	2 MI E OF FABENS	⛲🚻🗑🍼♿📞	TP
	4/5	E/W	4 MI E OF VAN HORN	⛲🚻🗑🍼♿	TP
	6	E	26 MI W OF FT. STOCKTON	⛲🚻🗑🍼♿	TP
	7	W	26 MI W OF FT. STOCKTON	⛲🚻🗑🍼♿	TP
	8/9	E/W	50 MI E OF FT. STOCKTON	⛲🚻🗑🍼♿	TP
	10/11	E/W	7 MI W OF SONORA	⛲🚻🗑🍼♿ 📺	TP
	12/13	E/W	6 MI E OF KERRVILLE	⛲🚻🗑🍼♿📞📺	TP, VM
	14/15	E/W	7 MI E OF SAN ANTONIO	⛲🚻🗑🍼♿📞📺	TP
	16/17	E/W	7 MI W OF LULING	⛲🚻🗑🍼♿📞📺	TP, VM
	18/19	E/W	5 MI W OF COLUMBUS	⛲🚻🗑🍼♿📞	TP, VM
	20/21	E/W	10 MI E OF HOUSTON	⛲🚻🗑🍼♿📞	TP
	22/23	E/W	12 MI W OF ORANGE	⛲🚻🗑🍼♿ 📺	TP, VM
	24	W	EAST OF ORANGE	⛲🚻🗑🍼♿📞 🏠	TP
20	25/26	E/W	13 MI W OF MONAHANS	⛲🚻🗑🍼♿	TP
	27/28	E/W	5 MI E OF MIDLAND	⛲🚻🗑🍼♿📞📺	TP
	29	E	3 MI E OF COAHOMA	⛲🚻🗑🍼	TP
	30	W	3 MI W OF WESTBROOK	⛲🚻🗑🍼	TP
	31/32	E/W	27 MI W OF ABILENE	⛲🚻🗑🍼♿	TP, VM
	33/34	E/W	10 MI E OF ABILENE	⛲🚻🗑🍼♿	TP
	35/36	E/W	18 MI W OF WEATHERFORD	⛲🚻🗑🍼♿	TP, VM
	37/38	E/W	43 MI E OF DALLAS	⛲🚻🗑🍼♿📞	TP, VM
	39/40	E/W	10 MI E OF CANTON	⛲🚻🗑🍼♿📞📺	TP, VM
	41/42	E/W	10 MI W OF MARSHALL	⛲🚻🗑🍼♿📞	TP, VM
	43	W	AT LA STATE LINE	⛲🚻🗑🍼♿📞📺🏠	TP
27	44/45	N/S	5 MI S OF HALE CENTER	⛲🚻🗑🍼♿	TP
30	46/47	E/W	4 MI W OF MT. VERNON	⛲🚻🗑🍼♿	TP

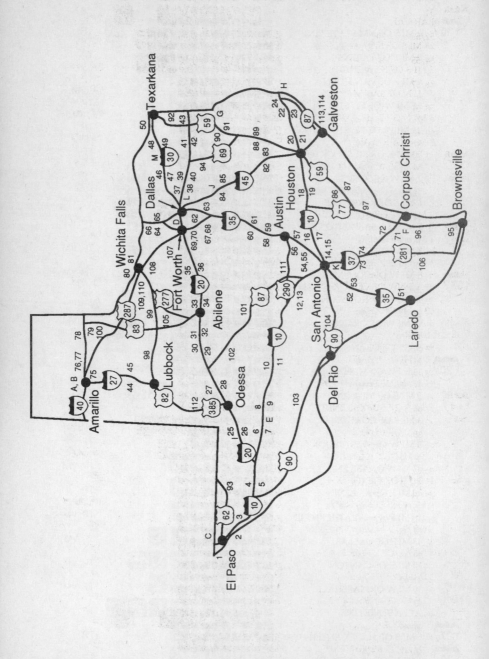

Site	Dir	Location	Facilities	Notes
48/49	E/W	11 MI W OF NEW BOSTON		TP, VM
50	W	1 MI W OF AR STATE LINE		TP
(35) 51	N	LAREDO		TP
52/53	N/S	23 MI S OF SAN ANTONIO		TP, VM
54/55	N/S	7 MI S OF NEW BRAUNFELS		TP, VM
56/57	N/S	7 MI N OF SAN MARCOS		TP, VM
58/59	N/S	3 MI N OF ROUND ROCK		TP, VM
60/61	N/S	3 MI S OF SALADO		TP, VM
(35E) 62/63	N/S	10 MI S OF WAXAHACHIE		TP
(35) 64/65	N/S	5 MI S OF GAINESVILLE		TP, VM
66	S	2 MI S OF OK STATE LINE		TP
(35W) 67/68	N/S	1 MI E OF ITASCA		TP
69/70	N/S	5 MI S OF BURLESON		TP
(37) 71/72	N/S	19 MI NW OF CORPUS CHRISTI		TP, VM
73/74	N/S	13 MI N OF THREE RIVERS		TP
(40) 75	E	AMARILLO		TP
76/77	E/W	16 MI E OF AMARILLO		TP
78/79	E/W	13 MI W OF SHAMROCK		TP
(44) 80/81	N/S	3 MI S OF BURKBURNETT		TP
(45) 82/83	N/S	9 MI N OF HUNTSVILLE		TP, VM
84/85	N/S	16 MI S OF CORSICANA		TP, VM
(59) 86/87	N/S	11 MI E OF VICTORIA		TP
88/89	N/S	9 MI N OF LIVINGSTON		TP, VM
90/91	N/S	5 MI S OF NACOGDOCHES		TP
92	N/S	6 MI NE OF LINDEN		TP
(62) 93	N/S	10 MI SW OF NM STATE LINE		TP
(69) 94	N/S	4 MI N OF JACKSONVILLE		TP
(77) 95	N/S	HARLINGEN		TP
96	N/S	20 MI S OF KINGSVILLE		TP

Texas

Route	#	Dir	Location	Facilities		
	97	N/S	10 MI S OF REFUGIO	picnic, restroom, trash, water, handicap		TP
82	98	E/W	4 MI E OF CROSBYTON	picnic, restroom, trash, water, handicap		TP
	99	W	5 MI E OF BENJAMIN	picnic, restroom, trash, water, handicap		TP
83	100	N/S	5 MI N OF WELLINGTON	picnic, restroom, trash, water, handicap		TP
87	101	N/S	6 MI W OF EDEN	restroom, trash, water, handicap		TP
	102	N/S	15 MI E OF STERLING CITY	picnic, restroom, trash, water, handicap		TP
90	103	E/W	LANGTRY	restroom, trash, water, handicap	shelter	TP
	104	E/W	5 MI E OF BRACKETTVILLE	picnic, restroom, trash, water, handicap		TP
277	105	N/S	10 MI S OF HASKELL	picnic, restroom, trash, water, handicap		TP
281	106	N/S	9 MI S OF FALFURRIAS	picnic, restroom, trash, water, handicap		TP
287	107	N	7 MI N OF DECATUR	picnic, restroom, trash, water, handicap		TP
	108	S	2 MI SE OF HENRIETTA	picnic, restroom, trash, water, handicap		TP
	109/110	N/S	2 MI NW OF IOWA PARK	picnic, restroom, trash, water, handicap		TP
290	111	E/W	20 MI E OF FREDERICKBURG	picnic, restroom, trash, water, handicap		TP
385	112	N/S	10 MI N OF ANDREWS	picnic, restroom, trash, water, handicap		TP
87	113/114	N/S	AT FERRY LANDING	picnic, restroom, trash, water, handicap, phone		TP

TEXAS SERVICE STATIONS WITH RV DUMP FACILITIES

A. Amarillo

Name of Business: Flying J Travel Plaza
Location: I-40, Exit 76 (Frontage Rd.).
Hours of Operation: 24 hours per day.
RV Information: No charge for use of RV Dump. Waterfill and diesel fuel available. No propane.
Station Type: Truck stop (Conoco).

B. Amarillo

Name of Business: Amarillo 76 Auto/Truck Stop
Location: I-40, Exit 74 (Whitaker Rd.).
Hours of Operation: 24 hours per day.
RV Information: No charge for use of RV Dump. Waterfill and diesel fuel available. No propane.
Station Type: Truck stop (Unocal 76)

C. Anthony

Name of Business:	Flying J Travel Plaza
Location:	I-10, Exit 0 (Mountain Pass Rd.).
Hours of Operation:	24 hours per day.
RV Information:	No charge for use of RV Dump. Waterfill, propane and diesel fuel available.
Station Type:	Truck stop (Conoco).

D. Dallas

Name of Business:	Flying J Travel Plaza
Location:	I-20, Exit 472 (Bonnie View Rd.)
Hours of Operation:	24 hours per day.
RV Information:	No charge for use of RV Dump. Waterfill, propane and diesel fuel available.
Station Type:	Truck stop (Conoco).

E. Fort Stockton

Name of Business:	7-D EXXON
Location:	I-10, Exit 261 (7-D Rd.).
Hours of Operation:	24 hours per day.
RV Information:	No charge for use of RV Dump. Waterfill and diesel fuel available. No propane.
Station Type:	Truck stop (EXXON).

F. Kingsville

Name of Business:	Get"N" Go Travel Center
Location:	US-77 Bypass.
Hours of Operation:	24 hours per day.
RV Information:	No charge for use of RV Dump. Waterfill and diesel fuel available. No propane.
Station Type:	Truck stop (Diamond Shamrock).

G. Nacogdoches

Name of Business:	Cactus Jack
Location:	NW Loop 224.
Hours of Operation:	5 A.M. to 10 P.M. M-F, 6 A.M. to 10 P.M. Sat, 8 A.M. to 10 P.M. Sun.
RV Information:	No charge for use of RV Dump. Waterfill and diesel fuel available. No propane.
Station Type:	Truck stop (Phillips 66).

H. Orange

Name of Business:	Flying J Travel Plaza
Location:	I-10, Exit 873 (TX-62).
Hours of Operation:	24 hours per day.
RV Information:	No charge for use of RV Dump. Waterfill,

propane and diesel fuel available.
Station Type: Truck stop (Conoco).

I. Pecos

Name of Business: Flying J Travel Plaza
Location: I-20, Exit 42 (US-80 & 285).
Hours of Operation: 24 hours per day.
RV Information: No charge for use of RV Dump. Waterfill and diesel fuel available. No propane.

Station Type: Truck stop (Conoco).

J. Rice

Name of Business: Lucky Lady Truck Stop
Location: I-45, Exit 238 (FM-1603).
Hours of Operation: 24 hours per day.
RV Information: No charge for use of RV Dump if remaining at RV park on property overnight. Waterfill and diesel fuel available. No propane.

Station Type: Truck stop (Fina).

K. San Antonio

Name of Business: Flying J Travel Plaza
Location: I-10, Exit 583 (Foster Rd.).
Hours of Operation: 24 hours per day.
RV Information: No charge for use of RV Dump. Waterfill, propane and diesel fuel available.

Station Type: Truck stop (Conoco).

L. Terrell

Name of Business: Rip Griffin Ambest
Location: I-20, Exit 503 (Wilson Rd.).
Hours of Operation: 24 hours per day.
RV Information: No charge for use of RV Dump. Waterfill and diesel fuel available. No propane.

Station Type: Truck stop (Texaco).

M. Winfield

Name of Business: Good Time Fuel Stop
Location: I-30, Exit 153 (Spur Rd.).
Hours of Operation: 6 A.M. to midnight.
RV Information: $3.00 charge for use of RV Dump. Diesel fuel available. No waterfill or propane. RV park on property.

Station Type: Truck stop (Citgo).

UTAH

"Beehive State"

Capital: Salt Lake City		**Largest City:** Salt Lake City	
Population: 1,722,850		**Area:** 82,096 sq. mi.	
Highest Point: 13,528 ft.		**Lowest Point:** 2000 ft.	

Date of Statehood: January 4, 1896

GENERAL INFORMATION

Additional Information On Services

- **Rest Area Hours.** Rest Areas are open 24 hours per day, seven days per week. Areas 25, 27, 29, 30, & 31 are closed in winter.
- **Welcome Center Hours.** Welcome centers are staffed approximately 8 hours per day.
- **Tourist Information.** For tourist information call 1-801-538-1030.

Rest Area Usage Rules

- **Overnight Parking.** Overnight parking is permitted.
- **Camping.** Camping is not permitted.
- **Stay Limit.** No published limit.

Driving In Utah

- **Emergencies.** For highway emergencies call 911 (may not be operable in all counties) or dial the highway patrol at 1-801-965-4505.
- **Open Container.** Open containers of alcoholic beverages in the passenger compartment of the vehicle are not permitted.
- **Seat Belts.** Seat belts are required for all front seat occupants. Children under 2 must be in a child restraint system. Children 2 through 8 must be in a child restraint system or seat belt.
- **Helmets.** Motorcycle operators and passengers under 18 must wear helmets and eye protection.
- **Road Conditions.** Dial 1-801-964-6000 in Utah or 1-800-492-2400 from out of state.

UTAH REST AREAS

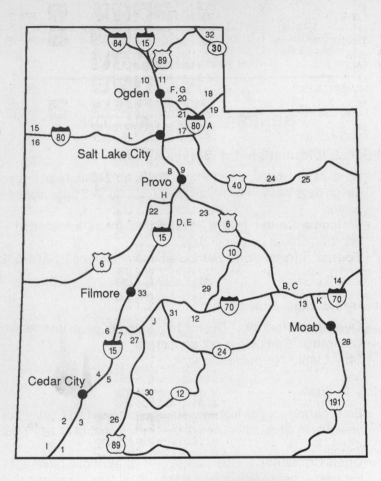

🛡️15	1 N 3 ST GEORGE	⛺	🚻	🚮	⛽	♿	📞		🏠 PW, TP
	2/3 N/S 45 2 MI S OF KANARRAVILLE	⛺	🚻	🚮	⛽	♿	📞		PW, TP
	4/5 N/S 88 LUNT PARK	⛺	🚻	🚮	⛽	♿	📞		PW, TP
	6 N 127 PINE CREEK	⛺	🚻	🚮	⛽	♿	📞		
	7 S 136 DOG VALLEY	⛺	🚻	🚮	⛽	♿	📞		TP
	8/9 N/S 277 AMERICAN FORK	⛺	🚻	🚮	⛽	♿	📞		PW, TP
	10 S 369 BRIGHAM	⛺	🚻	🚮	⛽	♿	📞		🏠 PW, TP
	11 N 363 PERRY	⛺	🚻	🚮	⛽	♿	📞		PW, TP

Route	No.	Name	Dir.	Mile	Facilities	Notes
70	12	IVIE CREEK	E	84	🏕🚻🗑🍼♿	PW, TP
	13	CRESCENT JCT	E	180	🏕🚻🗑🍼♿📞 🏠	PW, TP
	14	THOMPSON	W	187	🏕🚻🗑🍼♿📞 🏠	PW, TP
80	15/16	SALT FLATS	E/W	10	🏕🚻🗑🍼♿📞	TP
	17	SILVER CREEK	W	147	🏕🚻🗑🍼♿	PW, TP
	18	ECHO CANYON	W	171	🏕🚻🗑🍼♿📞 🏠	PW, TP
	19	ECHO CANYON	E	171	🏕🚻🗑🍼♿📞	PW, TP
84	20/21	MT GREEN	E/W	92	🏕🚻🗑🍼♿	TP
6	22	SILVER CITY	E/W	0	🏕🚻🗑🍼♿📞	
	23	TUCKER	E/W	203	🏕🚻🗑🍼♿	TP
40	24	PINION RIDGE	E/W	70	🏕🚻🗑🍼♿	TP
	25	ROOSEVELT	E/W	115	🏕🚻🗑🍼	
89	26	SHINGLE CREEK	N/S	95	🏕🚻🗑🍼♿	
	27	HOOVERS	N/S	184	🏕🚻🗑🍼♿	
191	28	KANE SPRINGS	N/S	10	🏕🚻🗑🍼♿📞	PW, TP
10	29	EMERY	N/S	12	🏕🚻🗑🍼	
12	30	PINES	E/W	10	🏕🚻🗑🍼♿📞	
24	31	OAK SPRINGS	E/W	35	🏕🚻🗑🍼♿	
30	32	BEAR LAKE	E/W	124	🏕🚻🗑🍼 📞	TP
99	33	FILMORE	E/W	3	🏕🚻🗑🍼♿📞	

UTAH SERVICE STATIONS WITH RV DUMP FACILITIES

A. Coalville

Name of Business: Holiday Hills
Location: I-80, Exit 164 (Frontage Rd.).
Hours of Operation: 6 A.M. to 12 P.M.
RV Information: $3.00 charge for use of RV Dump. Waterfill, propane and diesel fuel available.
Station Type: Truck stop (Phillips 66).

B. Green River
Name of Business:	Gary's Chevron
Location:	I-70, Exit 158 (Bus. I-70).
Hours of Operation:	24 hours per day.
RV Information:	No charge for use of RV Dump. Waterfill and diesel fuel available. No propane.
Station Type:	Service station with mini-mart (Chevron).

C. Green River
Name of Business:	West Winds Truck Stop
Location:	I-70, Exit 162 (US 6 & 50 E).
Hours of Operation:	24 hours per day.
RV Information:	No charge for use of RV Dump ($5.00 if fuel not purchased). Waterfill, propane and diesel fuel available.
Station Type:	Truck stop (Sinclair).

D. Nephi
Name of Business:	Tri-Mart Fuel Stop
Location:	I-15, Exit 222 (Main St.).
Hours of Operation:	24 hours per day.
RV Information:	No charge for use of RV Dump. Waterfill and diesel fuel available. No propane.
Station Type:	Truck stop (Texaco).

E. Nephi
Name of Business:	Circle C Car/Truck Plaza
Location:	I-15, Exit 222 (Main St.)
Hours of Operation:	24 hours per day.
RV Information:	No charge for use of RV Dump. Waterfill, propane and diesel fuel available.
Station Type:	Truck stop (Sinclair).

F. Ogden
Name of Business:	Flying J Travel Plaza
Location:	I-15, Exit 346 (21st St.).
Hours of Operation:	24 hours per day.
RV Information:	No charge for use of RV Dump. Waterfill, propane and diesel fuel available.
Station Type:	Truck stop (Conoco).

G. Ogden
Name of Business:	21st St. Auto Fuel Plaza
Location:	I-15, Exit 346 (21st St.).
Hours of Operation:	24 hours per day.
RV Information:	No charge for use of RV Dump. Waterfill and

diesel fuel available. No propane.

Station Type: Truck stop (Chevron/Conoco).

H. Payson

Name of Business: Fuel America
Location: I-15, Exit 254 (North Main St.)
Hours of Operation: 24 hours per day.
RV Information: No charge for use of RV Dump ($2,00 if fuel not purchased). Waterfill, propane and diesel fuel available.
Station Type: Truck stop (Phillips 66).

I. Richfield

Name of Business: Flying J Fuel Stop
Location: I-70, Exit 38 or 40 (North Main ST.).
Hours of Operation: 24 hours per day.
RV Information: $2.00 charge for use of RV Dump. Propane and diesel fuel available. No waterfill.
Station Type: Truck stop (Independent).

J. Saint George

Name of Business: Cash Saver
Location: I-15, Exit 6 (St. George Blvd. west, then right on Bluff St.).
Hours of Operation: 24 hours per day.
RV Information: No charge for use of RV Dump ($2.50 if fuel not purchased). Waterfill, propane and diesel fuel available.
Station Type: Truck stop (Premium Oil).

K. Thompson Springs

Name of Business: Rogers Roost Auto/Truck Stop
Location: I-70, Exit 185 (Rogers Rd.).
Hours of Operation: 24 hours per day (6 A.M. to 10 P.M. winter).
RV Information: No charge for use of RV Dump ($3.00 if fuel not purchased). Waterfill, propane and diesel fuel available.
Station Type: Truck stop (Phillips 66).

L. Tooele

Name of Business: Salt Lake City Auto Truck Plaza
Location: I-80, Exit 99 (Lake Point Rd.).
Hours of Operation: 24 hours per day.
RV Information: No charge for use of RV Dump. Waterfill and diesel fuel available. No propane.
Station Type: Truck stop (Shell/Unocal 76).

VERMONT

"Green Mountain State"

Capital: Montpelier	**Largest City:** Burlington	
Population: 562,758	**Area:** 9,609 sq. mi.	
Highest Point: 4,393 ft.	**Lowest Point:** 95 ft.	
	Date of Statehood: March 4, 1791	

GENERAL INFORMATION

Additional Information On Services

- **Rest Area Hours.** Rest Areas are open 10 A.M. Saturday through Thursday and 7 A.M. to 11 P.M. on Friday.
- **Welcome Center Hours.** Welcome centers at areas 11 and 12 are staffed from 8 A.M. to 8 P.M. Centers at 27 and 28 operate the same hours as the rest area. All facilities have a phone outside of the building for 24 hour use.
- **Tourist Information.** For tourist information call 1-802-223-3443.

Rest Area Usage Rules

- **Overnight Parking.** No overnight parking.
- **Camping.** Camping is not permitted.
- **Stay Limit.** No published limit.

Driving In Vermont

- **Emergencies.** For highway emergencies call 911 (may not be operable in all counties) or dial the highway patrol at 1-802-229-9191.
- **Open Container.** No open container law, but it is an offense for the driver to consume alcoholic beverages on the highway.
- **Seat Belts.** Children 1 and under must be in a child restraint system. Children 1 through 5 must be in a child restraint system in the front seat or a seat belt in the rear.
- **Helmets.** Motorcycle operators and passengers must wear helmets.
- **Road Conditions.** Dial 1-802-229-9191.

VERMONT REST AREAS

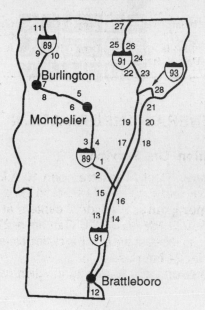

			Mile	Facilities		
89	1/2 SHARON	N/S	9	🏕️ 🚻 🚮 💧 ♿ ☎		TP
	3/4 RANDOLPH	N/S	34	🏕️ 🚻 🚮 💧 ♿ ☎		TP
	5/6 WATERBURY	N/S	66	🏕️		TP
	7/8 WILLISTON	N/S	82	🏕️ 🚻 🚮 💧 ♿ ☎		TP
	9/10 GEORGIA	N/S	110	🏕️ 🚻 🚮 💧 ♿ ☎		TP
	11 HIGHGATE	S	130	🏕️ 🚻 🚮 💧 ♿ ☎	🏠	TP
91	12 GUILFORD	N	.3	🏕️ 🚻 🚮 💧 ♿ ☎	🏠	TP
	13/14 SPRINGFIELD	N/S	39	🏕️		TP
	15/16 HARTLAND	N/S	68	🏕️ 🚻 🚮 💧 ♿ ☎		TP
	17/18 BRADFORD	N/S	100	🏕️ 🚻 🚮 💧 ♿ ☎		TP
	19/20 RYEGATE	N/S	114	🏕️		TP
	21 BARNET	N	122	🏕️		TP
	22 LYNDON	S	141	🏕️ 🚻 🚮 💧 ♿ ☎		TP
	23 WHEELOCK	N	143	🏕️		TP

Exit	Dir	Mile	Facilities	Lodging	
24 GLOVER	N	154	🏕️		TP
25 COVENTRY	S	167	🏕️		TP
26 COVENTRY	N	167	🏕️ 🚻 🗑️ ⛽ ♿ 📞		TP
27 DERBY	S	177	🏕️ 🚻 🗑️ ⛽ ♿ 📞	🏠	TP
93 28 WATERFORD	N	1	🏕️ 🚻 🗑️ ⛽ ♿ 📞	🏠	TP

VIRGINIA

"Old Dominion State"

Capital:	Richmond	Largest City:	Norfolk
Population:	6,187,358	Area:	40,767 sq. mi.
Highest Point:	5,729 ft.	Lowest Point:	Sea level

Date of Statehood: June 25, 1788

GENERAL INFORMATION

Additional Information On Services

- **Rest Area Hours.** Rest Areas are open 24 hours per day, seven days per week.
- **Welcome Center Hours.** Welcome center hours are 8 A.M. to 5 P.M., 7 days per week except on major holidays.
- **Tourist Information.** For tourist information call 1-804-786-4484.

Rest Area Usage Rules

- **Overnight Parking.** No overnight parking.
- **Camping.** Camping is not permitted.
- **Stay Limit.** Stay limit 2 hours.

Driving In Virginia

- **Emergencies.** For highway emergencies call 911 (may not be operable in all counties) or dial the highway patrol at 1-800-552-9965. State Police also monitor CB channel 9.
- **Open Container.** No open container law, but it is an offense to consume alcoholic beverages while driving.
- **Seat Belts.** Seat belts are required for all front seat occupants. Children 4 and under or less than 40 pounds must be in a child restraint system.
- **Helmets.** Motorcycle operators and passengers must wear helmets.
- **Road Conditions.** Dial 1-800-367-ROAD. Also use this number to report safety hazards on the highway.

VIRGINIA REST AREAS

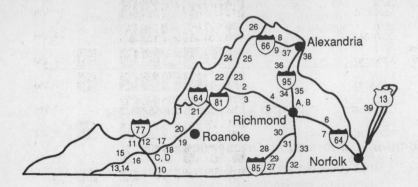

⑥④	1 COVINGTON	E	2	🏕️ 🚻 🗑️ 🍼 ♿ 📞					🏠	
	2/3 CHARLOTTEVILLE	E/W	105/113	🏕️ 🚻 🗑️ 🍼 ♿ 📞						TP, VM
	4/5 OILVILLE	E/W	169	🏕️ 🚻 🗑️ 🍼 ♿ 📞						TP, VM
	6/7 NEW KENT	E/W	214	🏕️ 🚻 🗑️ 🍼 ♿ 📞						TP, VM
⑥⑥	8 GAINESVILLE	W	49	🏕️ 🚻 🗑️ 🍼 ♿ 📞					🏠	TP, VM
	9 GAINESVILLE	E	49	🏕️ 🚻 🗑️ 🍼 ♿ 📞						TP, VM
⑦⑦	10 AT NC STATE LINE	N	0	🏕️ 🚻 🗑️ 🍼 ♿ 📞					🏠	TP, VM
	11 BLAND	S	60	🏕️ 🚻 🗑️ 🍼 ♿ 📞					🏠	TP, VM
	12 BLAND	N	60	🏕️ 🚻 🗑️ 🍼 ♿ 📞						TP, VM
⑧①	13 AT TN STATE LINE	N	0	🏕️ 🚻 🗑️ 🍼 ♿ 📞					🏠	TP, VM
	14 BRISTOL	N	13	🏕️ 🚻 🗑️ 🍼 ♿ 📞						TP, VM
	15 SMYTH	S	54	🏕️ 🚻 🗑️ 🍼 ♿ 📞						TP, VM
	16 RURAL RETREAT	N	61	🏕️ 🚻 🗑️ 🍼 ♿ 📞						TP, VM
	17/18 RADFORD	N/S	108	🏕️ 🚻 🗑️ 🍼 ♿ 📞						TP, VM
	19 CHRISTIANSBURG	N	129	🏕️ 🚻 🗑️ 🍼 ♿ 📞						TP, VM
	20 BUCHANAN	S	158	🏕️ 🚻 🗑️ 🍼 ♿ 📞						TP, VM
	21 FAIRFIELD	S	199	🏕️ 🚻 🗑️ 🍼 ♿ 📞						TP, VM
	22/23 MY. SIDNEY	N/S	232	🏕️ 🚻 🗑️ 🍼 ♿ 📞						TP, VM
	24/25 NEW MARKET	N/S	262	🏕️ 🚻 🗑️ 🍼 ♿ 📞						TP, VM

	Direction	Mile	Location	Facilities	Notes
	26 S	320	WINCHESTER	(icons)	TP, VM
85	27 N	1	AT NC STATE LINE	(icons)	TP, VM
	28/29 N/S	32	ALBERTA	(icons)	TP, VM
	30/31 N/S	55	DINWIDDIE	(icons)	TP, VM
95	32 N	0	AT NC STATE LINE	(icons)	TP, VM
	33 N	35	CARSON	(icons)	TP, VM
	34/35 N/S	108	LADYSMITH	(icons)	TP, VM
	36 S	132	FREDERICKSBURG	(icons)	TP, VM
	37/38 N/S	156	DUMFRIES	(icons)	TP, VM
13	39 S	1	NEW CHURCH	(icons)	VM

VIRGINIA SERVICE STATIONS WITH RV DUMP FACILITIES

A. Ashland

Name of Business: Speed and Briscoe 76 Auto/Truck Plaza
Location: I-95, Exit 89 (Lewistown Rd.).
Hours of Operation: 24 hours per day.
RV Information: No charge for use of RV Dump ($5.00 if fuel not purchased). Waterfill and diesel fuel available. No propane.
Station Type: Truck stop (Unocal 76).

B. Doswell

Name of Business: All American Travel Plaza
Location: I-95, Exit 98 (VA-30 E).
Hours of Operation: 24 hours per day.
RV Information: $5.00 charge for use of RV Dump. Waterfill and diesel fuel available. No propane. RV park on property.
Station Type: Truck stop (Texaco).

C. Wytheville

Name of Business: Wilderness Road 76 Auto/Truck Stop
Location: I-77, Exit 41 and I-81, Exit 72 (Perrersferry Rd.).
Hours of Operation: 24 hours per day.

| RV Information: | No charge for use of RV Dump. Waterfill and diesel fuel available. No propane. |
| Station Type: | Truck stop (Unocal 76). |

D. Wytheville

Name of Business:	Flying J Travel Plaza
Location:	I-81 & 77, Exit 77 (VA-24).
Hours of Operation:	24 hours per day.
RV Information:	No charge for use of RV Dump. Waterfill, propane and diesel fuel available.
Station Type:	Truck stop (Conoco).

WASHINGTON

"Evergreen State"

Capital: Olympia	Largest City: Seattle
Population: 4,866,692	Area: 65,570 sq. mi.
Highest Point: 14,411 ft.	Lowest Point: Sea Level

Date of Statehood: November 11, 1889

GENERAL INFORMATION

Additional Information On Services

- **Rest Area Hours.** Rest Areas are open 24 hours per day, seven days per week. Many rest areas have free coffee available.
- **Welcome Center Hours.** Welcome centers are staffed 8 A.M. to 5 P.M. from May through Labor Day weekend.
- **Tourist Information.** For tourist information call 1-800-544-1800 for travel packets or call 1-206-586-2102 or 1-206-586-2088.

Rest Area Usage Rules

- **Overnight Parking.** Overnight parking permitted.
- **Camping.** Camping is not permitted.
- **Stay Limit.** Parking limited to 8 hours.

Driving In Washington

- **Emergencies.** For highway emergencies call 911 (may not be operable in all counties) or dial the highway patrol at 1-800-283-7801. To report drunk drivers, call 1-800-28-DRUNK in western Washington and 1-800-22-DRUNK in eastern Washington. For water emergencies, the Coast Guard can be reached at 1-206-442-5886. To report forest fires, call 1-800-562-6010.
- **Open Container.** Open containers of alcoholic beverages in the passenger compartment of the vehicle are not permitted.
- **Seat Belts.** Seat belts are required for all occupants. Children under 5 must be in a child restraint system.
- **Helmets.** Motorcycle operators and passengers must wear helmets.
- **Road Conditions.** Dial 1-900-407-7277 for mountain pass reports and 1-900-407-7623 for other road conditions.

WASHINGTON REST AREAS

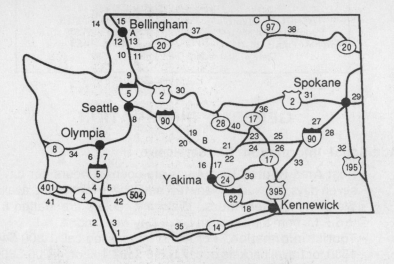

5	1 AT OR STATE LINE	N	0		🚻	▽	🍼	♿	📞			🏠	TP
	2/3 GEE CREEK	N/S	12	🏕	🚻	▽	🍼	♿	📞	📟	🏠		TP
	4/5 TOUTLE RIVER	N/S	55	🏕	🚻	▽	🍼		📞				TP
	6/7 MAYTOWN/SCATTER CREEK	N/S	92	🏕	🚻	▽	🍼	♿	📞				TP
	8 SEA TAC	N	140	🏕	🚻	▽	🍼	♿	📞	📟			TP
	9 SILVER LAKE	S	188	🏕	🚻	▽	🍼	♿	📞	📟			TP
	10/11 SMOKEY POINT	N/S	207	🏕	🚻	▽	🍼	♿	📞	📟			TP
	12 BOW HILL	S	238	🏕	🚻	▽	🍼		📞				TP
	13 BOW HILL	N	238	🏕	🚻	▽	🍼	♿	📞				TP
	14 CUSTER	S	268	🏕	🚻	▽	🍼	♿	📞			🏠	TP
	15 CUSTER	N	268	🏕	🚻	▽	🍼	♿	📞				TP
82	16/17 SELAH CREEK	E/W	23	🏕	🚻	▽	🍼		📞	📟			TP
	18 PROSSER	E	80	🏕	🚻	▽	🍼	♿	📞				TP
90	19/20 INDIAN JOHN HILL	E/W	89	🏕	🚻	▽	🍼	♿	📞	📟			TP
	21/22 RYE GRASS	E/W	125	🏕	🚻	▽	🍼		📞				TP
	23/24 WINCHESTER	E/W	162	🏕	🚻	▽	🍼		📞	📟			TP

#	Dir	Mile	Name	Facilities	
25	W	180	SCHRAG	🏕🚻🛢🔥📞☎	TP
26	E	180	SCHRAG	🏕🚻🛢🔥📞	TP
27	W	242	SPRAGUE LAKE	🏕🚻🛢🔥♿📞	TP
28	E	242	SPRAGUE LAKE	🏕🚻🛢🔥📞☎	TP
29	W	299	SPOKANE RIVER	🏕🚻🛢🔥📞🏠	TP
(2) 30	E/W	82	NASON CREEK	🏕🚻🛢🔥♿📞☎	TP
31	E/W	238	TELFORD	🏕🚻🛢🔥📞	TP
(195) 32	N/S	60	HORN SCHOOL	🏕🚻🛢🔥📞	TP
(395) 33	N/S	67	HATTON COULEE	🏕🚻🛢🔥♿📞	TP
(8) 34	E	2	ELMA	🏕🚻🛢🔥📞☎	TP
(14) 35	E/W	74	CHAMBERLAIN LAKE	🏕🚻🛢🔥📞	TP
(17) 36	N/S	89	BLUE LAKE	🏕🚻🛢🔥	TP
(20) 37	E/W	162	WASHINGTON PASS	🏕🚻🛢🔥♿🏠	TP
38	E/W	316	SHERMAN PASS	🏕🚻♿	TP
(24) 39	E/W	43	VERNITA TOLL	🏕🚻🛢🔥📞☎	TP
(28) 40	E/W	25	QUINCY VALLEY	🏕🚻🛢🔥♿	TP
(401) 41	N/S	1	MEGLER FERRY	🏕🚻🛢🔥♿📞🏠	TP
(504) 42	E/W	33	NORTH FORK RIDGE	🏕🚻🛢🔥♿📞🏠	TP

WASHINGTON SERVICE STATIONS WITH RV DUMP FACILITIES

A. Bellingham

Name of Business:	Yorky's #6
Location:	I-5, Exit 258 (Bennett Ave.).
Hours of Operation:	24 hours per day.
RV Information:	No charge for use of RV Dump. Waterfill and diesel fuel available. No propane.
Station Type:	Truck stop (EXXON).

B. Cle Elum

Name of Business:	Willette's Shell Service
Location:	I-90, Exit 84 & 85 (Rt. 903).
Hours of Operation:	6 A.M. to 10 P.M.
RV Information:	$2.00 charge for use of RV Dump. Waterfill, propane and diesel fuel available.
Station Type:	Truck stop (Shell).

C. Oroville

Name of Business:	Moser's Petroleum
Location:	US-97 (North end of town).
Hours of Operation:	6 A.M. to 7 P.M. (RV dump closed in winter)
RV Information:	$6.00 charge for use of RV Dump. Waterfill, propane and diesel fuel available.
Station Type:	Truck stop (EXXON).

WEST VIRGINIA

"Mountain State"

Capital: Charleston	**Largest City:** Huntington	
Population: 1,793,477	**Area:** 24,282 sq. mi.	
Highest Point: 4,863 ft.	**Lowest Point:** 247 ft.	
Date of Statehood: June 20, 1863		

GENERAL INFORMATION

Additional Information On Services

- **Rest Area Hours.** Rest Areas are open 24 hours per day, seven days per week. RV dump stations are closed in winter months.
- **Welcome Center Hours.** Welcome centers are staffed from 8:30 A.M. to 4:45 P.M. seven days per week.
- **Toll Road Plazas.** Areas 7, 8 and 9 are commercial plazas.
- **Tourist Information.** For tourist information call 1-800-CALL WVA.

Rest Area Usage Rules

- **Overnight Parking.** No overnight parking.
- **Camping.** Camping is not permitted.
- **Stay Limit.** No published limit.

Driving In West Virginia

- **Emergencies.** For highway emergencies call 1-304-746-2222 for the highway patrol.
- **Open Container.** Open containers of alcoholic beverages in the passenger compartment of the vehicle are governed by individual jurisdictions. However, throughout the state, the seal can not be broken on hard liquor.
- **Seat Belts.** Children 3 and under must be in a child restraint system. Children 9 and under must be in a seat belt.
- **Helmets.** Motorcycle operators and passengers must wear helmets.
- **Road Conditions.** Dial the local state police number.

WEST VIRGINIA REST AREAS

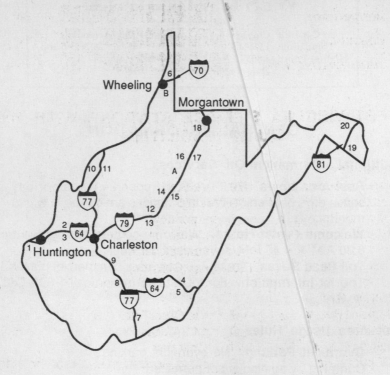

(64)	1 E HUNTINGTON	⛺	🚻	🚮	🍼	♿	📞		🏠	TP, VM
	2/3 E/W HURRICANE	⛺	🚻	🚮	🍼	♿	📞	📠		TP, VM
	4 W WHITE SULPHUR SPRINGS	⛺	🚻	🚮	🍼	♿	📞		🏠	TP, VM
	5 E WHITE SULPHUR SPRINGS	⛺	🚻	🚮	🍼	♿	📞	📠		TP, VM
(70)	6 W WHEELING	⛺	🚻	🚮	🍼	♿	📞	📠	🏠	TP, VM
(77)	7 N BLUESTONE TRAVEL PLAZA	⛺	🚻	🚮	🍼	♿	📞	📠	🏠	EX, RR, SK, TC, TP, VM
	8 S BECKLEY TRAVEL PLAZA	⛺	🚻	🚮	🍼	♿	📞	📠		EX, MF, SB, SK, TB, TC, TP, VM
	9 N MORTON TRAVEL PLAZA	⛺	🚻	🚮	🍼	♿	📞	📠	🏠	EX, RR, SK, TC, TP, VM
	10 S MINERAL WELLS	⛺	🚻	🚮	🍼	♿	📞	📠	🏠	TP, VM
	11 N MINERAL WELLS	⛺	🚻	🚮	🍼	♿	📞	📠		TP, VM
(79)	12/13 N/S SERVIA	⛺	🚻	🚮	🍼	♿	📞	📠		TP, VM
	14/15 N/S ASPINALL	⛺	🚻	🚮	🍼	♿	📞	📠		TP, VM

16/17 N/S CLARKSBURG		TP, VM
18 S MORGANTOWN		TP, VM
19 N BUNKER HILL		TP, VM
20 S 3 MI N OF FALLING WATER		TP, VM

WEST VIRGINIA SERVICE STATIONS WITH RV DUMP FACILITIES

A. Jane Lew

Name of Business:	I-79 Truck Stop
Location:	I-79, Exit 105 (Jane Lew Rd.).
Hours of Operation:	24 hours per day.
RV Information:	$10.00 charge for use of RV Dump. Waterfill, propane and diesel fuel available.
Station Type:	Truck stop (Chevron).

B. Valley Grove

Name of Business:	Dallas Pike Citgo Truck Stop
Location:	I-70, Exit 11 (Dallas Pike).
Hours of Operation:	24 hours per day.
RV Information:	$20.00 charge for use of RV Dump. Waterfill and diesel fuel available. No propane.
Station Type:	Truck stop (Citgo).

WISCONSIN

"Badger State"

Capital:	Madison	Largest City:	Milwaukee
Population:	4,891,769	Area:	56,154 sq. mi.
Highest Point:	1,951 ft.	Lowest Point:	581 ft.

Date of Statehood: May 29, 1848

GENERAL INFORMATION

Additional Information On Services

- **Rest Area Hours.** Rest Areas are open 24 hours per day, seven days per week.
- **Welcome Center Hours.** Welcome centers are open year-round. From October through April the centers operate from 8 A.M. to 4 P.M. Tuesday through Saturday. From May through September the centers are staffed from 8 A.M. to 6 P.M. seven days per week.
- **Tourist Information.** For tourist information call 1-800-432-TRIP.

Rest Area Usage Rules

- **Overnight Parking.** No overnight parking.
- **Camping.** Camping is not permitted.
- **Stay Limit.** No published limit.

Driving In Wisconsin

- **Emergencies.** For highway emergencies call 911 (may not be operable in all counties) or dial the local police or local number for the highway patrol.
- **Open Container.** Open containers of alcoholic beverages in the passenger compartment of the vehicle are not permitted.
- **Seat Belts.** Seat belts are required for all occupants. Children under 2 must be in a child restraint system. Children 2 through 4 must be in a child restraint system or seat belt.
- **Helmets.** Motorcycle operators and passengers 18 and under must.
- **Road Conditions.** Dial 1-800-762-3947.

WISCONSIN REST AREAS

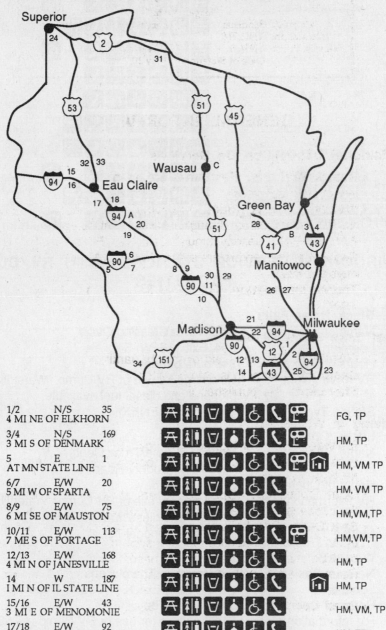

🛑**43**	1/2 N/S 35 4 MI NE OF ELKHORN	⛫	🚹	🗑	🍼	♿	☎	🚏	FG, TP
	3/4 N/S 169 3 MI S OF DENMARK	⛫	🚹	🗑	🍼	♿	☎	🚏	HM, TP
🛑**90**	5 E 1 AT MN STATE LINE	⛫	🚹	🗑	🍼	♿	☎	🚏 🏠	HM, VM TP
	6/7 E/W 20 5 MI W OF SPARTA	⛫	🚹	🗑	🍼	♿	☎		HM, VM TP
	8/9 E/W 75 6 MI SE OF MAUSTON	⛫	🚹	🗑	🍼	♿	☎		HM,VM,TP
	10/11 E/W 113 7 ME S OF PORTAGE	⛫	🚹	🗑	🍼	♿	☎	🚏	HM,VM,TP
	12/13 E/W 168 4 MI N OF JANESVILLE	⛫	🚹	🗑	🍼	♿	☎		HM, TP
	14 W 187 I MI N OF IL STATE LINE	⛫	🚹	🗑	🍼	♿	☎	🏠	HM, TP
🛑**94**	15/16 E/W 43 3 MI E OF MENOMONIE	⛫	🚹	🗑	🍼	♿	☎		HM, VM, TP
	17/18 E/W 92 3 MI SE OF OSSEO	⛫	🚹	🗑	🍼	♿	☎		HM, TP
	19/20 E/W 132 15 MI SE OF BLACK RIVER FALLS	⛫	🚹	🗑	🍼	♿	☎		HM, TP

Route	Exit	Dir	Mile	Location	Info
	21/22	E/W	262	22 MI E OF MADISON	S: HM, TP N: TP
	23	W	347	AT IL STATE LINE	HM, TP
2	24	S	14	SE EDGE OF SUPERIOR	FG, HM, TP
12	25	N	454	AT IL STATE LINE	FG, TP
41	26/27	N/S		2 MI S OF LOMIRA	S: FG N: FG, HM
	28	N/S		MARION	GT, TP
51	29	N	117	4 MI N OF WESTFIELD	N: HM
	30	S	149	3 MI S OF COLOMA	
	31	N/S		.5 MI S OF US-2	GT, HM, TP
53	32/33	N/S		28 MI NW OF CHIPPEWA FALLS	N: FG, HM S: FG
151	34	N/S		HWY 11 INTERCHANGE	TP

WISCONSIN SERVICE STATIONS WITH RV DUMP FACILITIES

A. Black River Falls

Name of Business: Black River Crossing Oasis
Location: I-94, Exit 116 (WI-54).
Hours of Operation: 24 hours per day.
RV Information: No charge for use of RV Dump. Waterfill, propane and diesel fuel available.
Station Type: Truck stop (CENEX).

B. Little Chute

Name of Business: Moasis 76 Auto/Truck Center
Location: US-41 and County Road N.
Hours of Operation: 24 hours per day.
RV Information: No charge for use of RV Dump. Waterfill, propane and diesel fuel available.
Station Type: Truck stop (Unocal 76).

C. Wausau

Name of Business: Rib Mountain Travel Center
Location: US-51 & 29, Exit 188 (County Road N).
Hours of Operation: 24 hours per day.
RV Information: $4.00 charge for use of RV Dump ($7.50 if fuel not purchased). Waterfill, propane and diesel fuel available.
Station Type: Truck stop (Amoco).

WYOMING

"Equality and Cowboy State"

Capital: Cheyenne   **Largest City:** Cheyenne
Population: 453,588   **Area:** 97,914 sq. mi.
Highest Point: 13,084 ft.   **Lowest Point:** 3,125 ft.
Date of Statehood: July 10, 1890

GENERAL INFORMATION

Additional Information On Services

- **Rest Area Hours.** Rest Areas are open 24 hours per day, seven days per week. Area 12 is subject to closure during winter.
- **Welcome Center Hours.** Welcome centers at areas 14 and 18 are staffed from 7 A.M. to 7 P.M. between May and October, closed in winter. The remaining centers are open year-round from 8 A.M. to 5 P.M. with extended summer hours of 7 A.M. to 7 P.M.
- **Tourist Information.** For tourist information call 1-307-777-7777.

Rest Area Usage Rules

- **Overnight Parking.** No overnight parking.
- **Camping.** Camping is not permitted.
- **Stay Limit.** No published limit.

Driving In Wyoming

- **Emergencies.** For highway emergencies call the highway patrol at 1-800-442-9090.
- **Open Container.** No open container law, but the driver may not drink alcoholic beverages.
- **Seat Belts.** Seat belts are required for all front seat occupants. Children 3 and under or less than 40 pounds must be in a child restraint system.
- **Helmets.** Motorcycle operators and passengers 18 and under must wear helmets.
- **Road Conditions.** Between October and April, dial these numbers:
  Northcentral: 1-800-442-2535; Northeast: 1-800-442-2555; Eastcentral: 1-800-442-2565; Southeast: 1-800-442-8321; Southwest: 1-800-442-7850.

WYOMING REST AREAS

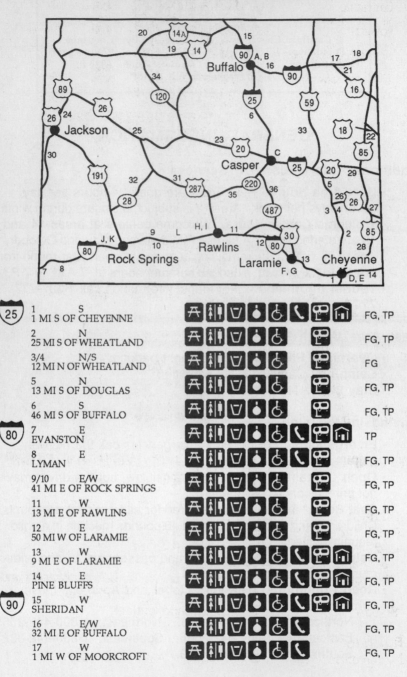

Route	No.	Dir.	Location	Services	Notes
25	1	S	1 MI S OF CHEYENNE	🏕 🚻 🗑 ⛽ ♿ 📞 🏤 🏠	FG, TP
	2	N	25 MI S OF WHEATLAND	🏕 🚻 🗑 ⛽ ♿ 🏤	FG, TP
	3/4	N/S	12 MI N OF WHEATLAND	🏕 🚻 🗑 ⛽ ♿ 🏤	FG
	5	N	13 MI S OF DOUGLAS	🏕 🚻 🗑 ⛽ ♿ 🏤	FG, TP
	6	S	46 MI S OF BUFFALO	🏕 🚻 🗑 ⛽ ♿ 🏤	FG, TP
80	7	E	EVANSTON	🏕 🚻 🗑 ⛽ ♿ 📞 🏤 🏠	TP
	8	E	LYMAN	🏕 🚻 🗑 ⛽ ♿ 📞 🏤	FG, TP
	9/10	E/W	41 MI E OF ROCK SPRINGS	🏕 🚻 🗑 ⛽ ♿ 🏤	FG, TP
	11	W	13 MI E OF RAWLINS	🏕 🚻 🗑 ⛽ ♿ 🏤	FG, TP
	12	E	50 MI W OF LARAMIE	🏕 🚻 🗑 ⛽ ♿ 🏤	FG, TP
	13	E	9 MI E OF LARAMIE	🏕 🚻 🗑 ⛽ ♿ 📞 🏤 🏠	FG, TP
	14	E	PINE BLUFFS	🏕 🚻 🗑 ⛽ ♿ 📞 🏤 🏠	FG, TP
90	15	W	SHERIDAN	🏕 🚻 🗑 ⛽ ♿ 📞 🏤 🏠	FG, TP
	16	E/W	32 MI E OF BUFFALO	🏕 🚻 🗑 ⛽ ♿ 📞	FG, TP
	17	W	1 MI W OF MOORCROFT	🏕 🚻 🗑 ⛽ ♿ 📞	FG, TP

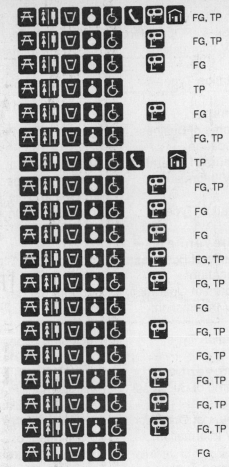

Route	Exit	Direction	Location	Notes
	18	E/W	1 MI E OF SUNDANCE	FG, TP
14	19	E/W	GREYBULL	FG, TP
14A	20	E/W	POWELL	FG
16	21	E/W	20 MI SO OF NEWCASTLE	TP
18	22	E/W	35 MI S OF NEWCASTLE	FG
20	23	E/W	49 MI W OF CASPER	FG, TP
26	24	N/S	JACKSON	TP
	25	E/W	37 MI W OF RIVERTO	FG, TP
	26	E/W	30 MI NW OF TORRINGTON	FG
	27	E/W	9 MI NW OF TORRINGTON	FG
85	28	N/S	24 MI NE OF CHEYENNE	FG, TP
	29	E/W	LUSK	FG, TP
89	30	N/S	10 MI N OF AFTON	FG
287	31	E/W	39 MI SE OF LANDER	FG, TP
28	32	E/W	SOUTH PASS	FG, TP
59	33	N/S	43 MI N OF DOUGLAS	FG, TP
120	34	N/S	37 MI NW OF THERMOPOLIS	FG, TP
220	35	E/W	52 MI SW OF CASPER	FG, TP
487	36	N/S	42 MI N OF MEDICINE BOW	FG

WYOMING SERVICE STATIONS WITH RV DUMP FACILITIES

A. Buffalo

Name of Business: Big Horn Travel Plaza
Location: I-25, Exit 299 (US-16).
Hours of Operation: 24 hours per day.
RV Information: No charge for use of RV Dump. Waterfill and diesel fuel available. No propane.
Station Type: Truck stop (Independent).

B. Buffalo

Name of Business: Buffalo CENEX Auto/Truck Stop

Location: I-25, Exit 299 (US-16).
Hours of Operation: 24 hours per day.
RV Information: No charge for use of RV Dump. Waterfill and diesel fuel available. No propane.
Station Type: Truck stop (CENEX).

C. Casper

Name of Business: Flying J Travel Plaza
Location: I-25, Exit 185 (Wyoming Blvd.)
Hours of Operation: 24 hours per day.
RV Information: No charge for use of RV Dump. Waterfill, propane and diesel fuel available.
Station Type: Truck stop (Conoco).

D. Cheyenne

Name of Business: Conoco Truck Stop
Location: I-25, Exit 9 (W. Lincoln Way).
Hours of Operation: 24 hours per day.
RV Information: No charge for use of RV Dump. Diesel fuel available. No waterfill or propane.
Station Type: Truck stop (Conoco).

E. Cheyenne

Name of Business: Flying J Travel Plaza
Location: I-25, Exit 7 (College Dr.).
Hours of Operation: 24 hours per day.
RV Information: No charge for use of RV Dump. Waterfill, propane and diesel fuel available.
Station Type: Truck stop (Conoco).

F. Laramie

Name of Business: Foster's Handy Truck Stop
Location: I-80, Exit 310 (Curtis St.).
Hours of Operation: 24 hours per day.
RV Information: No charge for use of RV Dump. Waterfill and diesel fuel available. No propane.
Station Type: Truck stop (Independent).

G. Laramie

Name of Business: Foster's Country Corner
Location: I-80, Exit 310, (Snowy Range Rd.).
Hours of Operation: 24 hours per day.
RV Information: No charge for use of RV Dump. Waterfill,

propane and diesel fuel available.
Station Type: Truck stop (Independent).

H. Rawlins

Name of Business: Flying J Travel Plaza
Location: I-80, Exit 209 (Johnson Rd.).
Hours of Operation: 24 hours per day.
RV Information: No charge for use of RV Dump. Waterfill, propane and diesel fuel available.
Station Type: Truck stop (Independent).

I. Rawlins

Name of Business: Rip Griffin Truck Service Center
Location: I-80, Exit 214 (Higley Blvd.).
Hours of Operation: 24 hours per day.
RV Information: No charge for use of RV Dump. Waterfill and diesel fuel available. No propane.
Station Type: Truck stop (Texaco).

J. Rock Springs

Name of Business: Tri-Mart Conoco
Location: I-80, Exit 107 (9th St.).
Hours of Operation: 5 A.M. to 11:30 P.M. (10:30 P.M. in winter)
RV Information: No charge for use of RV Dump ($3.00 if fuel not purchased). Waterfill and diesel fuel available. No propane.
Station Type: Truck stop (Conoco).

K. Rock Springs

Name of Business: Flying J Travel Plaza
Location: I-80, Exit 104 (Stagecoach Dr.).
Hours of Operation: 24 hours per day.
RV Information: No charge for use of RV Dump. Waterfill, propane and diesel fuel available.
Station Type: Truck stop (Conoco).

L. Wamsutter

Name of Business: Wamsutter Conoco Service
Location: I-80, Exit 173 (Mc Cormick Rd.).
Hours of Operation: 6 A.M. to 7 P.M., closed Sunday.
RV Information: No charge for use of RV Dump ($7.50 if no fuel purchased). Waterfill and diesel fuel available. No propane.
Station Type: Truck stop (Conoco).

Canada Rest Areas

ALBERTA

Capital:	Edmonton	**Largest City:**	Edmonton
Population:	2,237,724	**Area:**	255,285 sq. mi.
Highest Point:	12,294 ft.	**Lowest Point:**	686 ft.

Made a Province: September 1, 1905

GENERAL INFORMATION

Additional Information On Services

- **Rest Area Hours.** Areas 1, 2, 3, 9, 19, 20, 29, 35 and 38 are rest areas with modern facilities that operate from approximately 7 A.M. to 11 P.M. Areas 4, 5, 6, 7, 11, 12, 14, 15, 21, 22, 25, 30, 36 and 37 are Provincial Recreation Areas which serve only as day use areas or rest areas. The remaining areas are provincial parks and recreation areas, most of which have day use areas and also have a number of other recreational opportunities.
- **Welcome Center Hours.** Welcome centers are staffed between May and September.
- **Tourist Information.** For tourist information call 1-800-222-6501 within Alberta; 427-4321 in Edmonton; and 1-800-661-8888 throughout the United States and Canada.

Rest Area Usage Rules

- **Overnight Parking.** No overnight parking.
- **Camping.** Camping is not permitted at rest areas or day use areas.
- **Stay Limit.** No published limit.

Driving In Alberta

- **Emergencies.** For highway emergencies call 911 (may not be operable in all areas) or dial the local police or local number for the Royal Canadian Mounted Police.
- **Open Container.** Open containers of alcoholic beverages in the passenger compartment of the vehicle are not permitted.
- **Seat Belts.** Seat belts are required for all occupants. Children

must be properly restrained.
- **Helmets.** Motorcycle operators and passengers must wear helmets and have the headlight on.
- **Road Conditions.** Dial 1-800-661-8888 throughout the United States and Canada; 1-800-222-6501 within Alberta; and 427-4321 in Edmonton.

ALBERTA REST AREAS

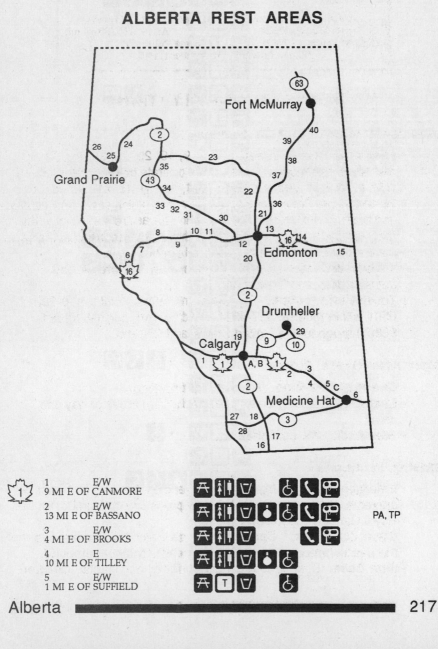

	1	E/W 9 MI E OF CANMORE
	2	E/W 13 MI E OF BASSANO
	3	E/W 4 MI E OF BROOKS
	4	E 10 MI E OF TILLEY
	5	E/W 1 MI E OF SUFFIELD

PA, TP

#	Dir	Location	Notes
6	E/W	3 MI E OF DUNMORE	
6	E/W	7 MI W OF HINTON	
7	E/W	12 MI E OF HINTON	
8	E/W	9 MI W OF EDSON	
9	E/W	13 MI E OF EDSON	TP
10	E/W	1 MI W OF NOJACK	
11	E/W	1 MI W OF GAINFORD	
12	E/W	1 MI W OF SPRUCE GROVE	
13	E/W	1 MI E OF ANDROSSAN	
14	E/W	1 MI E OF RANFURLY	
15	E/W	3 MI W OF KITSCOTY	
16	N/S	6 MI S OF CARDSTON	
17	N/S	NEAR CARDSTON	
18	N/S	2 MI W OF FORT MACLEOD	
19	N/S	4 MI S OF CROSSFIELD	PA, PW, TR, TP
20	N/S	13 MI S OF LEDUC	
21	N/S	3 MI S OF VIMY	
22	E/W	N OF ROCHESTER ACCESS RD	
23	E/W	10 MI E OF KINUSO	
24	N/S	DUNVEGAN BRIDGE	
25	N/S	3 MI N OF WOKING	
26	E/W	3 MI W OF DEMMITT	
27	E/W	9 MI W OF COLEMAN	
28	E/W	2 MI W OF LUNDBRECK	
29	E/W	ROSEDALE	SK, TR
30	E/W	S OF MAYERTHORPE	
31	E/W	12 MI N OF WHITECOURT	
32	E/W	30 MI N OF WHITECOURT	
33	E/W	11 MI S OF FOX CREEK	

34 N/S 8 MI N OF FOX CREEK		
35 N/S 1 MI S OF VALLEYVIEW		TP
36 N/S 3 MI N OF NEWBROOK		
37 N/S 4 MI W OF BOYLE		
38 N/S 17 MI N OF RTE 55		TP
39 N/S 60 MI N OF WANDERING RIVER		
40 N/S 21 MI S OF FORT MCMURRAY		

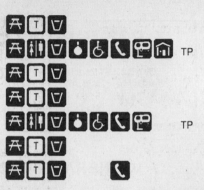

ALBERTA SERVICE STATIONS WITH RV DUMP FACILITIES

A. Calgary
Name of Business: Husky Car/Truck Stop
Location: Trans Canada Hwy. #1 to Barlow Trail to32nd Ave. NE.
Hours of Operation: 24 hours per day.
RV Information: No charge for use of RV Dump. Waterfill (closed in winter), propane and diesel fuel available.
Station Type: Truck stop (Husky).

B. Calgary
Name of Business: Road King Truck Stop
Location: Hwy. 2 (Deerfoot Trail) and Barlow Trail.
Hours of Operation: 24 hours per day.
RV Information: No charge for use of RV Dump. Waterfill, propane and diesel fuel available.
Station Type: Truck stop (Shell).

C. Redcliff
Name of Business: Trans Canada Truckstop
Location: South Highway Dr. and Trans Canada Hwy. #1.
Hours of Operation: 24 hours per day.
RV Information: No charge for use of RV Dump. Waterfill, propane and diesel fuel available.
Station Type: Truck stop (ESSO).

BRITISH COLUMBIA

Capital: Victoria   Largest City: Vancouver
Population: 2,883,367   Area: 365,974 sq. mi.
Highest Point: 15,300 ft.   Lowest Point: Sea Level
Made a Province: July 20, 1871

GENERAL INFORMATION

Additional Information On Services

- **Rest Area Hours.** Rest Areas are open 24 hours per day, seven days per week. Areas in the northern and eastern sections are closed in winter.
- **Tourist Information.** For tourist information call 1-800-663-6000.

Rest Area Usage Rules

- **Overnight Parking.** No overnight parking.
- **Camping.** Camping is not permitted.
- **Stay Limit.** No published limit.

Driving In British Columbia

- **Emergencies.** For highway emergencies call 911 (may not be operable in all areas) or dial the local police or local number for the Royal Canadian Mounted Police.
- **Open Container.** No open container law, but it is an offense to consume alcoholic beverages on the highway. Containers will be confiscated.
- **Seat Belts.** Seat belts are required for all occupants. Children 4 and under or under 40 pounds must be in a child restraint system.
- **Helmets.** Motorcycle operators and passengers must wear helmets.
- **Road Conditions.** Dial 1-800-663-4997.

BRITISH COLUMBIA REST AREAS

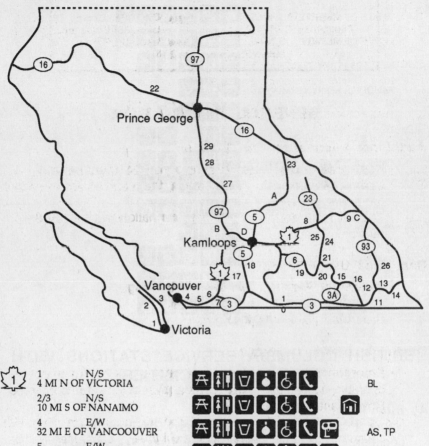

🍁 1	1 4 MI N OF VICTORIA	N/S	🍽	🚻	🗑	🚰	♿	📞		BL
	2/3 10 MI S OF NANAIMO	N/S	🍽	🚻	🗑	🚰	♿	📞	🏠	
	4 32 MI E OF VANCOOUVER	E/W	🍽	🚻	🗑	🚰	♿	📞	📺	AS, TP
	5 43 MI E OF VANCOUVER	E/W	🍽	🚻	🗑	🚰	♿	📞	📺	
	6/7 5 MI W OF HOPE	E/W	🍽	🚻	🗑	🚰	♿	📞		TP
	8 14 MI W OF REVELSTOKE	E/W	🍽	🚻						
	9 13 MI W OF GOLDEN	E/W	🍽	🚻						
③	10 18 MI E OF OSOYOOS	E/W	🍽	🚻	🗑					
	11 15 MI E OF CRESTON	E/W	🍽	🚻	🗑					PA
	12 5 MI NE OF YAHK	N/S	🍽	🚻	🗑					
	13 7 MI SE OF CRANBROOK	N/S	🍽	🚻	🗑					
	14 22 MI W OF FERNIE	E/W	🍽	🚻	🗑					

Route	No.	Dir.	Location	Notes
3A	15	E/W	BALFOUR FERRY TERMINAL	
	16	E/W	KOOTENAY BAY	
5	17	N/S	48 MI S OF MERRITT	TP
	18	N/S	41 MI S OF MERRITT	TP
6	19	E/W	NEEDLES FERRY TERMINAL	
	20	N/S	FAUQUIER FERRY TERMINAL	
	21	N/S	11 MI S OF NAKUSP	BL
16	22	E/W	21 MI E OF VANDERFOOF	
	23	E/W	4 MI E OF HWY 5	
23	24	N/S	GALENA BAY TERMINAL	
	25	N/S	SHELTER BAY FERRY TERM.	
93	26	N/S	18 MI N OF KIMBERLY	TP
97	27	N/S	8 MI N OF 100 MILE HOUSE	HM
	28	N/S	46 MI S OF QUESNEL	
	29	N/S	22 MI S OF QUESNEL	

BRITISH COLUMBIA SERVICE STATIONS WITH RV DUMP FACILITIES

A. Blue River

Name of Business: Blue River Husky Car/Truck Stop
Location: Highway 5 South and Yellowhead Hwy.
Hours of Operation: 24 hours per day.
RV Information: No charge for use of RV Dump. Waterfill, propane and diesel fuel available.
Station Type: Truck stop (Husky).

B. Cache Creek

Name of Business: Husky Car/Truck Stop
Location: Trans Canada Hwy. #1 and Hwy. 97.
Hours of Operation: 24 hours per day.
RV Information: No charge for use of RV Dump ($4.00 if fuel not purchased). Waterfill (closed in winter), propane and diesel fuel available.
Station Type: Truck stop (Husky)

C. Golden

Name of Business:	Golden Husky Car/Truck Stop
Location:	Trans Canada Hwy. #1 and Hwy. 95.
Hours of Operation:	24 hours per day.
RV Information:	No charge for use of RV Dump. Waterfill, propane and diesel fuel available.
Station Type:	Truck stop (Husky).

D. Kamloops

Name of Business:	Kamloops Travel Center
Location:	Trans Canada Hwy. #1 W, Exit 366 (Copperhead Dr.).
Hours of Operation:	24 hours per day.
RV Information:	No charge for use of RV Dump. Waterfill, propane and diesel fuel available.
Station Type:	Truck stop (Petro Canada).

MANITOBA

Capital: Winnipeg	Largest City: Winnipeg
Population: 1,026,241	Area: 251,000 sq. mi.
Highest Point: 2,729 ft.	Lowest Point: Sea Level
Made a Province: July 15, 1870	

GENERAL INFORMATION

Additional Information On Services

- **Rest Area Hours.** Rest Areas are open 24 hours per day during the open season.
- **Welcome Center Hours.** Welcome centers at areas 1, 8 and 17 are staffed from 8 A.M. to 9 P.M. from mid-May through early September. The welcome center at area 31 is staffed from early March through mid November, 9 A.M. to 5 P.M. Hours are extended from mid-May through early September to 8 A.M. to 9 P.M.
- **Tourist Information.** For tourist information call 1-800-665-0040.

Rest Area Usage Rules

- **Overnight Parking.** No overnight parking.
- **Camping.** Camping is not permitted.
- **Stay Limit.** No published limit.

Driving In Manitoba

- **Emergencies.** For highway emergencies call 911 (may not be operable in all areas) or dial the local police or local number for the Royal Canadian Mounted Police.
- **Open Container.** Open containers of alcoholic beverages in the passenger compartment of the vehicle are not permitted.
- **Seat Belts.** Seat belts are required for all front seat occupants. Children 5 and under or under 50 pounds must be in a child restraint system.
- **Helmets.** Motorcycle operators and passengers must wear helmets.
- **Road Conditions.** Dial 1-204-945-3704.

MANITOBA REST AREAS

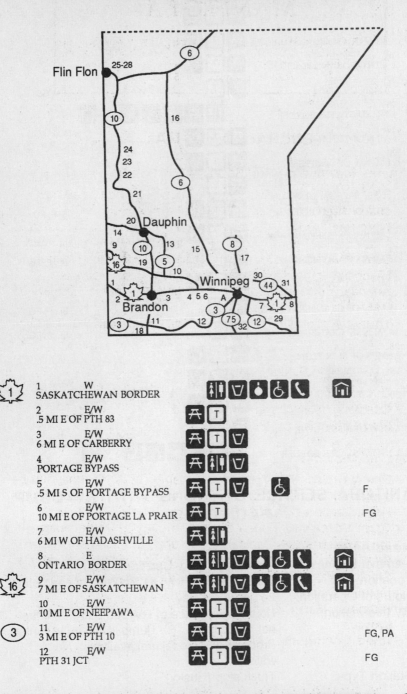

(1)	**1** W SASKATCHEWAN BORDER	🚻	🗑	🍼	♿	📞		🏠
	2 E/W .5 MI E OF PTH 83	🍴	T					
	3 E/W 6 MI E OF CARBERRY	🍴	T	🗑				
	4 E/W PORTAGE BYPASS	🍴	🚻	🗑				
	5 E/W .5 MI S OF PORTAGE BYPASS	🍴	T	🗑		♿		F
	6 E/W 10 MI E OF PORTAGE LA PRAIR	🍴	T					FG
	7 E/W 6 MI W OF HADASHVILLE	🍴	🚻					
	8 E ONTARIO BORDER	🍴	🚻	🗑	🍼	♿	📞	🏠
(16)	**9** E/W 7 MI E OF SASKATCHEWAN	🍴	🚻	🗑	🍼	♿	📞	🏠
	10 E/W 10 MI E OF NEEPAWA	🍴	T	🗑				
(3)	**11** E/W 3 MI E OF PTH 10	🍴	T	🗑				FG, PA
	12 E/W PTH 31 JCT	🍴	T	🗑				FG

Route	#	Dir	Location	Facilities	Codes
(5)	13	N/S	12 MI N OF MCCREARY	picnic / restrooms / trash	
	14	E/W	10 MI W OF GRANDVIEW	picnic / T / trash	FG
(6)	15	N/S	1 MI N OF ERIKSDALE	picnic / T / trash / camera	FG
	16	N/S	2 MI S OF GRAND RAPIDS	picnic / T / trash	C, FG
(8)	17	N/S	11 MI N OF GIMLI	picnic / T	SN, GS
(10)	18	N/S	UNITED STATES BORDER	restrooms / trash / water / handicap / phone / shelter	
	19	N/S	5 MI N OF TCH 16A JCT	picnic / T / trash	
	20	N/S	21 MI NW OF DAUPHIN	picnic / T / trash	
	21	N/S	1 MI N OF COWAN	picnic / T	
	22	N/S	1 MI W OF BIRCH RIVER	picnic / T / trash	C, F, FG
	23	N/S	15 MI N OF MAFEKING	picnic / T / trash	
	24	N/S	16 MI N OF MAFEKING	picnic / T / trash	BL, F, FG
	25	N/S	9 MI N OF CRANBERRY PORTGE	picnic / T / trash	BL, F
	26	N/S	11 MI N OF CRANBERRY PORTG	picnic / T	BL, F, FG
	27	N/S	14 MI N OF CRANBERRY PORTG	picnic / T	BL, F, FG
	28	N/S	11 MI S OF FLIN FLON	picnic / T / trash	PA
(12)	29	N/S	7 MI N OF PTH 89	picnic / T / trash	FG
(44)	30	E/W	3 MI W OF PTH 11	picnic / T / trash	FG
	31	E/W	6 MI W OF WEST HAWK	picnic / T	FG
(75)	32	N/S	UNITED STATES BORDER	restrooms / trash / water / handicap / phone / shelter	

MANITOBA SERVICE STATIONS WITH RV DUMP FACILITIES

A. Headingly

Name of Business:	Headingly Husky Car/Truck Stop
Location:	Trans Canada Hwy. #1 W (West of perimeter)
Hours of Operation:	24 hours per day.
RV Information:	No charge for use of RV Dump ($3.00 if fuel not purchased). RV dump is closed in winter. Propane and diesel fuel available. No waterfill.
Station Type:	Truck stop (Husky).

NEW BRUNSWICK

Capital: Fredericton	**Largest City:** St. John
Population: 696,403	**Area:** 28,348 sq. mi.
Highest Point: 2,690 ft.	**Lowest Point:** Sea Level

Made a Province: July 1, 1867

GENERAL INFORMATION

Additional Information On Services

- **Rest Area Hours.** Rest Areas open mid-June thru mid-September.
- **Welcome Center Hours.** Open mid-June thru mid-September.
- **Tourist Information.** For tourist information call 1-800-561-0123 within the United States and 1-800-442-4442 within New Brunswick.

Rest Area Usage Rules

- **Overnight Parking.** No overnight parking.
- **Camping.** Camping or sleeping outside of vehicle is not permitted.
- **Stay Limit.** Parking limited to 4 hours.

Driving In New Brunswick

- **Emergencies.** For highway emergencies call 911 (not operable in all areas) or the Royal Canadian Mounted Police at 1-800-442-9722.
- **Open Container.** Open containers of alcoholic beverages in the passenger compartment of the vehicle are not permitted.
- **Seat Belts.** Seat belts are required for all occupants. Children must be properly secured in a child restraint system or seat belt.
- **Helmets.** Motorcycle operators and passengers must wear helmets.
- **Road Conditions.** Dial 1-800-561-4063.

NEW BRUNSWICK REST AREAS

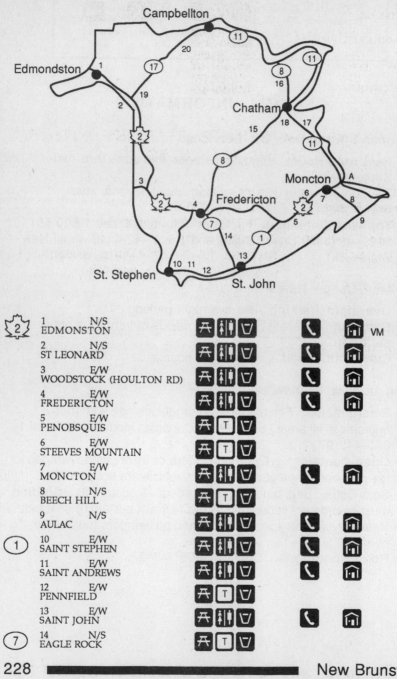

⛰2	1 N/S EDMONSTON	⛱ 🚻 🗑		📞	🏠	VM
	2 N/S ST LEONARD	⛱ 🚻 🗑		📞	🏠	
	3 E/W WOODSTOCK (HOULTON RD)	⛱ 🚻 🗑		📞	🏠	
	4 E/W FREDERICTON	⛱ 🚻 🗑		📞	🏠	
	5 E/W PENOBSQUIS	⛱ T 🗑				
	6 E/W STEEVES MOUNTAIN	⛱ T 🗑				
	7 E/W MONCTON	⛱ 🚻 🗑		📞	🏠	
	8 N/S BEECH HILL	⛱ T 🗑				
	9 N/S AULAC	⛱ 🚻 🗑		📞	🏠	
①1	10 E/W SAINT STEPHEN	⛱ 🚻 🗑		📞	🏠	
	11 E/W SAINT ANDREWS	⛱ 🚻 🗑		📞	🏠	
	12 E/W PENNFIELD	⛱ T 🗑				
	13 E/W SAINT JOHN	⛱ 🚻 🗑		📞	🏠	
⑦7	14 N/S EAGLE ROCK	⛱ T 🗑				

(8) 15   N/S BLACKVILLE

16   N/S GREYSTONE

(11) 17   N/S CHATHAM

18   N/S SAINT MARGARETS

(17) 19   E/W SAINT LEONARD

20   E/W GLENWOOD

NEW BRUNSWICK SERVICE STATIONS WITH RV DUMP FACILIITES

B. Aulac

Name of Business:	Aulac Irving Big Stop
Location:	Trans Canada Hwy. #2 and Hwy. 16
Hours of Operation:	24 hours per day.
RV Information:	No charge for use of RV Dump. Waterfill, propane and diesel fuel available.
Station Type:	Truck stop (Irving).

NEWFOUNDLAND

Capital: St. John's	**Largest City:** St. John's
Population: 567,681	**Area:** 156,185 sq. mi.
Highest Point: 5,600 ft.	**Lowest Point:** Sea Level

Made a Province: March 31, 1949

GENERAL INFORMATION

Additional Information On Services

- **Rest Area Hours.** Newfoundland has no system of rest areas. The listing below consist of a sampling of day use areas, open from dawn to dusk, at Provincial Parks along the selected highways. Day use is free.
- **Welcome Center Hours.** Welcome centers shown here are comfort stations at Provincial Parks. They are staffed from dawn to dusk.
- **Tourist Information.** For tourist information call 1-800-563-6353.

Rest Area Usage Rules

- **Overnight Parking.** No overnight parking.
- **Camping.** Camping is not permitted at day use areas.
- **Stay Limit.** No published limit.

Driving In Newfoundland

- **Emergencies.** For highway emergencies call 911 (may not be operable in all areas) or dial the local police or local number for the Royal Canadian Mounted Police.
- **Open Container.** Open containers of alcoholic beverages in the passenger compartment of the vehicle are not permitted.
- **Seat Belts.** Seat belts are required for all occupants. Children under 40 pounds must be in a child restraint system.
- **Helmets.** Motorcycle operators and passengers must wear helmets.
- **Road Conditions.** Dial the Provincial Department of Highways.
  St. John's: 1-709-729-3796   Avalon: 1-709-729-2391
  Clarenville: 1-709-466-7952   Grand Falls: 1-709-489-2293
  Deer Lake: 1-709-635-2162

NEWFOUNDLAND REST AREAS

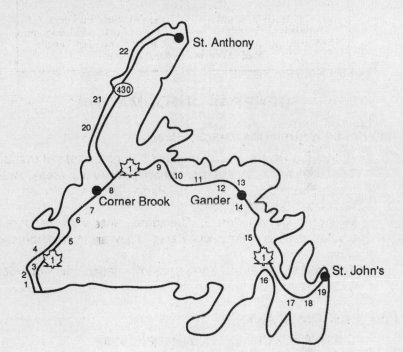

 1   N/S
CHEESEMAN (CAPE RAY)   ⊞ T ⊽

2   N/S
MUMMICHOG (TOMPKINS)   ⊞ T ⊽

3   N/S
GRAND CODROY (DOYLES)   ⊞ ⚥ ⊽   ♿ ☎ ▣ ⌂

4   N/S
CRABBES RIV (ST FINTAN'S)   ⊞ T ⊽

5   N/S
BRACHOIS (ST GEORGE'S)   ⊞ ⚥ ⊽   ♿ ☎ ▣ ⌂

6   N/S
BLUE PONDS (CORNER BROOK)   ⊞ T ⊽

7   N/S
STAG LAKE (CORNER BROOK)   ⊞ T ⊽

8   N/S
PASADENA BEACH (PASADENA)   ⊞ T ⊽

9   E/W
INDIAN RIVER (SPRINGDALE)   ⊞ T ⊽

10   N/S
CATAMARAN (BADGER)   ⊞ T ⊽

11   E/W
BEOTHUCK (GRAND FALLS)   ⊞ T ⊽

12   E/W
NOTRE DAME (LEWISPORT)   ⊞ T ⊽   ▣

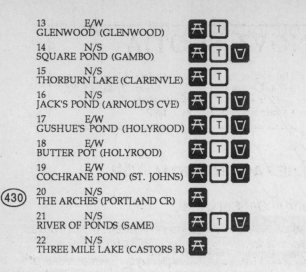

13	E/W GLENWOOD (GLENWOOD)	⛺	T		
14	N/S SQUARE POND (GAMBO)	⛺	T	🚽	
15	N/S THORBURN LAKE (CLARENVLE)	⛺	T		
16	N/S JACK'S POND (ARNOLD'S CVE)	⛺	T	🚽	
17	E/W GUSHUE'S POND (HOLYROOD)	⛺	T	🚽	🎥
18	E/W BUTTER POT (HOLYROOD)	⛺	T	🚽	🎥
19	E/W COCHRANE POND (ST. JOHNS)	⛺	T	🚽	
430) 20	N/S THE ARCHES (PORTLAND CR)	⛺			
21	N/S RIVER OF PONDS (SAME)	⛺	T	🚽	
22	N/S THREE MILE LAKE (CASTORS R)	⛺			

NOVA SCOTIA

Capital: Halifax	**Largest City:** Halifax
Population: 847,442	**Area:** 21,425 sq. mi.
Highest Point: 1,745 ft.	**Lowest Point:** Sea Level
Made a Province: July 1, 1867	

GENERAL INFORMATION

Additional Information On Services

- **Rest Area Hours.** Nova Scotia has no system of rest areas. The listing below consist of a sampling of day use areas at Provincial Parks along the selected highways. These areas are open from dawn to dusk, from mid-May through mid-October as a minimum. There are no fees associated with day use; adjacent parks offer a variety of recreational opportunities, in most cases.
- **Tourist Information.** For tourist information call 1-800-565-0000.

Rest Area Usage Rules

- **Overnight Parking.** No overnight parking.
- **Camping.** Camping is not permitted.
- **Stay Limit.** No published limit.

Driving In Nova Scotia

- **Emergencies.** For highway emergencies call 911 (may not be operable in all areas) or dial the local police or local number for the Royal Canadian Mounted Police.
- **Open Container.** Open containers of alcoholic beverages in the passenger compartment of the vehicle are not permitted.
- **Seat Belts.** Seat belts are required for all occupants. Children under 40 pounds must be in a child restraint system.
- **Helmets.** Motorcycle operators and passengers must wear helmets.
- **Road Conditions.** Dial 1-902-424-4247.

NOVA SCOTIA REST AREAS

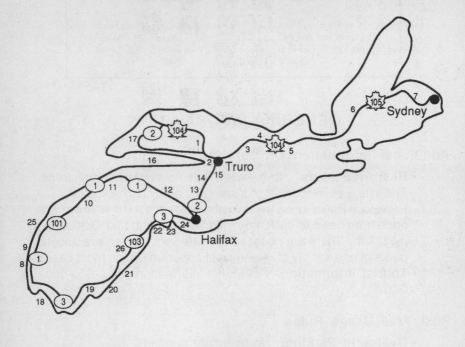

<image 104> 1 N/S WENTWORTH	A	T	⊔	♿	▣
2 E/W MCELMOND'S POND	A	T	⊔		
3 E/W SALT SPRINGS	A	T	⊔		▣
4 E/W GREEN HILL	A	T	⊔		
5 E/W BEAVER MTN	A	T	⊔		▣
6 E/W WHYCOCOMAGH	A	T	⊔		▣
7 E/W DALEM LAKE	A	T	⊔		
(1) 8 N/S MAVILETTE BEACH	A	T	⊔		
9 N/S SMUGGLERS COVE	A	T	⊔		
10 E/W CLAIRMONT	A	T	⊔		
11 E/W COLDBROOK	A	T	⊔		
12 E/W MOUNT UNIACKE	A	T	⊔		
(2) 13 N/S LAURIE	A	T	⊔		▣

	14 N/S OAKFIELD	⊼ T ⊔	♿	
	15 N/S SHUBENACADIE	⊼ T ⊔	♿	
	16 E/W FIVE ISLANDS	⊼ T ⊔	♿	⊞
	17 N/S NEWVILLE LAKE	⊼ T ⊔		
③	18 E/W GLENWOOD	⊼ T ⊔		
	19 E/W THE ISLANDS	⊼ T ⊔	♿	⊞
	20 E/W SABLE RIVER	⊼ T ⊔		
	21 N/S SUMMERVILLE BEACH	⊼ T ⊔	♿	
	22 E/W GRAVES ISLAND	⊼ T ⊔		⊞
	23 E/W EAST RIVER	⊼ T ⊔		
	24 E/W LEWIS LAKE	⊼ T ⊔	♿	
⑩¹ 101	25 N/S SAVARY	⊼ T ⊔		
⑩³ 103	26 N/S FANCY LAKE	⊼ T ⊔		

ONTARIO

Capital: Toronto	**Largest City:** Toronto
Population: 8,625,107	**Area:** 412,582 sq. mi.
Highest Point: 2,275 ft.	**Lowest Point:** Sea Level
Made a Province: July 1, 1867	

GENERAL INFORMATION

Additional Information On Services

- **Rest Area Hours.** Rest Areas are open from dawn to dusk from mid-May through mid-October.
- **Welcome Center Hours.** Welcome centers are staffed at least 8 hours per day.
- **Freeway Service Centers.** Areas 11 through 34 are freeway service centers. All operate on a 24 hour basis and all have diesel fuel and service bays (seasonal). Rest areas are immediately adjacent to the service centers.
- **Tourist Information.** For tourist information call 1-416-965-4008 from Toronto and 1-800-ONTARIO from elsewhere in Canada and the United States.

Rest Area Usage Rules

- **Overnight Parking.** No overnight parking.
- **Camping.** Camping is not permitted.
- **Stay Limit.** No published limit.

Driving In Ontario

- **Emergencies.** For highway emergencies call 911 (may not be operable in all areas) or dial the local police or local number for the Ontario Provincial Police.
- **Open Container.** Open containers of alcoholic beverages in the passenger compartment of the vehicle are not permitted.
- **Seat Belts.** Seat belts are required for all occupants. Children under 50 pounds must be in a child restraint system.
- **Helmets.** Motorcycle operators and passengers must wear helmets.
- **Radar Dectors.** Radar detectors are prohibited and will be confiscated.
- **Road Conditions.** Dial 1-416-235-1110.

ONTARIO REST AREAS

(6)	1 N/S 8 MI S OF DURHAM	🏕	🚻	🗑					
	2 N/S 3 MI N OF DURHAM	🏕	🚻	🗑					
	3 N/S 1 MI S OF MAR	🏕	🚻	🗑					
	4 N/S 3 MI N OF MILLER LAKE	🏕	🚻	🗑					
(10)	5 N/S 1 MI N OF FLESHERTON	🏕	🚻	🗑					
(17)	6 N/S BATCHAWANA BAY	🏕	🚻	🗑					FG
(21)	7 N/S 1 MI N OF TIVERTON	🏕	🚻	🗑					
(26)	8 E/W 3 MI E OF WOODFORD	🏕	🚻	🗑					
(89)	9 E/W 3 MI E OF CONN	🏕	🚻	🗑					
	10 E/W 2 MI E OF VIOLET HILL	🏕	🚻	🗑					FG
(401)	11 W 2 MI W OF CHATHAM EXIT	🏕	🚻	🗑	🍼	♿	☎		HN, PC, TP
	12 E 2 MI E OF TILBURY EXIT	🏕	🚻	🗑	🍼	♿	☎		HN, KFC, SH, TP
	13 W 3 MI W OF DUTTON EXIT	🏕	🚻	🗑	🍼	♿	☎		McD, PC, TP

#	Dir	Location	Facilities	Services
14	E	3 MI E OF WESTLORNE EXIT	🏕 🚻 ⛲ 🛢 ♿ ☎	HN, SH, TP, WD
15	W	3 MI W OF WOODSTOCK EXIT	🏕 🚻 ⛲ 🛢 ♿ ☎	BK, ES, TP
16	E	3 MI E OF INGERSOL EXIT	🏕 🚻 ⛲ 🛢 ♿ ☎	ES, HN, TP, WD
17	W	6 MI W OF GUELPH EXIT	🏕 🚻 ⛲ 🛢 ♿ ☎	McD, PC, TP
18	E	3 MI E OF CAMBRIDGE EXIT	🏕 🚻 ⛲ 🛢 ♿ ☎	McD, PC, TP
19	E	1 MI E OF MISSISSAUGA EXIT	🏕 🚻 ⛲ 🛢 ♿ ☎ 🏠	HN, SH, TP, WD
20	W	3 MI W OF NEWTONVILLE EXIT	🏕 🚻 ⛲ 🛢 ♿ ☎	BK, ES, TP
21	E	1 MI E OF NEWTONVILLE EXIT	🏕 🚻 ⛲ 🛢 ♿ ☎	ES, HN, TP, WD
22	W	4 MI W OF TRENTON EXIT	🏕 🚻 ⛲ 🛢 ♿ ☎	HN, SH, TP, WD
23	E	3 MI E OF BRIGHTON EXIT	🏕 🚻 ⛲ 🛢 ♿ ☎	McD, PC, TP
24	W	3 MI W OF ODESSA EXIT	🏕 🚻 ⛲ 🛢 ♿ ☎	McD, PC, TP
25	E	4 MI E OF ODESSA EXIT	🏕 🚻 ⛲ 🛢 ♿ ☎	ES, HN, KFC, TP
26	W	5 MI W OF BROCKVILE EXIT	🏕 🚻 ⛲ 🛢 ♿ ☎	ES, HN, TP, WD
27	E	4 MI E OF MALLORYTOWN EXIT	🏕 🚻 ⛲ 🛢 ♿ ☎	ES, HN, TP, WD
28	E	4 MI E OF MORRISBURG EXIT	🏕 🚻 ⛲ 🛢 ♿ ☎	HN, KFC, SH, TP
29	W	5 MI W OF INGLESIDE EXIT	🏕 🚻 ⛲ 🛢 ♿ ☎	ES, HN, KFC, TP
30	W	1 MI W OF QUEBEC BORDER	🏕 🚻 ⛲ 🛢 ♿ ☎	SH, TP, WD
(400) 31	S	3 MI S OF KING	🏕 🚻 ⛲ 🛢 ♿ ☎	BK, ES, TP
32	N	2 MI N OF MAPLE	🏕 🚻 ⛲ 🛢 ♿ ☎	HN, PC, TP, WD
33	S	5 MI S OF THORNTON	🏕 🚻 ⛲ 🛢 ♿ ☎	McD, PC, TP
34	N	2 MI N OF THORNTON	🏕 🚻 ⛲ 🛢 ♿ ☎	McD, PC, TP
(417) 35	W	1 MI W OF QUEBEC BORDER	🏕 🚻 ⛲ 🛢 ♿ ☎ 🏠	

ONTARIO SERVICE STATIONS WITH RV DUMP FACILITIES

A. Dorchester

Name of Business: Sean's 5th Wheel Truck Stop
Location: Hwy. 401, Exit 199 (Dorchester Rd.).
Hours of Operation: 24 hours per day.
RV Information: No charge for use of RV Dump. Diesel fuel

	and propane available. No waterfill.
Station Type:	Truck stop (Independent).

B. Windsor

Name of Business:	Windsor Husky Car/Truck Stop
Location:	Hwy. 401, Exit 14 (County Road 46)
Hours of Operation:	24 hours per day.
RV Information:	No charge for use of RV Dump. Waterfill, diesel fuel and propane available.
Station Type:	Truck stop (Husky).

PRINCE EDWARD IS.

Capital: Charlottetown	**Largest City:** Charlottetown
Population: 129,765	**Area:** 2,184 sq. mi.
Highest Point: 465 ft.	**Lowest Point:** .Sea Level
Made a Province: July 1, 1873	

GENERAL INFORMATION

Additional Information On Services

- **Rest Area Hours.** Prince Edward Island has no system of rest areas. The listing below consist of a sampling of day use areas at Provincial Parks along the selected highways. These areas are open from dawn to dusk and there are no fees associated with day use.
- **Tourist Information.** For tourist information call 1-902-368-4444.

Rest Area Usage Rules

- **Overnight Parking.** No overnight parking.
- **Camping.** Camping is not permitted.
- **Stay Limit.** No published limit.

Driving In Prince Edward Island

- **Emergencies.** For highway emergencies call 1-902-566-7111 for the Royal Canadian Mounted Police.
- **Open Container.** Open containers of alcoholic beverages in the passenger compartment of the vehicle are not permitted.
- **Seat Belts.** Seat belts are required for all occupants. Children under 35 pounds must be in a child restraint system.
- **Helmets.** Motorcycle operators and passengers must wear helmets.
- **Road Conditions.** Dial 1-902-368-4770.

PRINCE EDWARD ISLAND REST AREAS

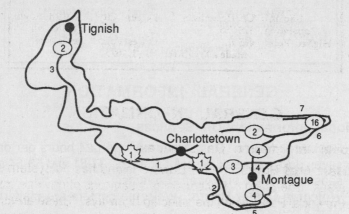

🍁 ①	1 STRATHGARTNEY	E/W	🏕 🚻 🗑		♿ ☎ 🏢
	2 LORD SELKIRK	N/S	🏕 🚻 🗑		☎ 🏢
②	3 BLOOMFIELD	N/S	🏕 🚻 🗑		
③	4 BRUDENELL	E/W	🏕 🚻 🗑		☎ 🏢
④	5 NORTHUMBERLAND	E/W	🏕 🚻 🗑		☎ 🏢
⑯	6 RED POINT	E/W	🏕 🚻 🗑		♿ ☎ 🏢
	7 CAMPBELL'S COVE	E/W	🏕 🚻 🗑		☎ 🏢

QUEBEC

Capital: Quebec	Largest City: Montreal
Population: 7,360,145	Area: 636,400 sq. mi.
Highest Point: 4,160 ft.	Lowest Point: .Sea Level
Made a Province: July 1, 1867	

GENERAL INFORMATION

Additional Information On Services

- **Rest Area Hours.** Rest Areas are open 24 hours per day, seven days per week. Areas 20, 28-32, 37-51 and 53-64 are seasonal and are only open in summer.
- **Welcome Center Hours.** Welcome centers are staffed at least 8 hours per day.
- **Service Centers.** Areas 2, 21 and 33 are service centers.
- **Kilometers.** Numbers in parenthesis in the data block indicate kilometers.
- **Tourist Information.** For tourist information call 873-2015 from the Montreal area and 1-800-363-7777 from elsewhere in Quebec, Canada and the United States.

Rest Area Usage Rules

- **Overnight Parking.** No overnight parking.
- **Camping.** Camping is not permitted.
- **Stay Limit.** Parking limited to 4 hours.

Driving In Quebec

- **Emergencies.** For highway emergencies call 911 (may not be operable in all counties) or dial the local police or local number for the highway patrol.
- **Open Container.** Open containers of alcoholic beverages in the passenger compartment of the vehicle are not permitted.
- **Seat Belts.** Seat belts are required for all occupants. Children under 5 must be in a child restraint system.
- **Helmets.** Motorcycle operators and passengers must wear helmets.
- **Road Conditions.** Dial 1-514-873-4121 in Montreal and 1-418-643-6830 in Quebec City.

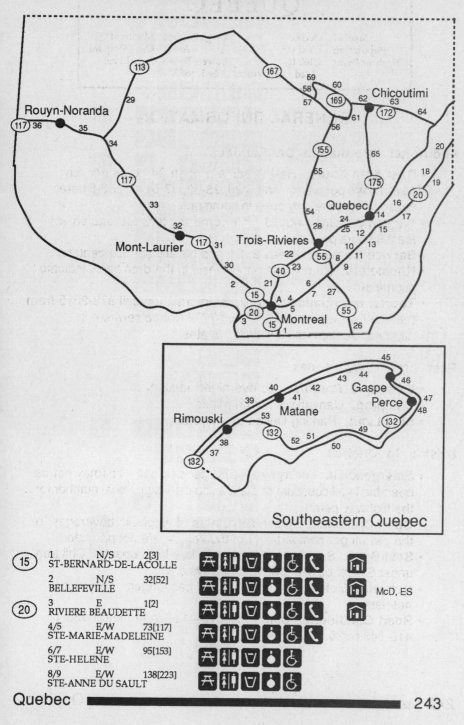

Southeastern Quebec

(15)	1 STE-BERNARD-DE-LACOLLE	N/S	2[3]							
	2 BELLEFEVILLE	N/S	32[52]							McD, ES
(20)	3 RIVIERE BEAUDETTE	E	1[2]							
	4/5 STE-MARIE-MADELEINE	E/W	73[117]							
	6/7 STE-HELENE	E/W	95[153]							
	8/9 STE-ANNE DU SAULT	E/W	138[223]							

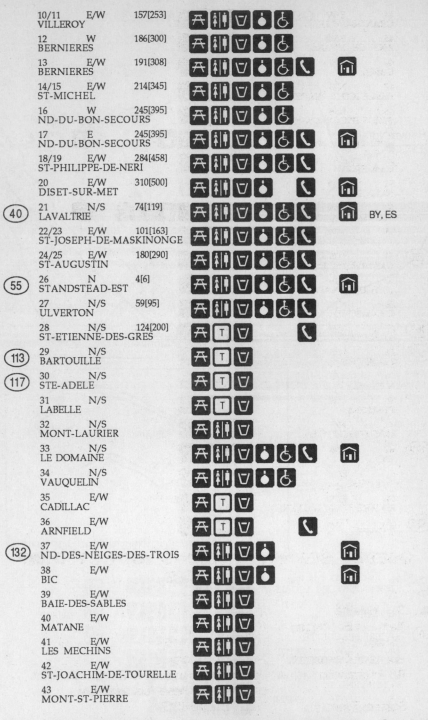

10/11 E/W 157[253] VILLEROY			
12 W 186[300] BERNIERES			
13 E/W 191[308] BERNIERES			
14/15 E/W 214[345] ST-MICHEL			
16 W 245[395] ND-DU-BON-SECOURS			
17 E 245[395] ND-DU-BON-SECOURS			
18/19 E/W 284[458] ST-PHILIPPE-DE-NERI			
20 E/W 310[500] DISET-SUR-MET			
(40) 21 N/S 74[119] LAVALTRIE			BY, ES
22/23 E/W 101[163] ST-JOSEPH-DE-MASKINONGE			
24/25 E/W 180[290] ST-AUGUSTIN			
(55) 26 N 4[6] STANDSTEAD-EST			
27 N/S 59[95] ULVERTON			
28 N/S 124[200] ST-ETIENNE-DES-GRES			
(113) 29 N/S BARTOUILLE			
(117) 30 N/S STE-ADELE			
31 N/S LABELLE			
32 N/S MONT-LAURIER			
33 N/S LE DOMAINE			
34 N/S VAUQUELIN			
35 E/W CADILLAC			
36 E/W ARNFIELD			
(132) 37 E/W ND-DES-NEIGES-DES-TROIS			
38 E/W BIC			
39 E/W BAIE-DES-SABLES			
40 E/W MATANE			
41 E/W LES MECHINS			
42 E/W ST-JOACHIM-DE-TOURELLE			
43 E/W MONT-ST-PIERRE			

44 E/W GRANDE-VALLEE	🏕	🚻	🗑	
45 E/W ANSE DE DETANG	🏕	🚻	🗑	
46 N/S GASPE	🏕	🚻	🗑	
47 N/S PERCE (COTE SURPRISE)	🏕	🚻	🗑	
48 N/S PERCE (PIC-DE-L'AURORE)	🏕	🚻	🗑	
49 E/W NEW RICHMOND	🏕	🚻	🗑	🔵 🏠
50 E/W CARLETON	🏕	🚻	🗑	
51 E/W NOUVELLE	🏕	🚻	🗑	
52 E/W POINTE-A-LA-CROIX	🏕	🚻	🗑	🔵 ♿ 📞 🏠
53 E/W VAL BRILLANT	🏕	T	🗑	
(155) 54 N/S GRANDES-PILES	🏕	T	🗑	
55 N/S LA BOSTONNAIS	🏕	T	🗑	
56 N/S CHAMBORD	🏕	🚻	🗑	
(167) 57 N/S ST-FELICIEN	🏕	T	🗑	
(169) 58 N/S ST-METHODE	🏕	🚻	🗑	
59 N/S MISTASSINI	🏕	T	🗑	
60 E/W PERIBONKA	🏕	🚻	🗑	
61 N/S METABETCHOUAN	🏕	🚻	🗑	
(172) 62 E/W VALIN	🏕	🚻	🗑	
63 E/W STE-ROSE-DU-NORD	🏕	T	🗑	
64 E/W RIVIERE STE-MARGUERITE	🏕	T	🗑	
(175) 65 N/S L'ETAPE	🏕	T	🗑	

QUEBEC SERVICE STATIONS WITH RV DUMP FACILITIES

A. St. Hilaire

Name of Business:	Gaz-O-Bar
Location:	Hwy. 20, Exit 115.
Hours of Operation:	24 hours per day.
RV Information:	No charge for use of RV Dump. Waterfill, propane and diesel fuel available.
Station Type:	Truck stop (ESSO).

Quebec ▬▬▬▬▬▬▬▬▬▬▬▬▬▬▬ 245

SASKATCHEWAN

Capital: Regina	**Largest City:** Regina
Population: 968,313	**Area:** 251,700 sq. mi.
Highest Point: 4,546 ft.	**Lowest Point:** 699 ft.
Made a Province: September 1, 1905	

GENERAL INFORMATION

Additional Information On Services

- **Rest Area Hours.** Seasonal rest areas and picnic facilities, numbers 2, 3, 5, 16, and 20, are located at the major entry points into Saskatchewan in conjunction with tourist reception/information centres. These are open from mid-May to Labour Day In addition, a number of Saskatchewan communities and regional parks along the main highways also provide picnic/rest areas. Presented in this section are some of the provincial parks, most of which are not along the main highways, but which can fill the rest area need. All areas shown are open year-round except for areas 14, 15, and 22, which are open from mid-May through Labour Day. Fees are associated with use in most areas.
- **Tourist Information.** For tourist information call 1-800-667-7191 in the United States and Canada and 787-2300 in Regina.

Rest Area Usage Rules

- **Camping.** Camping is permitted in most of these areas.
- **Stay Limit.** Varies.

Driving In Saskatchewan

- **Emergencies.** For highway emergencies dial 0 and ask for police.
- **Open Container.** Open containers of alcoholic beverages in the passenger compartment of the vehicle are not permitted.
- **Seat Belts.** Seat belts are required for all occupants. Children under 50 pounds must be properly secured in an approved car seat.
- **Helmets.** Motorcycle operators and passengers must wear helmets and eye protection.
- **Road Conditions.** Dial one of the following nine hotline numbers:

Moose Jaw	694-3860	North Battleford	446-7785
Prince Albert	953-3575	Regina	787-7623
Rosetown	882-5444	Saskatoon	933-8333
Swift Current	778-8355	Weyburn	848-2432
Yorkton	786-1666		

SASKATCHEWAN REST AREAS

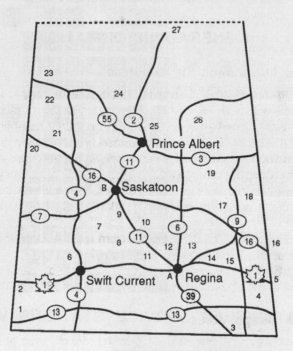

1 CYPRESS HILLS, 17 MI S OF
MAPLE CREEK ON HWY 21

2 MAPLE CREEK
24 MI E OF ALBERTA BORDER

3 NORTH PORTAL
US BORDER

4 MOOSE MOUTAIN, 14 MI N
OF CARLYLE

5 FLEMING
MANITOBA BORDER

6 SASKATCHEWAN LANDING,
13 MI S OF KYLE

7 DANIELSON, N END OF LAKE
DIEFENBAKER

8 DOUGLAS, 7 MI SE OF
ELBOW ON HWY 19

9 PIKE LAKE, 19 MI S OF
SASKATOON ON HWY 60

10 BLACKSTRAP, 20 MI SE OF
SASKATOON ON HWY 11

Saskatchewan

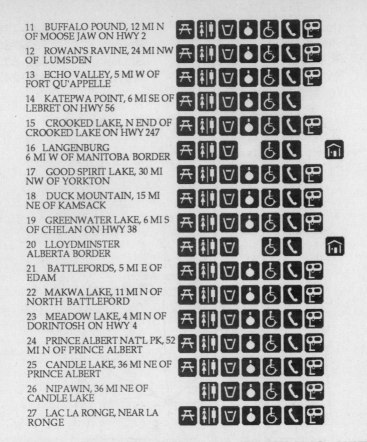

11 BUFFALO POUND, 12 MI N OF MOOSE JAW ON HWY 2							
12 ROWAN'S RAVINE, 24 MI NW OF LUMSDEN							
13 ECHO VALLEY, 5 MI W OF FORT QU'APPELLE							
14 KATEPWA POINT, 6 MI SE OF LEBRET ON HWY 56							
15 CROOKED LAKE, N END OF CROOKED LAKE ON HWY 247							
16 LANGENBURG 6 MI W OF MANITOBA BORDER							
17 GOOD SPIRIT LAKE, 30 MI NW OF YORKTON							
18 DUCK MOUNTAIN, 15 MI NE OF KAMSACK							
19 GREENWATER LAKE, 6 MI S OF CHELAN ON HWY 38							
20 LLOYDMINSTER ALBERTA BORDER							
21 BATTLEFORDS, 5 MI E OF EDAM							
22 MAKWA LAKE, 11 MI N OF NORTH BATTLEFORD							
23 MEADOW LAKE, 4 MI N OF DORINTOSH ON HWY 4							
24 PRINCE ALBERT NAT'L PK, 52 MI N OF PRINCE ALBERT							
25 CANDLE LAKE, 36 MI NE OF PRINCE ALBERT							
26 NIPAWIN, 36 MI NE OF CANDLE LAKE							
27 LAC LA RONGE, NEAR LA RONGE							

SASKATCHEWAN SERVICE STATIONS WITH RV DUMP FACILITIES

A. Regina

Name of Business:	Regina Husky Car/Truck Stop
Location:	Trans Canada Hwy. 1 E & Prince of Wales Dr.
Hours of Operation:	24 hours per day.
RV Information:	No charge for use of RV Dump. Waterfill, propane and diesel fuel available.
Station Type:	Truck stop (Husky).

B. Saskatoon

Name of Business:	Circle Drive Husky
Location:	Idylwyld Dr. N and Circle Dr.
Hours of Operation:	24 hours per day.
RV Information:	No charge for use of RV Dump. Waterfill, propane and diesel fuel available.
Station Type:	Truck stop (Husky).